Translating Anarchy

The Anarchism of Occupy Wall Street

Translating Anarchy

The Anarchism of Occupy Wall Street

Mark Bray

zero books

Winchester, UK
Washington, USA

First published by Zero Books, 2013
Zero Books is an imprint of John Hunt Publishing Ltd., Laurel House, Station Approach,
Alresford, Hants, SO24 9JH, UK
office1@jhpbooks.net
www.johnhuntpublishing.com
www.zero-books.net

For distributor details and how to order please visit the 'Ordering' section on our website.

ISBN: 978 1 78279 126 3

A CIP catalogue record for this book is available from the British Library.

Design: Stuart Davies

Printed and bound by CPI Group (UK) Ltd, Croydon, CR0 4YY

CONTENTS

Dedicated to the memory of Ida Braiman

Thank-You's

I would like to thank all of the Occupy organizers that were kind enough to grant me their time for an interview. Without you all, this project would have been impossible. I want to specifically send my appreciation to Marisa Holmes, Priscilla Grim, and Sofía Gallisa for introducing me to more fantastic people to interview. Thanks to Bill Scott for prompting me to write about the media and Occupy. Your invitation to discuss media issues was highly influential for the first chapter of this book. Thank you to Zero Books for giving me the opportunity to publish my work. And thanks to Eric R. McGregor and Jessica Lehrman for providing many of the photos in this book.

Thank you to all of the Rutgers faculty and students who supported OWS and my participation in the movement. Special thanks to my advisor, Temma Kaplan, for all of her guidance and support these past years. I also want to tip my cap to Matt Friedman for organizing OWS informational events on campus. Big shout-outs to my friends and comrades around the world who have been so warm and hospitable over the past years and taught me so much about their struggles: Sofia, Eliana, Tzissous, Vangelis, Malamas and everyone else with Alpha Kappa, Ellison, Mario and the Madrid CNT, Keisuke Narita and the Irregular Rhythm Asylum, Takesi and the Freeters' Union, and Fabien Delmotte. Special thanks to my brother Alfonso Pérez of the CIPO-RFM in Oaxaca for teaching me so much about the indigenous struggle and being such a great friend and comrade over the years. Special thanks to my sister Rudy Amanda Hurtado Garcés for being such a courageous freedom fighter. *Su apasionada búsqueda de la autodeterminación y autogestión de los pueblos ha sido una inspiración enorme.*

I am deeply indebted to my dear friends and comrades Abbey Volcano, Chris Spannos, and Harpreet K. Paul for taking the time to give me invaluable support and feedback throughout the writing of this book. Especially big hugs for Deric Shannon who really helped me navigate the uncertainties of the publishing process and gave me essential moral support.

I want to thank my wonderful Auntie Sue and Uncle Neil for their support of Occupy Wall Street. Neil, I really appreciated the time you took to discuss political strategy with me; it helped me reflect on some vitally important issues. Also thanks to Joyce and Bob Herman for visiting Liberty Square and taking the fight to the banks up in Rochester. Big hugs for Vanessa, Gigi, and Karina for their support. Karina, I've always appreciated your righteous indignation at injustice and your comradeship at all of the demonstrations over the years.

Finally, I'll conclude by thanking my incredible family. Mom, thank you so much for the pride you take in everything I do. Wearing your 99% pin and standing up for us in the newspaper really meant a lot to me. Emily, thank you for supporting my organizing and for being such a great friend over the years. You have helped me to become a more caring and compassionate person. Dad, thank you for always pushing me to be an independent thinker, inculcating me with a love of reading and writing, and making me comfortable with being the black sheep once in a while. And to Senia, the love of my life, without you this book, and everything else, would be unimaginable. ("It was a moment like this, do you remember?")

"It is often said that anarchists live in a world of dreams to come, and do not see the things which happen today. We see them only too well, and in their true colors, and that is what makes us carry the hatchet into the forest of prejudices that besets us."

Pyotr Kropotkin, 1896

Introduction

"Conquerors on Horseback are not Many-Legged Gods"

If the abolition of slave-manacles
began as a vision of hands without manacles,
then this is the year;
if the shutdown of extermination camps
began as imagination of a land
without barbed wire or the crematorium,
then this is the year;
if every rebellion begins with the idea
that conquerors on horseback
are not many-legged gods, that they too drown
if plunged in the river,
then this is the year.

So may every humiliated mouth,
teeth like desecrated headstones,
fill with the angels of bread.
—Martín Espada[1]

2011: for the first time in a long time people across the world said, "this is the year." From the revolutions of the Arab Spring to the student uprisings in Chile and Colombia, from the Spanish 15M Movement which spread to the squares of France, Greece, Israel, and Latin America to the rage of the dispossessed on the streets of London, to Occupy. Many of us never thought we would live to see a year that could be compared to 1989, 1968, or even 1848 with a straight face, but there it was in TIME Magazine. In an attempt to explain such a historic outpouring of resistance, mainstream commentators tended to reduce the origins of each movement to its context and political 'nature.' In their eyes the Arab Spring, entirely unthinkable to liberal and conservative warmongers who only years earlier had argued that regime change grows out the barrel of an American gun, made sense in the context of dictatorial regimes and a 'fanatical' political culture. The squares movements in southern Europe and the occasional Greek riot made sense in the context of their declining economies and 'entitled' political culture that was resistant to 'reasonable' cuts in life-sustaining social services.

So then where did Occupy come from and what did it mean to those who made it happen? The mainstream consensus was that Occupy Wall Street (OWS) was a liberal response to Obama's failure to do more to soften the blows of the economic crisis. Liberal pundits saw it as an intriguing cultural novelty, a 'sign of the times' in a post-historical world, and a welcome shot of adrenaline to a Democratic Party that had been drifting rightward for at least twenty years. More fundamentally, however, sympathetic mainstream observers saw it as an example of our cool-headed, pragmatic, post-60s American political culture briefly awakening from its hibernation in order to nudge our political system back into line before drifting back into the 4G dream world. The subtext read something like this: 'the world of jihadists, Molotov cocktails, dictators, and extremism is elsewhere. Here, we're rational, even-handed, and realistic. We're the mature ones in this world since our movements resolve things with words instead of fists, and reforms instead of insurrections.' In that sense, liberals attempted to recuperate Occupy into a self-congratulatory nationalist narrative that posits protest as the greatest indicator of the life of a 'democracy.'

But what the liberal pundits didn't realize was that Occupy Wall Street was about much more than 'patriotic protest' or acting as a 'corporate watchdog.' At its core, Occupy Wall Street was an anti-capitalist, anti-authoritarian movement run by organizers with predominantly anarchist and anarchistic politics.

Translating Anarchy is an insider's account of the central role of anarchist and anarchistic politics in the origins, praxis, and rapid ascent of Occupy Wall Street in New York. Although anarchism was thought to have died during the course of the global fratricide of the 20th century, it reemerged in exciting new forms across the world after the fall of the Berlin Wall and has become the fastest growing and most dynamic radical ideology of the 21st century. Over the past decades anarchists have played pivotal roles in numerous waves of global resistance including opposition to neo-liberalism and austerity, radical environmentalism, queer liberation, anti-militarism, prison abolition, information freedom, animal liberation, anti-racist and anti-fascist struggles, labor organizing, and many more. As Occupy Wall Street has demonstrated, it is impossible to understand where 21st century social movements are heading without taking the horizontalism, direct action, and mutual aid of anarchism into account. Whereas the American "New Left" of the 1960s and 70s was more strongly influenced by various strands of Marxism, the soul of today's radical left is imbued with the spirit of anarchism.

The centrality of anarchism in OWS was obvious to those who knew what to look for. The confluence of directly democratic general assemblies and spokescouncils, the consensus decision-making process, a strategic focus on direct action and occupation rather than electoral politics, and a reluctance to settle on a few reformist demands essentially branded the movement with a giant circle-A. That much was clear from the outside, but it was even more obvious from the inside. For almost the entire first year of OWS, I was one of the most active members of the Press Working Group (WG) and a regular participant in the Direct Action (DA) WG. As an organizer involved in the planning and public messaging of a wide variety of OWS actions, I came to understand the inner dynamics of the movement.

That insight allowed me to conduct 192 interviews between

December 2011 and February 2013 with the vast majority of the organizers that made Occupy Wall Street happen. As opposed to other studies that merely scratched the surface by interviewing "active movement supporters" who attended a large coalition march predominantly composed of non-OWS activists[2] or took an online survey,[3] *Translating Anarchy* is the first comprehensive study of the politics of the movement's core organizers in New York City. Such a study could only be carried out by an organizer because outside researchers wouldn't know who was really involved and to what extent, they wouldn't understand how the working groups, affinity groups, spokescouncils, caucuses, general assemblies, clusters and other bodies interacted with each other, and they wouldn't realize that there was a significant political divide between a mass of mainly liberal supporters and an overwhelmingly anarchist and anarchistic core. The most important finding for the purposes of this book is that 39%[4] of OWS organizers self-identified as anarchists and a further 33% had politics that were essentially anarchistic (anti-capitalist, anti-hierarchical, and direct action oriented) without using the label. That means that in total 72% of OWS organizers had explicitly anarchist or implicitly anarchistic politics.

So while most Occupy participants wanted to reform capitalism, most organizers wanted to destroy it (78% were anti-capitalist). However, as I discuss in Chapter 1, outside commentators tended to blur the distinction between participants and organizers and view the entirety of OWS as a homogeneous liberal mass of bodies in a park. That's part of the reason why journalists mistook OWS for a liberal love-fest. Another reason was that many of us strategically articulated our politics to the media and the general public in order to present an accessible, mainstream image to make our revolutionary anti-capitalist politics more digestible. So it's understandable that liberal journalists would interpret our rhetoric as a call for free expression and an improved social safety net, while in fact we used popular political discourse to make a case for an autonomous, non-electoral social movement working toward a non-capitalist economy that would replace the profit incentive with a prioritization of human need.

Since it wouldn't have gained massive popular support under an explicitly anarchist or anti-capitalist banner, Occupy Wall Street became a vehicle for 'translating anarchy' to a society that was generally receptive to many anarchist ideas but wary of its ideological trappings. Since many OWS anarchists refrained from using the 'a-word' when speaking to the general public, outside researchers wouldn't have noticed the prominence of anarchist ideas in the movement because they wouldn't have developed the kinds of personal relationships and trust necessary for some people to feel comfortable disclosing their revolutionary and insurrectionary aspirations. In contrast, I knew most of my interview subjects personally prior to interviewing them.

In conducting the interviews I limited myself to organizers involved in the occupation of Liberty Square (or "Liberty Plaza"; formerly known as Zuccotti Park) in one way or another. I did not interview people involved in Occupies in other cities or those involved in general assemblies in the outer boroughs that were not also involved in the main organizing hub revolving around Liberty Square. Therefore, while my results and arguments may bear some resemblance to the situation in other cities or with other groups, they are only intended to address the organizers of the groups, projects, and activities associated with the main body of Occupy Wall Street.

Although I didn't manage to speak with every OWS organizer, I interviewed the vast majority of those who were active over the first year of the movement and I made sure to speak with those who did not limit themselves to one working group or project but played important roles in the larger OWS community. I limited my interviews to those involved during the first year in part because I left the country shortly after the one year anniversary of OWS on September 17, 2012 to spend a year in Spain doing academic research, but also because whatever one might think of what remains of "Occupy Wall Street" as of this writing in March 2013, it is certainly quite different from what it was over the course of the first three months to a year of its existence. Certainly a lot of great work has been done, and is still being done, by those involved in Strike Debt, an OWS project focused on organizing around debt, Occupy Sandy, networks mobilized in response to Hurricane Sandy that outperformed FEMA and the Red Cross, and other projects. But these inspirational networks of Occupy projects and campaigns are very different quantitatively and qualitatively from what emerged in the fall of 2011, so I am limiting my focus to the first year of OWS with a special focus on the first three months. I speak about Occupy Wall Street in the past tense not to dismiss the work that is still being done, but rather because the entity that grabbed global headlines no longer exists in the same form.

While the logistics didn't work out to be able to speak with some people, only three organizers declined my interview request (because they disliked interviews). The majority of the interviews were conducted in person, often in Liberty, before or after a meeting, or at an OWS event, but a good number were conducted over the phone. Information from the interviews is cited in a note with the person's name as they asked me to list it (most were fine with their entire names, others asked me to use first names and a few preferred nicknames) followed by the date of the interview. The first time I speak about someone I interviewed, I list their age at the time of the interview in parentheses if they chose to share it. All translations from Spanish, French and Catalan are my own unless otherwise noted.

Translating Anarchy is fundamentally about the role of anarchists in Occupy Wall Street, but it also situates the movement within the history of social movements and anarchism more broadly. An important objective of this book is to clear up popular misunderstandings of anarchism and give new anarchists a broader understanding of the depth and diversity of the anarchist tradition. My experience as a political organizer and my research as an academic provide the foundation for the comparative and historical elements of the book. I am a member of the Industrial Workers of the World (IWW) labor union and have previous experience participating in the global justice movement, the anti-war movement, and student and immigrants' rights work, so that background informs my analysis of Occupy. In addition, I am a PhD Candidate in Modern European History and Women's and Gender History at Rutgers University where my dissertation research is on turn of the 20th century Spanish anarchism, human rights, state repression, and media (my academic background explains why I tend to use European historical examples). It's important to note that this book is not a history of Occupy Wall Street as a whole, and it omits many important topics that would have to be included in such a work. I touch upon notable episodes and dynamics in the movement's history, but only insofar as they relate to my broader political analysis of the organizers of OWS.

From a historical perspective, it's remarkable that Occupy Wall Street was a defining moment in the shift from the relatively hierarchical Marxist politics of the New Left to the new horizontal anarchist politics of the 21st century radical left, but the media could only think about it as a "liberal tea party" that might influence the 2012 presidential election. In Chapter 1, "Insight From Confusion: The Media and Occupy," I tackle the question of why the media was so confused about OWS and why journalists couldn't think beyond two narrow, pre-conceived ideological frameworks that I call *mimicry of the elite* and *communication with the elite*. Understanding the blockages in the media lens clarifies why they so thoroughly misinterpreted Occupy and sets the context for the project of *Translating Anarchy*. Readers exclusively interested in explicitly anarchist themes might want to jump to Chapter 2.

In Chapter 2, "'The Bane of Occupy Wall Street': Anarchism and the Anarchistic," I delve into the anarchism of Occupy Wall Street while providing a historical and ideological exposition of anarchism to clarify what anarchists are all about. It goes into more depth about the distinction between 'anarchist' and 'anarchistic' politics and argues that the scope and influence of anarchism in Occupy extended well beyond those who actively used the label. Moreover, Chapter 2 addresses anarchist and Occupy perspectives on capitalism and democracy and explores the strengths and weaknesses of consensus decision-making, our general assemblies and spokescouncils. Finally, it discusses the Occupy aversion to demands and examines the few instances when the media actually noticed traces of anarchism in the movement.

Chapter 3, "Translating Anarchy," reveals the strategic articulation of anarchist politics on the part of the anarchists and anti-authoritarians of Occupy Wall Street. Reflecting on my own process of radicalization, I offer some preliminary thoughts on how to shift popular perspectives in an anarchist direction before dissecting the various layers of Occupy media including the *Occupied Wall Street Journal*, the Occupy theory journal *Tidal*, and occupywallst.org. After delineating how the various layers of messaging managed to bring masses of liberals and progressives into anarchist forms of organizing, I discuss the anarchist origins of the '99%' slogan. Finally, I share some individual stories of organizers who became (or realized that they already were) anarchists under the radicalizing influence of OWS.

Chapter 4, "Why We Need a Revolution or: Beyond 'Socialism in One Park,'" explores anarchist and Occupy perspectives on tactics and strategy. Starting with debates surrounding electoral politics and the Obama presidency, it touches upon direct action and affinity groups before settling into the controversial debates surrounding 'violence,' 'diversity of tactics' and the infamous black bloc. Finally, Chapter 4 dives into the evolution/revolution debate about how to change society to argue that alternative institutions and withdrawal from capitalism cannot replace the class struggle.

After you put down this book, I hope you'll ask yourself whether perhaps it isn't the advocate of an economic system that leaves millions in lifelong poverty while burying the rich in redundant luxuries who is the truly dangerous 'extremist' and 'fanatic' in this world. Unfortunately, the capitalists responsible for the carnage of the economic crisis have managed to hold onto their power while their victims continue to suffer. But at least Occupy managed to tarnish the seemingly invincible allure of the American economic and political elite and broadcast inklings of an alternative. It performed the necessary task of showing people "that conquerors on horseback are not many-legged gods, that they too drown if plunged in the river" which is indeed how "every rebellion begins."

Chapter One

Insight from Confusion: The Media and Occupy

"These protests began almost two weeks ago now under this name 'Occupy Wall Street' and during that time a clear goal, a clear message has yet to really surface from these myriad demonstrators leaving many to ask 'what does Occupy Wall Street want?'"
—CNN Newsroom anchor Brooke Baldwin[1]

Why was the media so confused about Occupy Wall Street? What was so difficult to grasp about an anti-Wall Street protest in the wake the most catastrophic financial fraud in our lifetimes? Most of the organizers I knew were baffled. Our national approval rating was 43%, Congress's national approval rating was an all-time low of 9%, and *we* had to do a better job expressing our message to the public?[2] During the first week of the occupation of Liberty Square, there was very little media coverage of Occupy Wall Street. Some claimed this was a deliberate media blackout, but the same can be said for most demonstrations. We get inane segments like NBC Nightly News' "Making a Difference" which features individual tales of do-goodery rather than stories about community organizations or immigrant workers' centers that are *actually making a difference.*[3] But after the pepper-spraying of Chelsea Elliot and Jeanne Mansfield on September 24, 2011 and the arrests of over 700 marchers on the Brooklyn Bridge on October 1st, the media frenzy was in full swing and there was actually much more positive coverage than any of us could have expected.[4] However, as I've argued elsewhere,[5] the sympathetic coverage we received from seemingly liberal journalists didn't emerge from a shared understanding of the underlying nature and purpose of OWS.

As conservative CNN contributor Will Cain astutely noted in early October, "this Occupy Wall Street movement right now is just a Rorschach test, it's an inkblot test. People see in it what they want to see. It's a projection of what they already feel."[6] And so, many liberal journalists saw the liberal Tea Party that they wanted to see, but, as the days passed, their confusion didn't abate. If anything, it increased because OWS was not sitting down to join them at their tea party. Some of the confusion stemmed from the movement's resistance to electoral politics, but the confusion of mainstream journalists went much deeper than that.

Activist explanations for this lingering bewilderment generally focused on political bias or journalistic incompetence. A common opinion was that many mainstream journalists didn't want to understand our message because, no matter how liberal they may have been, they were our enemies. They willfully misrepresented it. Corporate news outlets would never accurately report on grassroots social movements because they were part of the same machinery that we were working to dismantle. We could do our best to nudge the coverage in our favor here and there, but ultimately we couldn't trust the corporate media to cover an anti-corporate movement.

Another perspective was that some mainstream reporters were too incompetent to understand Occupy Wall Street. Even when some journalists wanted to write accurate, un-biased articles, it was often clear that they knew nothing about non-electoral politics or social movements, and were completely unqualified for the task before them. Some reporters really didn't understand what we were doing, and no amount of talking points about how 'education is a human right' or comparisons to the anti-nuclear movement were going to change that. Activists, of course, recognized this incompetence as a banal byproduct of the politics of the corporate media, which wouldn't promote accurate coverage of social movements.

In contrast, liberal and conservative mainstream critics offered a much more straightforward explanation for the media's confusion: the message of Occupy Wall Street was actually confusing. Of course much of the confusion came from the unconventional nature of the idea of occupying a park, the movement's countercultural elements, and its emphasis on direct democracy. But if you take this confusion more seriously and make the effort to dig beneath the superficial pundit chatter about smelly hippies and muddled messaging, it becomes evident that there are some startling paradoxes at the heart of the rhetoric of Occupy Wall Street.

Unlike most, I think that both the activists *and* the mainstream critics were correct in their explanations of the media confusion. The activists were correct because there were some journalists who were willfully confused because they opposed our politics, and even more reporters, I would argue, who wanted to understand us but lacked the information and motivation to think beyond the confines of the dominant political culture. However, I would also argue that there was a profound insight at the heart of the media's confusion. Mainstream journalists may have been the products of news corporations and larger social structures that work to systematically delegitimize non-electoral politics, but in their befuddlement they were actually on to something. They realized that there was a missing piece at the center of the Occupy puzzle, but made the mistake of assuming that it simply didn't exist. In truth, they didn't know what we wanted because we didn't tell them.

Journalism: The Narrative Form of Capitalism

To get to the insights of the mainstream critics it's important to take some time to explore why journalists were confused and what they were confused about because, paradoxically, their insights stemmed from their confusion. Journalists who deliberately sought to misrepresent the rhetoric of OWS out of a conscious political bias reveal much less about the dominant political culture than those whose confusion followed from an unconscious tendency to fall into familiar patterns of thought. For that reason, I will ask why so many mainstream journalists who had some desire to understand Occupy Wall Street simply couldn't, and what that reveals about the strategic gaps in our self-presentation.

One of the most apparent reasons for the confusion of many reporters was that they knew very little if anything about where our strategies of organizing or methods of action came from. They had no context. Although a minor incident, the following anecdote exemplified this phenomenon for me. On November 30, 2011, we demonstrated against the war profiteers who met at the "Aerospace & Defense Finance Conference" near Madison Square Park. There was a picket line scheduled that morning, so I showed up early to greet any press that arrived. The first journalist there was a young woman working for FM News 101.9 in New York. After I spent a minute describing the day's protest she said, "I was reading the post on your website about this protest and there was this word I saw a lot that I didn't understand." Peaking my curiosity, I asked her which word and she answered "militarism." I was so surprised that it took me a moment to start explaining the term for her. Yes, our anti-war statement would be presented to the city by someone who didn't know what 'militarism' meant. To be fair, most reporters like this woman simply have to show up, ask us what we're doing to get a five second sound bite, and leave. Anyone could carry out that kind of reporting. But it's indicative of a larger trend I noticed among many journalists covering OWS. It would have taken very little effort for them to rectify their lack of knowledge about the movements that preceded Occupy or the history of direct democracy, for example, if they had tried. Simply spending a couple of hours on Google would have greatly enhanced the quality of their coverage, but they usually had no professional incentive to spend the time.

The total lack of preparation was evident on the one-year anniversary of OWS when we publicized the map of our plan of attack on the financial district. It showed four convergence points that would lead to eight intersections around the Wall Street area. I arrived an hour early on September 17, 2012 to do press work, and of the dozens of reporters I spoke with, only about 20% had taken the time to look at the map on the front page of our website. They had very little idea of what was going on. The reporters were like college students rolling out of bed and coming to class without having done the reading. The most egregious example from that day was the report from Sean Hennessey of CBS 2 in New York live from an empty Foley Square at 6PM where he reported that our "rally" for the afternoon had been cancelled.[7] Actually, Foley Square was our backup location, and as he was speaking there were thousands of people packed into Zuccotti. If he had looked at our website or press releases he would have known this, but accuracy wasn't important enough to him to bother. The 101.9 reporter could have figured out what 'militarism' meant on her own, but it wasn't worth her time.

Why not? There are several factors that come to mind. For now, I'll just focus on one but I'll touch upon others later in this chapter. The most obvious factor is that most readers/viewers/listeners don't care about the accuracy of minor details or the greater context of protest, so journalists don't bother learning them. News outlets are corporations driven by the profit incentive, and therefore aim to sell the most marketable product. The unfortunate reality is that most media consumers would rather read about Occupy in relation to 'crazy hippies,' or, at best, in terms of strict policy matters than read about consensus process or watch a news segment connecting the origins of Occupy to the global justice movement. Regardless of how you explain this consumer preference, it's pretty hard to deny it (although I think that there are a lot more people who would like to learn about the larger context of OWS than the corporate news estimates). Many activists argue that beneath it all most people are really starving for this information and that their 'real' interests are being stifled by the media; that they are essentially being 'brainwashed.' On the other hand, a standard capitalist response would point out that if enough people wanted to read about the origins of the spokescouncil model and its use in Chiapas, Mexico, then journalists would be falling over each other to write that story; but people don't want to read about that, so the stories aren't written—simple supply and demand, nothing insidious behind the scenes.

I agree that there is no Dr. Evil behind the scenes fine-tuning his brainwashing machine to unleash on the hapless public (although Rupert Murdoch might be close) and that consumer preferences wouldn't magically transform themselves overnight if the coverage changed. Certainly MSNBC and Fox News, for example, push their respective liberal and conservative agendas through their networks and craft specific messages to influence their viewers, but it's really missing the larger point to reduce the complex relationship between media producers and consumers to a 'conspiracy of the 1%.'

To get a fuller understanding of the complex dialogue between media producers and consumers as it played out in Occupy Wall Street, it's critical to understand the historical development of journalism. As historical sociologist Jean Chalaby argues in *The Invention of Journalism*, journalism emerged as its own unique form of discourse in the second half of the 19th century in Great Britain and the United States, primarily in response to changes in print capitalism. Early 19th century forms of printed public discourse explicitly sought to convince the reader of the writer's opinion and were often tied to political parties or workers' organizations. However, this political motivation for publishing shifted mid-century as new developments in print technology enhanced the potential profitability of the industry, making newspapers one of the first commodities to be mass-produced. Over time, newspaper production became more and more capital-intensive and the level of competition increased causing a consolidation of media outlets and a desire to expand readership. The best way for a paper to get more readers was to divorce itself from any specific affiliation and portray itself as an independent voice of public opinion and common sense. So was born the discourse of journalistic objectivity.[8]

By portraying itself as objective and above the fray of partisan interest, journalistic discourse forged a foundation of legitimacy to speak from. Rather than speaking from a clearly expressed perspective, newspapers came to speak with the voice of society as a whole.[9] In turn, the claim that the newspaper was merely reflecting the will of the greater society actually allowed it to forge public opinion. A modern parallel would be when Fox News anchors state, for example, "These days, people are saying that teachers are being paid too much" without citing any sources. Of course, those anchors are the "people" saying those things, and the more they say it the more their viewers repeat it.

The project of grounding media credibility in the ability to speak on behalf of society was aided by the invention of the opinion poll by press baron William Stead. Stead realized that the poll would allow journalists to "speak with an authority far superior to that possessed by any other person." Public opinion as expressed by these polls has been understood as a disparate accumulation of isolated individual opinions, as a collection of signs lining Zuccotti, rather than the expression of a collective outlook or a protest movement.[10] Opinion polls have provided a populist veneer for the atomization of the population, inhibiting the imagination of collective struggle. Publishers used the polls to support their political interests through the dissemination of supposedly universal moral standards. Chalaby states that

> the supposed universal validity of moral categories also allowed journalists to express opinions on politics and elected officials with categories taken as valid in the political sphere but which were not openly politically connoted.[11]

Objectivity has allowed the media to portray itself as 'of the people' yet independent from them. It has allowed journalists (in the service of corporate news media) to tap into the long-standing Western philosophical tradition of striving toward a disembodied position of absolute truth.[12] Yet, with the expansion of the rhetoric of democracy and popular politics in the 19th century truth was increasingly associated with the masses. Therefore, that disembodied objective stance ironically gained its legitimacy from its grounding in 'the people.' The more a news outlet was 'of the people' as a whole, without reference to 'divisive' social issues like class and race, the greater was its ability to see above the people to understand the truth. The argument being made here is not that newspapers would be better if all articles were oriented around unabashed moralizing, but rather that no text is neutral. Objectivity becomes a political discourse when it is used to obscure an underlying partiality.

The partiality that persisted after the "invention of journalism" was not only about what retrospectively might be considered explicit political bias, but also about what kind of information was provided to whom. Market influences enhanced the homogeneity of the media's political orientation while increasing the heterogeneity of the quality and tone of its content along class lines. In the 1820s and 1830s, before technology allowed newspapers to become truly profitable, working class and upper class papers had a similar quality of information and tone of delivery. Yet, when the industry was consolidated into the hands of a relatively small number of press barons, the reading public was divided into the "information-rich and information-poor" which reinforced class society.[13] In addition, around the turn of the century the topics of sports, society news (social engagements of the rich), sensational news, and human interest stories served to reduce coverage of politics and color the way political issues were reported. These new journalistic foci led coverage to focus more on the quirks of politicians than the issues, and presented politics as being no less important than sensational stories. A modern-day parallel would be when you're watching a thirty second segment about the corporate negligence behind the BP oil spill and suddenly the broadcast shifts to a discussion of Kim Kardashian's new cat. I imagine that many readers have had this happen while watching the news and felt a jolt from it. The point is not that there should never be a place for television programming about cats, and that every program should be serious, but that this format of information dissemination subtly equates the two. As Noam Chomsky and Edward S. Herman point out in *Manufacturing Consent*, "the steady advance, and cultural power, of marketing and advertising has caused 'the displacement of a political public sphere by a depoliticized consumer culture.'"[14] Moreover, the emphasis on the lives of prominent individuals and the development of the human interest story allowed the political focus to center on 'good' or 'bad' elites without addressing the underlying system. As historian Martin Conboy argues,

> the popular press allowed a modicum of public outrage against the foibles of the privileged and the abuses of the powerful without doing anything to either analyze a system which produced such abuse or to scrutinize the economic and institutional structures that enabled newspapers to make money[15]

The scholarship of Chalaby, Conboy, Chomsky and Herman

demonstrates how the news preferences of media consumers, like the preferences of all consumers, are historical constructs that have emerged out of specific technological, economic, and historical circumstances. The capitalist argument that consumers are simply autonomous agents who make personal choices apart from their context is another iteration of the classical Western tradition of disembodied truth discussed earlier. It is another variant of the ahistorical 'objectivity' that undergirds journalism. The long trajectory of print capitalism makes it clear that the ignorance of most mainstream journalists about Occupy and non-electoral politics in general is simply a product of market imperatives that have gradually sculpted the preferences of media consumers in accordance with the maintenance of class rule. Perhaps Chalaby put it best when he argued that "journalism is not only an invention of the market economy, but... the narrative form that capitalism took to become a historical force."[16] Therefore, if journalism is a discursive form that trivializes politics, individualizes identity, and segregates information along class lines while hiding behind capitalist 'objectivity,' it's no surprise that journalists walked into Occupy with some serious blinders on.

The best way to explore the other factors behind the confusion of the mainstream media is to situate them in terms of the elements of Occupy Wall Street that these journalists were confused about. Fundamentally, I argue that journalists were confused because they tried to assess the movement in terms of two central standards of conduct in the dominant political culture: *mimicry of the elite* and *communication with the elite*. In the context of Occupy, I understand 'the elite' to be politicians, influential government officials, and Wall Street level capitalists. In addition, I recognize that there are various liberal and conservative shades of the dominant political culture, but my goal here is to address what they have in common.

Mimicry of the Elite

One of the main standards of political conduct in this country is the degree to which a group or movement apes the political culture of the elite. If we are to be taken seriously, they tell us, we must fashion ourselves in their image. Politics is understood as a predictable, stable performance. Groups and movements like OWS can audition for a part in the political drama before a row of political and financial judges, but their performance is evaluated based on its costumes, delivery, and fealty to the script. What does the scripted performance entail? To get a sense of its parameters, I will address two of the main areas of media confusion: the tactic of occupation and our lack of official leaders.

One of the most boring and tiresome aspects of doing press work for OWS during the first two weeks of October was the complete lack of imagination from the reporters asking the same handful of questions over and over. One of the most popular was: 'What does camping in a park have to do with Wall Street, and when are you going home?' Some conservative journalists portrayed the occupation as nothing more than a "squalid, crime-infested sleep-in,"[17] but even sympathetic reporters were of the opinion that we would be taken more seriously if we left the park and turned ourselves into a 'real' organization or protest movement. Even many commentators who initially praised the occupation eventually said it was time to get down to the 'real' task of politics. The occupation made us seem immature, irresponsible, uninformed and anything but serious. Moreover, the countercultural element of Occupy Wall Street invited equal parts derision and fascination. There was an endless stream of stories about every aspect of cultural minutiae in Zuccotti from the yoga, to the drum circle, to the shrine on the west side of the park. Some journalists used the counterculture to attack us, others eventually celebrated aspects of it but it was never considered politically useful although, like the occupation as a whole, it garnered attention. If we had dressed in a 'presentable fashion' and staged single-event demonstrations, we were told, we would have been taken much more seriously. But, if it was such a bad idea to occupy a park and dance around like hippies in the pursuit of social justice, then why was the media there? Because, fundamentally, they were covering us out of a desire for sensationalism rather than political insight. There was a minor conflict between their political moralizing and their thirst for ratings.

The first time I really thought about this inner conflict within the corporate media between advocating boring political work and actually covering 'reckless' direct action was in 2007 when I was living in Providence, RI and organizing with the Industrial Workers of the World (IWW). We organized a small, unpermitted march in solidarity with Wobbly (IWW) foodstuffs workers in New York that blocked the right lane of traffic on a busy Saturday afternoon. When the police arrived, they brutally attacked one of the marchers leaving her with a gruesome knee injury. In response, over the next weeks I organized the press campaign in her favor and did a number of interviews for the Rhode Island media including a long radio appearance on conservative WPRO in Providence. During that interview, the host was berating us for our negligence in daring to block traffic and I asked him straightforwardly whether I would have been invited on his program to speak about the struggles of immigrant foodstuffs workers in New York if the march had quietly marched single-file down the sidewalk. His supposed fury at our public disruption melted away as he revealed a wide, knowing smile. "No, of course not," he responded.

Journalists at Zuccotti smiled in the same way when I responded to their question about the purpose of the occupation with a question of my own: 'Would every major news agency in the world be here if we had a normal one day demonstration and then went home?' There was something so strange about having a reporter from CNN ask me how our actions could make a difference when their very presence was proof that they already were. The same issue emerged regarding our protest tactics more generally. On May Day 2012, I spoke to a reporter from CBS Channel 2 in New York who asked me why we were protesting. My response was,

> the only way that we can really get our voice out is by getting out onto the street, by demonstrating in the tradition of so many protest movements before because you wouldn't be interviewing me if we were doing an online petition. You're here because we're out in the streets.[18]

The market for sensational news (even blocking traffic or delaying commuters) creates an opening for public expression within a corporate media that advocates un-newsworthy political action for dissident groups. The moralizing and the horror are actually two sides of the same coin, and neither could exist without the other. If horror didn't emerge from stepping out of line, then there would be no incentive to behave. If unusual political and cultural acts weren't moralized, then they wouldn't titillate viewers and spike ratings. Media scholar Gadi Wolfsfeld pointed out that there are two ways to get the media's attention: elites can go through the front door, while the back door is "designed for the poorer actors and the entrance fee is often paid for in (what could be labeled) the 'dues of disorder.'"[19] The media eagerly accepted our disruptive "dues" despite the need to scold us for them.

The final irony of the media's confusion about our occupation was that while we were in Liberty Square, journalists couldn't understand how a social movement could be based out of a park, but, after the eviction on November 15, 2011, they couldn't understand how Occupy Wall Street could exist without the park. Part of that was our fault since many organizers made the movement about the park above all else. Nevertheless, the catch-22 of the media's take on the occupation emerged because they never really understood how the tactic fit into our overall political strategy (which they couldn't discern anyway).

* * *

> Writing about Occupy Wall Street is a journalist's nightmare... you have to owe up to the challenge of writing about a communal protest movement where there are no clear "leaders" and no official "organizers." For those of us weaned on writing about top-down hierarchial [sic] organizations with CEOs, presidents, advisory boards and parliaments, it's a challenge.
>
> -Neal Ungerleider, *Fast Company*[20]

As a non-hierarchical movement we were described, and often described ourselves, as a 'leaderless' movement. Some organizers tried to infuse the Occupy discourse with the term 'leaderful' instead to emphasize how our structure actually allowed space for anyone with the motivation to take on a leadership role, but this word never really caught on outside of movement circles. Neal Ungerleider's quote demonstrates how confusing it was for the media to hear many voices rather than one, and how they would have preferred to reduce our message to the character and biography of our potential leader rather than the content of our collective message. As much as we tried to explain our commitment to direct democracy to the press, they always assumed that there really were leaders behind the scenes, and that it was their job to sniff them out, or that it was only a matter of time before such leaders would emerge.

One afternoon in early October, a journalist came up to me and said, "I'm looking for Grim." "Who?" I responded. "Grim. All I know is the name is Grim. Supposedly Grim's the one behind all of this." "Oh," I replied, "I'm not sure who that is but I can tell you that there is no one person behind anything." "Thanks, I'll keep looking." It was evident which part of my answer they were focused on. Later, I would learn that 'Grim' was Priscilla Grim, one of the indefatigable editors of the *Occupied Wall Street Journal* and organizers of the 'We are the 99%' Tumblr with Chris (29) from the Kitchen Working Group. She would be the first to tell you that she was far too busy working on the newspaper, Tumblr, and other projects to have considered directing the entire movement even if she had wanted to.

Jerry Ceppos, dean of journalism at LSU gave journalists the following advice, "I know some members say the groups are 'leaderless.' But I have trouble believing this is an entirely organic movement that grew without a leader. I'd push hard to see if there are leaders and to profile them."[21] Reporters took his advice. Some went the easy route of assuming that Kalle Lasn of Adbusters was "The Brains Behind 'Occupy Wall Street,'"[22] although his only contribution was a ballerina poster, while others took the time to identify some OWS organizers and arbitrarily imbue their efforts with hierarchical qualities. Neal Ungerleider of *Fast Company* took the latter route in "The Stealth Leaders of Occupy Wall Street," where he made the head-scratching argument that the New York City General Assembly (NYCGA) was a discrete group of organizers that were pulling the strings of the protest behind the scenes. Anyone with even the slightest knowledge of the movement would realize that there were different people at every General Assembly (GA), and many of the most dedicated organizers rarely had the time or energy to attend even in early October. Bill O'Reilly, like many other Fox News commentators, took the laziest, least informed route of arguing that, "This isn't a spontaneous demonstration against crony capitalism. If it were, they would be in front of the White House. This is organized by the unions, backed up by George

Soros and the MoveOn people…"[23]

A lot of the confusion had to do with the semantics of the word 'leader.' A 'basic' definition of the term would refer to someone who takes an especially active role in a project. Based on that definition we had many leaders; hence 'leaderful.' A more 'mainstream' definition might describe someone who takes active participation based on some recognized official role in a hierarchical chain of command. Based on that definition we were 'leaderless.' Some conservative journalists would collapse the two definitions onto each other and use the accuracy of one definition to demonstrate the supposed applicability of the other. They would argue that since we clearly had some people who were more active than others, we had leaders (use of the 'basic' definition); and since it can be demonstrated that we had leaders, we therefore had hierarchy since leaders are emblematic of hierarchy (subtle insertion of the 'mainstream' definition). This subterranean rationale was apparent in stories like the *National Post*'s "Occupy Wall Street plagued by the hierarchy it seeks to destroy" which argued that we had "so-called 'facilitators' pretending they are not self-appointed leaders just so the movement can proclaim itself leaderless."[24] Anyone who has witnessed the excruciating and thankless task of facilitating a large Occupy meeting would understand how senseless it is to argue that the movement acts upon the whims of its facilitators.

There was an unquestioned assumption that leaders, in the hierarchical sense, are essential to political action. In early October, CNN anchor Carol Costello asked Georgetown professor Michael Kazin, "If someone, like a strong leader, would become the voice of this movement, uhh, I guess I'll ask it this way: who would that strong voice be who could focus these protesters and turn it into a real, powerful movement?"[25] The first thing to note is the conflation between hierarchy, the "real," and the "powerful."[26] In a world of hierarchical power, hierarchy, power and reality are constructed as naturally inseparable. Beyond that, however, one can observe the shift in tense halfway through her question. While part of the issue is that she struggled to find the phrasing that she was looking for, at a subconscious level it is telling that she started to ask the question from the perspective that the emergence of a "strong leader" was a hypothetical possibility, and then shifted to a phrasing that asked not "if" a leader would emerge but who it would be.

Movements can only be taken seriously once they become mirrors in which the elite can recognize themselves. The *mimicry of the elite* is an assimilatory standard that makes dissent less threatening by narrowing the differences between resistance and acquiescence, but it's also more than that. Like the "supposed universal validity" of "moral categories" a century earlier, *mimicry of the elite* presents itself as an independent, universal standard of conduct based on 'common sense' rather than a set of values emanating from a specific source of authority. That way, the elite are presented as the most talented players of the game rather than the ones who arbitrarily re-write the rules to solidify their positions of power. Like the journalistic discourse of 'objectivity' and capitalist arguments about consumer preferences, this political standard taps into the Western tradition of universal philosophical abstraction to erase tangible, contextual power dynamics.

Communication with the Elite

Another byproduct of our lack of formal leadership was that elites felt like they couldn't communicate with us. It was not uncommon for some prominent official to want to have a backdoor meeting with the 'real' leaders of OWS. Instead we would tell them to come address the General Assembly like everyone else, but they shied away from such public, unscripted meetings. Not only are dissident groups expected to comport themselves in the 'orderly' hierarchical fashion of the elite, they are also expected to communicate with them in the proper manner through the proper channels. Once your message has been suitably conveyed, it is judged on its merits, in abstraction, as an idea under consideration rather than as an expression of power. Here, I will focus on two specific aspects of our *communication with the elite*: demands and elections.

When *Adbusters* put out the famous poster of the ballerina balancing on the Wall Street Bull in front of masses of black-clad, gas mask-wearing rioters launching the call for "#OCCUPY-WALLSTREET" in July 2011, the top of the poster asked "What is our one demand?" Already, before the organizing had even started, the movement was saddled with the question of having a single overarching demand. But the confusion around demands wasn't primarily about the *Adbusters* question because many who critiqued us for our lack of demands didn't even know about the *Adbusters* poster. Rather, this consternation was the product of the central role that demands play in the process of *communication with the elite* within the dominant political culture. In Chapter 2, I'll explore the reasons why OWS never settled on a short official set of demands, but, for now, the focus will be on why that decision caused such distress for the media.

"Thus comes the greatest critique of the movement: It has no demands. Even if the power elites wanted to yield to the protesters, what would they do?"[27] If the goal is to communicate a certain request to the elite for their consideration, then this is the question to ask. After all, what can you expect them to do if they don't know what you want? So, did we ever collectively describe what we wanted? Not exactly, but there was the "Declaration of the Occupation of New York City" created by those who happened to attend the General Assembly on September 29, 2011, which listed many of our collective grievances such as: illegal foreclosures, workplace discrimination, a poisoned food supply, a lack of privacy, the torture of animals, attacks on workers' rights, student debt, corporate personhood, a lack of press freedom, the manufacture of weapons of mass destruction, and colonialism.[28] Implicit in each grievance was a corresponding demand, so was this sufficient? No, it wasn't because embedded within the media demand for 'demands' were the criteria that they be few in number (there were 23 bullet points in the Declaration and countless other issues that emerged from the park) and that they seek to adjust the existing state of affairs as little as possible. The underlying assumption that dominates the etiquette of *communication with the elite* is that there is only a small realm of political tinkering that has not yet been completely mastered after the *End of History*[29] and the triumph of neo-liberal capitalism. If a set of demands or grievances does not confine itself to that discrete sphere of acceptable dissent, it is rendered unintelligible in the media and invalidated entirely. Journalists would often list a dozen demands they encountered at Liberty Square, but they wouldn't usually describe OWS as having 'many demands,' they would describe it as having 'no demands.' If a group's *communication with the elite* is not articulated in the proper form, it is rendered invisible. To be 'realistic,' we are told, is not to 'demand the impossible,' but to limit our critique to a couple items, thereby tacitly acknowledging that there really aren't that many issues to address, and orient our demands around what already exists as much as possible. We should literally sculpt our vision of a better world into a replica of the one we're living in. The subtext of this *communication with the elite* is that although the immediate message from the 'proper' dissident is a complaint, the fact that it focuses on such a minor grievance implicitly reaffirms the larger political system by implying that everything else is just and equitable. Protest is enveloped in tribute.

Mainstream pundits only put the question in reverse and ask why elites are not properly communicating with the people in terms of the foibles of specific candidates in the context of elections where the popular audience is a passive focus group whose only speech option is a 'yes' or a 'no.' In the tradition of the journalistic de-politicization of public discourse that Chalaby describes, political issues are reduced to the character of the candidate. It turns into the 'would you like to have a beer with this guy?' test.

In his article for *Forbes* "The 'Occupy Wall Street' Communications Gap," Ken Makovsky essentially highlights the importance of *communication with the elite,*

> One of the principles of good communications is—communicate. Be strategic and be clear. Right now, the Occupy Wall Street (OWS) movement, which is spreading throughout the US and the world has something to say to business and government, however mushy its goals and confusing its messages.[30]

It was simply incomprehensible that we wouldn't contort our behavior to meet the standard of *communication with the elite*. The assumption was that we wanted to say something to Wall Street with the hope that it would change their behavior. It never really occurred to them that perhaps our message was not directed at the bankers.

But surely we *must* have been trying to express something to the politicians, right? Arguably the main political reason for the hype around OWS in the first months was the idea that it would influence the elections. Although it was a social movement the media could only interpret it through the lens of electoral politics, which meant that the burning question was whether OWS would become the "liberal Tea Party." On October 6, 2011, liberal strategist Steve Rosenthal said "you don't have to be a genius to see that you can overlay what is going on with Occupy Wall Street to energize and mobilize a Democratic base. So from that standpoint, it has enormous potential."[31] That's why prominent Democratic politicians like Al Gore and Nancy Pelosi endorsed Occupy, and even Obama said that Occupy was "giving voice" to those upset with "how our financial system works."[32] As much as we tried to explain that there were already third parties, like the Green Party, and that we sought to operate as an external force of pressure rather than a political party, it was unfathomable that we would not conform to the standard of *communication with the elite* through electoral channels. Some reporters, it seemed, hadn't even contemplated any alternative form of change.

To resist this narrative, we often made historical references to previous American examples of extra-parliamentary resistance such as the Civil Rights Movement, Labor Movement, and Women's Movement. These precedents afforded us a small opening to argue our point, but the way that these movements have been remembered limited their rhetorical efficacy. Essentially, they are all remembered as exceptions from a distant past whose evils have been remedied, rendering the tactics that spurred them obsolete. Racism as a major social phenomenon is over, they say. 'Women' are equal, and workers can earn their way into the middle class if they try hard enough. All legitimate grievances can be communicated through legitimately democratic channels. Of course, many of the same people who attack us today would have attacked those movements in the past, but that element of continuity is lost. During my interview with Poppy Harlow of CNN for their piece looking back on the first year of the movement, I described OWS as working off of the legacy of past movements. Right as I started to make this argument she cut me off and asked in disbelief, "You think you're the same as these past movements?" I replied that we are in very different circumstances but have a number of areas of continuity.[33] For her and many others, those past movements belong to a mythologized past and have been irreversibly severed from what many radicals think of as a trans-historical struggle.

Interestingly enough, the process of mythologizing past

struggle for the purpose of de-legitimizing current organizing happened within the first months of OWS. For example, Bill Maher (who happens to be from my hometown) came out in support of OWS initially, but by June he said that it had lost its power "because the people who originally started, I think they went home, and now, I think it's these anarchist stragglers." And he also said "douchebags," "get a job."[34] In mid-November Mayor Quan of Oakland said that "the people who originally founded the encampments are either no longer there or no longer in control."[35] Bill O'Reilly made a somewhat similar comment in late October when he claimed that there had been "sincere protesters but they're long gone."[36] Occupy had become so mainstream that even O'Reilly was forced to concede that it had tapped into legitimate grievances but like Maher he mythologized the origins of OWS to discredit it.

As my research demonstrates, the vast majority of the people who organized Occupy Wall Street from August through October were still organizing into the winter. What becomes evident here, though, is how the misrepresentation of history, even on a small scale, cordons off the resistance of the past from the struggles of the present. In the present "it's time for Occupy Wall Street to actually participate in the American political process" as Maher argues, by doing "boring stuff, like canvassing neighborhoods, raising money, running candidates for office, manning phone banks, and making a baby with John Edwards."[37] Little does Maher know that we spent plenty of time doing all of those things except running candidates and procreating with John Edwards. Nevertheless, it shows that the present must be about elections, even if the past was about direct action and civil disobedience.

'Movement as Protest,' 'Protest as Election'

Yet, the election mentality transcends the ballot and the segregation of past struggles from present resistance. It produces two subtle forms of political re-valuing that make all forms of political action more like elections. They are what I refer to as *movement as protest* and *protest as election*.

Let's start with *movement as protest*. What is a protest? There are a number of different interpretations, but for my purposes I will use the term 'protest' as it is understood in society: as a petitioning of authorities wherein the sole focus of the act is its impact on its target, and if the target does not relent, that is the end of the story. Often movements engage in acts of protest, but, in this context, I consider a movement to be a network of groups and organizations that aspires toward the construction of some form of counter-power. The idea behind the concept of the movement is that if a protest or any other form of political action fails, the struggle continues. It differs drastically from the popular understanding of a protest as a discrete, individual speech act. This was clear in an article that described my role as an OWS organizer in great detail, yet still included the statement that I went to "Zuccotti Park about 50 times to support protests."[38] It portrays politics as a series of isolated actions. It's on par with saying 'I went to the beach 50 times last year.' Popular discourse puts movements into the framework of a series protests with a short shelf life rather than a continuous body of struggle.

This argument becomes a little clearer with the introduction of the second concept: *protest as election*. Coverage of protests portrays them as a collection of isolated individuals coming together to express themselves. That is why so many stories include the personal anecdotes of attendees rather than a political analysis of the strategy or tactics of the organizers behind the action. The human-interest story stands in for politics. Any voice is just as relevant as any other in explaining this event, although a similar methodology wouldn't be followed with coverage of a hierarchical body because, for the media, a protest is just a live-action opinion poll. It's a moving pie chart designed to better inform those in positions of power. The act of collective assembly is understood in a liberal framework, in a Habermasian public sphere where the free market of ideas allows any sort of opinion

Police raid Liberty Square in the early morning hours of Nov. 15, 2011. Photo by Minister Erik McGregor.

The Liberty encampment reduced to rubble. Photo by Minister Erik McGregor.

to be expressed and adopted without reference to power. This was apparent when Mayor Michael Bloomberg reversed his initial position that we could continue our movement because New York was the "most tolerant, open city in the world,"[39] and argued after the eviction that OWS would "have to occupy the space with the power of their arguments."[40]

Bloomberg's comment embodies the ethos of an atomized liberalism that considers abstract ideas to be the source of political change. On May Day 2012 Bloomberg made his distaste for protest politics explicit when he said, "if you want to change things I'm not sure why protesting does things [sic]. Go and try to do something and make it better."[41]

A movement becomes a protest because power is taken out of the equation. A protest becomes an election because it is only comprehended as an upward looking appeal to the elite and is only interpreted as an assemblage of a body of public opinion in favor of a position (understood as a stand-in for a candidate). As an election, a protest is considered a short-term public referendum to be decided solely based on the number of bodies in your camp. Elites will act on your protest if they agree and you have made a well-reasoned argument, and they will decline if they disagree. The dynamic of *protest as election* was unmistakable in the commentary of liberal supporters who attempted to defend Occupy from the accusation that it lacked clear messaging by agreeing that the message was muddled but that "it's the job of the politicians actually to formulate a clear policy."[42] In one of the earliest prominent liberal commentaries, Paul Krugman defended the supposedly confusing nature of OWS by claiming that, "it's really the job of policy intellectuals and politicians to fill in the details."[43] It's a way for sympathetic liberals to surgically remove what they like from Occupy as they discard the rest. As I described in an article on Krugman's anti-democratic liberalism,

For Krugman, we aren't a social movement as much as an

> exceptionally raucous and colorful bloc of public opinion; a parade of concerned citizens fated to remain spectators to loci of power. From this perspective, the only acceptable role for extra-parliamentary collective action is to serve as nerve endings in a body whose brain is composed of "policy intellectuals," like Krugman, "and politicians."[44]

Once the timetable has expired, your protest/election is over and the results are to be tallied. If you lose, that's just 'democracy' since the majority wasn't with you. Sorry! Better luck next time. Once the 'election' is over, it's over. If you persist, you are portrayed as a loser who needs to 'get a life.' That's why commentators have gauged the success of OWS almost exclusively based on crowd size (with each demonstrator representing a vote in the abstract public sphere), and why they were quick to pronounce the movement a failure because the window for social change, like an election cycle, has a definitive point of termination.

The urgency of the journalists to come to a conclusion on Occupy Wall Street was indicative of the pervasive nature of the *protest as election*. As early as September 29, 2011, the subtitle of an article from the *Los Angeles Times* read "almost two weeks into an anti-greed sit-in, the 'leaderless resistance movement' is at a crossroads."[45] On October 3, the subtitle for a CNN video read, "despite growing media attention, the Wall Street protests haven't sparked any changes."[46]

This hyper-accelerated timetable condensed our window of coverage and played an important role in the quality of coverage we received. These journalists were on very tight deadlines and often worked on several assignments at once. Day after day as I sat in Liberty in the fall of 2011, I would see a news van pull up along the south side of the park. The reporter and cameraman would get out, track down a couple of people for some sound bites in accord with their pre-arranged story angle, and then leave. If the first person they spoke with didn't say what they wanted to hear, they'd move onto someone else. Frequently I could tell that they wanted to wrap up their coverage by lunch and had no interest in delving deeper to find out what was actually going on that day. One of the main motivations for organizing the Press Working Group was to facilitate the process of finding diverse, articulate people to speak with journalists to counteract the overwhelming tendency of the media to film the most countercultural, least informed person possible. By the second week in October, we had extensive lists of people of all professions, backgrounds, and experiences ready to feed to journalists. One morning in October, a reporter from WPIX Channel 11 in New York came over and said he needed a teacher, a student and an unemployed person by 11:30 AM. Go! Reporters came to rely so thoroughly on our Press table along the north wall of the park next to the Peoples' Library that when there was no one there for a moment they would freak out.

I remember speaking to one reporter after the other and marveling at how novel they thought Occupy was. For most organizers with some experience, it was simply an inflated version of tactics, strategies and actions that we had practiced for years, but the media presented it as some sort of alien artifact discovered in a crater without any known precedents. At the time many of us realized that, ironically, this lack of general information about the greater context of struggle in the country greatly helped our momentum by presenting us as a fascinating new phenomenon to behold. If, instead, a more knowledgeable public had looked at us and said 'oh, they're reliving the global justice movement in a park,' then that's all we would have been doing. Yet, later on it occurred to me that the real irony of the situation was that even if reporters were well informed about the context from which OWS emerged, and maybe some were more than they let on, it was in their interests to present it as the hot new trend to enhance their ratings. During the peak of the media frenzy, there was a brief window of time when it was actually mutually beneficial for Occupy to be considered new and exciting. Context would have been counterproductive.

The desire to present the newest news possible, and make that new news seem as new as possible, is not new. In fact, the "fetishism of the present," whose corollary is the uprooting of historical context, dates back to technological developments in printing and communication in the second half of the 19th century.[47] However, this tendency has been greatly accelerated by social media and the 24-hour cable news cycle. While in past decades most news stories came with expiration dates in terms of reader interest, today social media and cable news stimulate the fervor of a news item at its peak while hastening its expiration date. They condense coverage into a shorter, more intense timeframe. It was an instance when the market pressure of novelty and the political standard of the *protest as election* converged to set the movement on a lightning-fast pace, which proved to be a blessing and a curse.

* * *

As much as the media tried to squeeze us into the conceptual boxes at their disposal, Occupy Wall Street would not follow the rules of the *mimicry of the elite* and *communication with the elite*. The movement wouldn't appoint leaders, organize a short 'pragmatic' set of demands, or engage in elections. To liberal sympathizers, this was merely a product of youthful exuberance and idealism. Liberal and conservative pundits looked at the countercultural element of the movement as a source of nostalgia or idiocy, but neither took the cultural element seriously. For those who took our language seriously and were astute enough to recognize the fact that we were intentionally operating outside of the rules of political engagement, it was clear that something was amiss.

Stephen Moore of the *Wall Street Journal* pointed out that "the message is kind of contradictory. On the one hand they say 'down with Wall Street, down with businesses, down with profit, down with corporations.' Well, where do they think jobs come from?"[48] And he's right. Within a capitalist economy, jobs are generally created by sources of capital. To oppose profit and want jobs one must be advocating another form of economic organization. How could OWS be serious about working toward a world where everyone has enough food, shelter, education, and healthcare? Where would the money come from for that? "If you reject the mixed capitalist economy and representative democracy, how do you fit within a political coalition broadly aligned with the Democratic Party, even its left flank?"[49]

The pieces didn't quite fit in the Occupy puzzle, but the media couldn't understand why. So what is it that we weren't telling them? What did Occupy Wall Street want?

Chapter Two

"The Bane of Occupy Wall Street": Anarchism and the Anarchistic[1]

"There is no one demand. That's ridiculous. Unless that one demand was so incredibly radical like 'smash capitalism and the state at the same time.' That would be the one demand."
—Madeline Nelson, anarchist OWS organizer[2]

The destruction of capitalism and the construction of a classless, environmentally sustainable, democratic economy characterized by mutual aid and solidarity that prioritizes the fulfillment of human need. The development of forms of participatory and direct democracy grounded in local communities, groups, and bodies that empower individuals and collectivities. The elimination of all hierarchical social relations, whether founded in concepts of sexuality, race, gender, or any other.

That is what Occupy Wall Street wanted (and much of what anarchists want too).

Or at least that is what the vast majority of OWS organizers envisioned as the ultimate goal of their political struggle.

Not the Volker Rule. Not a Robin Hood tax. Not the Glass-Steagall Act. Not ending corporate personhood. Not an increased capital gains tax. Not repealing Citizens United. And certainly not re-electing Obama.

Some saw those reforms as steps in the process, but for most they were never the final targets. That is why the mainstream media, both liberal and conservative, could never really understand what we were doing. If we had been content with adjusting taxes for millionaires by 2% we would have gone about things completely differently, the way the media expected, but we didn't want a bigger slice of the pie, we were after the entire bakery. As Justine Tunney (27), self-described "tranarchist" and founder of the main OWS website (occupywallst.org) phrased it, "I believe that the hetero-normative, cis-normative, patriarchal, state-capitalist establishment is evil and must be destroyed."[3]

I am not, however, speaking about most of the supporters of the movement who attended an occasional General Assembly or marched with us. They were overwhelmingly liberal, and generally considered goals such as "getting money out of politics" to be their endgames. As I will discuss in more detail in Chapter 3, OWS succeeded because it managed to attract a thick outer layer of liberals and progressives around an inner core that was predominantly anarchist in character (anti-capitalist, anti-hierarchical, direct action oriented).[4] Without either element, Occupy Wall Street wouldn't have succeeded. Much of the media confusion stemmed from their unconscious tendency to think in terms of two concepts explored in Chapter 1: *movement as protest* and *protest as election*. Essentially, they reduced the organized element of the movement to a diffuse conglomeration of individuals grouped into a protest, and then saw the message and direction of OWS as the sum total of the opinions of all the bodies in Liberty Square (as if it were an election and each body was 'voting' for its political outlook). This outlook was part of why they glossed over the distinction between organizers and participants and Occupy's liberal outer shell and overwhelmingly anarchist core. Another was that we didn't tell them about it.

Given the democratic nature of OWS, and my relationships with fellow organizers, I knew that there was a very strong anarchist tendency among the people who made Occupy happen, but I wanted to investigate exactly how widespread it was. Therefore, between December 2011 and February 2013, I conducted interviews with 192 of the main organizers of Occupy Wall Street in New York. The interviews showed that 39% of OWS organizers self-identified as anarchists. As the remainder of this chapter will demonstrate, self-identifying as an anarchist can mean a variety of things, but it is indicative of a general current running through the movement in New York. That percentage was much higher than I expected, but I didn't think that erecting a stale binary between anarchists and non-anarchists really captured the pervasive nature of anarchist ideas within Occupy. As I analyzed the other 61% of interviews conducted with those who didn't label themselves anarchists, I came to see that anarchism had saturated the political atmosphere of OWS to a much wider degree than that 39% indicated. I noticed that 30% of organizers who did not self-identify as anarchists (34% of all organizers didn't identify with any overarching label) listed anarchism as an influential element in their overall thought. Examples included Ravi Ahmad (34), an organizer with the Tech Ops, Housing, and Outreach Working Groups who was often seen casually knitting during large meetings. Years ago, she

OWS medic tent, Nov. 12, 2011. Note the sign for the "Red and Black Cross" (colors of anarchism) and the anti-capitalist signs next to it. Photo by David Shankbone.

worked with the student front of the Communist Party of India where she occasionally upset the party hierarchy because she was "a Marxist with an anarchist streak."[5] Similarly, Rose Bookbinder (28), an organizer with the United Auto Workers, said that there were "parts of communism, socialism, and anarchism that I pull from."[6]

I also noticed that even those who strongly disagreed with anarchism often talked about it in contrast with their ideas, showing that it was nearly impossible to describe one's politics in terms of the movement without situating them in relation to anarchism. Despite media expectations, only three organizers described themselves as "progressive," and two described themselves as "liberal." I would argue that there were more organizers with progressive and liberal politics than those figures indicate, but the radical political climate made reformists more likely to not identify with a specific ideology, or self-identify as some sort of socialist. For example Karanja Wa Gaçuça (39), a former Wall Street analyst from Kenya who was laid off right as OWS started, said that before getting involved with the Press WG he identified as a liberal but he "found out that 'liberal' is a dirty word" so now he identifies as a socialist.[7] Overall, 7% of organizers identified as some sort of "socialist" and 9% identified as "left" or "radical." Perhaps the most creative political answer I heard was from Dennis Flores (36), a cop-watch organizer from Brooklyn involved in Occupy Sunset Park, who described his politics as "fuck the police."[8]

More importantly, though, I found that another 33% of all organizers had politics that were largely indistinguishable from most anarchists (although they used a different label or avoided one altogether): they were anti-capitalists in favor of direct democracy and opposed to hierarchy who considered direct action, rather than elections, to be the most effective route toward social change, but chose not to use the anarchist label. For the purposes of this book, I join Richard J. F. Day,[9] Cindy Milstein[10] and others in referring to these organizers as having 'anarchistic' politics, meaning that their politics were similar to anarchism (within the anarchist orbit, one might say) though they did not actively identify with anarchism. The degree to which the perspectives of a given 'anarchistic' organizer aligned with those of anarchism varied. While most were basically anarchists, others retained traces of non-anarchist perspectives alongside a more broadly anti-authoritarian outlook. So the category of the 'anarchistic' was not homogeneous or always an exact synonym for anarchism, but the outlooks of these organizers were closer to anarchism than other political orientations. In total, 72% of organizers had politics largely consistent with anarchism whether they were explicitly anarchist or implicitly anarchistic.

Here I would like to address two potential objections to my use of the label 'anarchistic.' First, it may be argued that a more general term, such as 'libertarian socialist,'[11] might be a more accurate umbrella term for those who didn't identify as anarchists since a number of organizers came to their positions through traditions distinct from anarchism. Certainly it would be misleading to argue that all anti-capitalist or directly democratic political outlooks are anarchist in orientation, especially since 10 organizers self-identified as some form of Marxist.[12] Yet, although anarchism certainly played a more significant role than any other discernible tendency in radicalizing OWS (many fewer spoke of anti-authoritarian Marxist theories, for example), my point is not that all of those under the umbrella of 'anarchistic' came to their perspective through anarchism, but rather that the politics they had developed were in many crucial ways exceedingly similar to those of anarchism. Therefore, it wouldn't be inaccurate to use a term like 'libertarian socialist' instead, but in the context of discussing anarchism and Occupy I am emphasizing the similarities that these people's politics have to anarchism specifically.

Another potential objection to the use of the term 'anarchistic' might be that if many of the people that fall into this category are opposed to labeling their politics, then why would I? Might it not be better to analyze the constituent features of their perspectives on their own and take them for what they are? One of my motivations for using the term 'anarchistic' is to demonstrate how the core ideas of anarchism have not only spread beyond a self-conscious identification with the ideology, but have often done so as a unit. For example, I found that 78% of all organizers were anti-capitalist and 82% were in favor of non-hierarchical direct democracy rather than representative government. This shows that only about 6% of organizers were anti-capitalist without being in favor of direct democracy, and only about 10% were in favor of direct democracy without being anti-capitalist. That means that regardless of the label, the rejection of the economic hierarchy of capitalism and the political hierarchy of representative government usually went hand in hand. My goal is not to plant the red and black flag where it doesn't belong, but rather to transcend description and actually analyze this process of political diffusion. In so doing, I have chosen to utilize the term 'anarchistic' as a conceptual term that emphasizes the proximity of many organizers to the ideas of anarchism although they may have eschewed labels of any kind. While my intent is not to engage in representation, "it is impossible to do analysis without imposition,"[13] and just because you don't label yourself doesn't mean that a given label doesn't necessarily describe you to some extent.

As with many other political ideas in different contexts, it is clear that anarchist ideas have exerted an influence within OWS that transcends those who actively identified with the label. Ideas, whether political, religious, or cultural, are usually not digested whole. More often, they are selectively adapted to pre-existing perspectives and values and certain elements are adopted and others discarded. As historian Antonio López Estudillo said of the first years of anarchism in Spain, "affirmation of anarchist ideas was very slow and always partial."[14] Therefore, if we want to talk about the influence of anarchism we cannot limit ourselves only to those who consciously place themselves within the circle-A box or even those whose ideas fall entirely within the classical anarchist tradition, but, to start out, we should have a decent idea of what that canonical tradition has been.

Anarchism: A (Trans)Historical Phenomenon

What is anarchism? What has anarchism been historically? My goal here is to try to address elements of continuity in the anarchist tradition over time while maintaining the fact that its parameters have continually shifted based on its context.

Thus far, I have described anarchism as a revolutionary,[15] non-hierarchical, direct action-oriented, form of socialism. Many descriptions of anarchism start with the origins of the word 'anarchy' from the Greek *αναρχία*, which literally means "without a leader."[16] For anarchists as well as Occupy Wall Street, 'leaderless' really implies that that everyone can lead (since the distinction between leaders and led has ended). At its foundation, anarchism is a rejection of all forms of hierarchy. As Luke Richardson (26), an anarchist organizer who spent much of his time working on media and the OWS radio show on WBAI, put it, "I look at most of the problems in the world as stemming from domination."[17] Instead of bonds of domination and hierarchy, anarchists strive to forge relationships based on solidarity, mutual aid, and free association. Although anarchists disagree about a variety of issues, they share a common vision of a world characterized by voluntary association free from the authoritarian coercion of the state.

Anarchists envision a society that promotes community and collective social participation without infringing upon the autonomy of the individual. As the influential Russian anarchist

Pyotr Kropotkin (1842-1921) wrote, it is "a synthesis of the two chief aims pursued by humanity since the dawn of its history—economic freedom and political freedom."[18] It could also be described as the doctrine that best combines what liberal political theorist Isaiah Berlin referred to as positive liberty (freedom to participate) and negative liberty (freedom to be left alone) in his influential "Two Concepts of Liberty." Anarchists consider classical liberal conceptions of political participation and individual autonomy to be empty as long as capitalism and the state persist, and they consider hierarchical, Soviet-style systems to be oppressive and inimical to the values of personal and collective autonomy. As the prominent Russian anarchist Mikhail Bakunin (1814-1876), "the demon of revolt,"[19] wrote, "freedom without socialism is privilege and injustice ... socialism without freedom is slavery and brutality."[20]

Born into a large, upper class Russian family, Bakunin nevertheless became an ardent, life-long revolutionary. After years of agitation against the Russian, Austro-Hungarian, and Prussian Empires, he was imprisoned and then exiled to Siberia. In 1861 he escaped, toothless from scurvy, and returned to revolutionary activity.[21] In the 1860s, he melded Pierre-Joseph Proudhon's (1809-1865) antipathy toward centralized authority with elements of Marx's critique of capitalism to help lay the foundation of the anarchist doctrine.[22] The distinct character of anarchism, as opposed to the other schools of socialism, made itself evident during the conflict between the followers of Bakunin and Karl Marx at the Hague Congress of the International Workingmen's Association (IWMA, often called the First International) in 1872 over the nature of hierarchy. Essentially Marx and his followers argued that internal hierarchy, in the form of a political party, was a necessary vehicle of struggle, and that during the revolution it was necessary to seize the hierarchical state apparatus and wield it against the capitalists, in the form of the 'dictatorship of the proletariat,' until they had been subdued and the state could 'wither away' to organically pave the way for the ultimate goal of a non-hierarchical communist society. Bakunin and his followers argued that the means of struggle had to reflect their political ends.

This perspective was echoed in the words of Amin Husain (36) who was part of the resistance to Israeli occupation in Palestine from the ages of 13-17. After quitting his job in corporate property financing and property law to join OWS full time,[23] he co-edited the theory journal *Tidal*, and was a tireless organizer with Facilitation, Direct Action (DA), Plus Brigades,[24] and other groups. An advocate of direct democracy and direct action who considered capitalism to be "racist and patriarchal," Amin made the classical anarchist argument that "movements that fight toward something, even when they win, tend to reproduce themselves."[25] If a hierarchical movement wins, it will inevitably recreate hierarchy. Like Amin, anarchists have argued that the vehicle of revolutionary struggle has to be non-hierarchical, and that the hierarchical structure of the state could never be utilized to create a non-hierarchical, stateless society. Bakunin argued that,

> No dictatorship can have any other aim but that of self-perpetuation, and it can beget only slavery in the people tolerating it; freedom can be created only by freedom, that is, by a universal rebellion on the part of the people and free organization of the toiling masses from the bottom up.[26]

Anarchists reject the proposition that economic or political liberty can exist in isolation. From the 19th into the 20th centuries anarchism spread widely across Europe (especially southern Europe) and the Americas and developed groups in North Africa, the Middle East, and East Asia. Anarchists played prominent roles in the labor movement, they promoted 'rational education' in contexts of high illiteracy,[27] they organized against war and militarism, and they challenged the institution of marriage and promoted 'free love.'[28] The initial wave of anarchist organizing in the 1870s and 1880s provoked harsh state repression and eliminated the option of mass-based, popular mobilization in some countries.[29] This repression, and the challenges of mass organizing, influenced the development of "propaganda by the deed"[30] which became fodder for the reactionary media to portray anarchists as "monsters in human form."[31]

By the turn of the 20th century, the prestige of "propaganda by the deed" had waned within anarchist circles and anarcho-syndicalism,[32] or revolutionary syndicalism (largely the same thing without the anarchist label), took off. Syndicalism came to distinguish itself by its strategy of industrial unionism, an organizing model that unites all workers within an industry regardless of skill into the same union, and its focus on the general strike as a revolutionary weapon. OWS organizer and anarcho-syndicalist Yoni Miller (18) explained that,

> Anarcho-syndicalism recognizes the transformative and empowering nature of direct action, but also that change requires massive participation of democratically organized movements, fighting illegitimate systems, and exemplifying through their organizational practice, what an alternative society looks like.[33]

As Yoni said, the anarcho-syndicalist union was designed to be a tool for everyday struggle as well as a foundation for the future society. The union was to 'build a new world in the shell of the old.' This model of struggle became quite popular. Marxist historian Eric Hobsbawm wrote, "between 1905 and 1914 the typical revolutionary in the West was likely to be some kind of revolutionary syndicalist who, paradoxically, rejected Marxism as the ideology of parties which used it as an excuse for not trying to make revolution."[34] Although some writers portray anarcho-syndicalism as an entirely new development in anarchist praxis, anarchists had practiced a similar kind of Bakuninist, broad-based, militant unionism in the 1870s.

In the early 20th century, anarcho-syndicalist and revolutionary syndicalist unions came to represent the most dynamic element in the international labor movement.[35] Traditionally, many historians of anarchism have ignored the anarchist inclination of syndicalism and have skipped from Kropotkin to the Spanish Revolution without recognizing just how massive syndicalism became. For example, in France, the *Confédération generale du travail* (CGT) laid the groundwork for revolutionary syndicalism with its anti-electoral 1906 Charter of Amiens and had a membership exceeding 800,000 in 1914. Meanwhile, in Portugal anarchists organized their own CGT, which had 90,000 members by 1922. In Italy, the *Unione Sindacale Italiana* (USI) had 800,000 members in 1920, and in Germany the *Freie Arbeiter Union Deutschlands* (FAUD) had 120,000 in 1922.

Across the Atlantic, in Latin America, the *Federación Obrera Regional Argentina* (FORA) split into two: the FORA-V, which was explicitly anarchist-communist, had 200,000 members by 1922 while the FORA-IX, which was not explicitly anarchist, had 70,000 members. In Mexico the COM/FORM federation had 150,000 members in 1916 and the Mexican CGT had 80,000 members in 1928-9, Paraguay had the anarcho-syndicalist *Federación Obrera Regional Paraguaya* (FORP), in Peru anarchists formed the *Federación Obrera Regional del Perú* (FORPe), and in Bolivia there was the anarcho-syndicalist *Federación Obrera Local* (FOL). Moreover, "anarchism became the most popular ideology of the Cuban labor movement,"[36] where the *Confederación Nacional Obrera de Cuba* (CNOC) had 200,000 members in 1925.

Across the Pacific, Chinese anarchists organized approximately 40 unions near Canton, and in Japan the anarcho-syndicalist *Zenkoku Jiren* had 15,000 members in 1926. In the United

States, the Industrial Workers of the World (IWW), the first interracial labor union to include both skilled and unskilled workers, had 100,000 members by 1917. There were also IWW branches in the UK, Canada, Australia, South Africa, Mexico, and Chile (which had 25,000 members in the early 20s). Long before OWS, the IWW coined the slogan "we are all leaders."[37] Whether they flew the red and black flag of anarchism or not, all of these unions, representing millions of people around the world, were committed to the principles of democratic, anti-capitalist workers' self-management, internationalism, anti-militarism, equality, and direct action rather than parliamentary politics.

The most important anarcho-syndicalist union historically was the Spanish *Confederación Nacional del Trabajo* (CNT), which reached a membership of more than a million during the Spanish Civil War and participated in the democratic collectivization of most of the industry and agriculture in eastern Spain from 1936-1939. The Spanish Revolution was certainly the most successful example of non-hierarchical socialism in practice. Thousands of workplaces were democratically collectivized and self-managed in federations with workers in other industries to coordinate production and consumption. Healthcare facilities were run by doctors and nurses, schools were run by teachers, telephone companies were run by telephone workers, and on and on. As George Orwell described in *Homage to Catalonia*, "It was the first time that I had ever been in a town where the working class was in the saddle. Practically every building of any size had been seized by the workers and was draped with red flags or with the red and black flag of the Anarchists..."[38] Noam Chomsky wrote, "production continued effectively; workers in farms and factories proved quite capable of managing their affairs without coercion from above..."[39] Ultimately, the Spanish Revolution was destroyed by Stalinist and fascist attacks as George Orwell personally observed. On their own, the workers' collectives were doing quite well considering the obstacles of the civil war. Their legacy played a crucial role in my own decision to adopt anarchism.

Prior to the Russian Revolution of 1917, and even after in many places such as Spain, the main current of global revolutionary politics was anarchism, whether explicitly or implicitly. Actually, Lenin's success in appealing to the Russian workers and peasants owed a great deal to the fact that he cloaked his authoritarian Marxist politics in anarchist clothing. Lenin and the Bolsheviks claimed that the peasants should directly control their land and the workers should directly control their factories. The slogan "All Power to the Soviets" was interpreted as a libertarian revolutionary slogan of federated, yet autonomous, local control. Many anarchists even considered Bolshevism to be a kind of Bakuninized Marxism.[40] However, after the Bolsheviks eliminated worker self-management by bringing back many pre-revolutionary managers, destroyed the Nabat Ukrainian anarchist federation and Nestor Makhno's anarchist army, and attacked the anti-authoritarian Kronstadt sailors in 1921, the libertarian promise of the revolution had vanished.

Following the Russian Revolution, non-hierarchical revolutionary socialism gradually started to decline in the face of the Bolshevik triumph. Yet, there were significant episodes of anarchist action before World War II such as the Spanish Revolution and the creation of a vast autonomous zone in the Shinmin province of Manchuria in 1929 by the Korean Anarchist Communist Federation (KACF). Within this zone, democratic councils were created for workers and peasants to self-manage the economy before Japanese forces defeated them in 1931.[41] In the 60s and 70s, though, there was a revival of anti-authoritarian politics. The Situationist International and May 1968 in France, the Italian and German autonomous movements of the 70s and 80s,[42] and the Provos of Amsterdam[43] are just a few examples. In southern Mexico Zapatista[44] and Magonista[45] indigenous groups have melded traditional forms of organization and anarchist practice to carve out autonomous zones free from state control since the 1990s. By the end of the 20th century, the flaws of authoritarian, statist forms of socialism had been exposed setting the stage for a new era of anarchist ascendency of which Occupy Wall Street has been the most prominent American example since the global justice movement (aka anti-globalization or alter-globalization movement) and the 'Battle of Seattle.'

However, it's important to note how anarchism has changed over the past century with the emergence of the distinction, elaborated by anarchist anthropologist and OWS organizer David Graeber among others, between a new "small-a" anarchism as opposed to classical "capital-A anarchism." As it is commonly understood, the difference between the two is that "capital-A" anarchists are more sectarian, they identify more strongly with class struggle politics, and they advocate larger-scale federal organizations operated by majority voting oriented around anarcho-syndicalist and anarcho-communist outlooks; while "small-a" anarchists organize decentralized networks run by consensus, place a greater emphasis on lifestyle choices and non-class politics like environmentalism, and have a stronger connection to counter-culture. Writing in 2002, Graeber considered the "small-a" anarchists to be "the real locus of historical dynamism right now."[46] And I think he was correct insofar as the "small-a" anarchism of black blocs, info-shops, and direct action networks was broadening the horizon of the movement and spurring a historic surge of anti-authoritarian politics. Yet, anarchist writer Uri Gordon is right to point out that the distinction between the two is often overstated since the "capital-A" movement is still quite large, with anarcho-communist organizations across the world and anarcho-syndicalist unions with thousands of members, and sectarianism can be found on both sides of the divide.[47] Also, many "capital-A" anarchists actually have fabulous politics around non-class oppression and some CNT unions in Madrid, for example, operate by consensus though the larger bodies use majority voting.

Historically, though, the divide has always existed in one form or another despite growing over the past decades. As long as there have been anarchists, they have come in a variety of shapes and sizes. Even in the 19th century there were anarchists into vegetarianism, abstaining from alcohol, free love, nudism, and other 'counter-cultural' pursuits who often tended to create agricultural communes and push for a 'withdrawal strategy,' and some of them belonged to "capital-A" organizations at the same time. Debates raged between advocates of large federations of workers groups and unions and others who argued that anarchists should focus on forming small collectives with only loose organizational ties. Many of the main dividing lines have existed for more than a century. The only reason that "capital-A" anarchism is thought of as a "dinosaur"[48] in comparison to a supposedly brand new "small-a" anarchism is that "capital-A" anarchism had so much more success and popular support, becoming the globally dominant revolutionary ideology before WWI, that it overshadowed the "small-a" anarchists of the 19th century and retrospectively came to be considered the only anarchism until the rebirth of its modern "small-a" variant.

I've known plenty of people with one foot in each camp and I've often felt like my anarchism was a little small for the "capital-A" crowd and a little big for the "small-a" crowd so I guess maybe I'm a "medium-a" anarchist insofar as I try to take the best from both sides of the divide. Nevertheless, the vast majority of the anarchists of OWS in New York could be easily categorized as "small-a" anarchists. When I asked them how they had originally gotten into anarchism, common answers included punk rock, living in collective houses, or involvement in groups like Food Not Bombs, but very few mentioned any of the "capital-A" groups.

Part of my argument in this book is that in order for American anarchism to continue its recent growth and make serious inroads in the struggles of the oppressed it needs to get bigger organizationally. We'll only really be able to spread anti-authoritarian ideas by getting more people involved.

The history of anarcho-syndicalism, specifically, points to the complexity of this issue. Historically, a large percentage, if not a majority, of the members of anarcho-syndicalist unions weren't ideologically committed to the entirety, or even necessarily the majority, of anarchist doctrine. Many people joined the CNT in Spain, for example, because they were the main union in their trade, or because they were the most successful union at winning pay raises or improved working conditions. This might cause some to dismiss the prominence of anarchist ideology in this period, but to me it shows that most people don't develop their politics through the communication of ideas in abstraction; they develop them in the context of struggle. That's why we need large outward-facing anarchist formations (whether explicitly or implicitly) that engage the broader society in forms of resistance. This is a theme that I will return to throughout the book, but it's worth emphasizing here that members of these unions formed their anti-authoritarian, anti-capitalist outlooks through their participation in struggles for their individual and collective betterment, and this process of ideological diffusion was often partial and intertwined with other religious, cultural and political influences. The vibrant history of anarcho-syndicalism shows that one of the best ways to get someone to think like an anarchist, at least in part, is to get them involved in movements, organizations, and situations where the pursuit of their interests has them acting like an anarchist. This is what Occupy Wall Street did.

Before moving on, I should address the fact that I didn't discuss tendencies associated with anarchism such as individualism,[49] mutualism,[50] or primitivism.[51] I think that they should be considered either (a) peripheral tendencies within a more broadly communal, anti-capitalist, ideology that maintains a nuanced perspective on the pros and cons of various forms of technology, or (b) beyond the parameters of anarchism. I don't think it's terribly important which of the two you prefer, though I advocate the latter. To me, anarchism is inherently communal and anti-capitalist, so I would exclude absolute individualism entirely and consider mutualism to be proto-anarchist. It is important, though, to recognize the influence that these ideas have had on the larger body of anarchist thought. Even anarchist communists celebrated the ideas of the individualists Max Stirner and Benjamin Tucker and that reverence shouldn't be overlooked. Nevertheless, they revered those aspects of individualism that complemented a broader communistic focus. Likewise, anarchism largely grew out of Proudhon's mutualism, but anarchists ended up taking elements from his thought, such as his opposition to the state and advocacy of worker self-management, while leaving others, such as his opposition to class struggle, and a market-based economic perspective. Elements of primitivist thought play an important role in the perspectives of many green anarchists, and there are instances when we should be wary of certain forms of technology, but those who are fine with billions of people dying in order to thin the population and return to some supposed 'state of nature' have nothing to do with a doctrine that prioritizes the needs of all. Primitivism is largely associated with the work of John Zerzan and groups in the Pacific Northwest, but as far back as the 1890s there was a Parisian group, *L'Etat Naturel* or the Natural State, which wanted to return to hunter-gatherer society without technology.[52]

Yet, for some Occupy anarchists, anarchism wasn't about a particular political stance as much as a more general rebellious outlook. For example, Rami Shamir (31) from Brooklyn got into anarchism through OWS. He had always had a rebellious outlook on life, but it wasn't until Occupy that he came to realize that his perspectives aligned with anarchism. He told me "I don't think of it as political but spiritual."[53] Similarly, Harrison 'Tesoura' Schultz (29), who gained some notoriety for speaking about anarchism on cable news, said "you can definitely talk about it as an ideal, as a set of precepts or something, but for me it's really an experience. It's this form of glee. It's almost a little sadistic."[54] For Jez (27), who was active in the Arts and Culture and Archives WGs, and Ed Mortimer (56), a medic from Connecticut, anarchism was about the absence of ideology. Jez explained that "anarchism is a word that doesn't have a clear ideology to me and I use it only to describe the fact that I'm critical of institutions,"[55] and Ed said that he was an anarchist "in the sense that I am me, and I don't follow any ideologies."[56] Instead, he told me that his political perspectives could range from right to left based on the issue.[57]

These perspectives are indicative of another interpretation of anarchism, which argues that it is a transhistorical phenomenon of resistance more generally that has always existed, in one form or another, across time and space. This differs markedly from a historical interpretation, which posits that anarchism is a specific ideology that emerged in the middle of the 19th century. In *Demanding the Impossible: A History of Anarchism* Peter Marshall claims that, "the first anarchist was the first person who felt the oppression of another and rebelled against it" and that "as a recognizable trend in human history, the thread of anarchism, in thought and deed, may be traced back several thousand years."[58] Yet he clarifies that "these manifestations are, strictly speaking, part of the prehistory of anarchism." Marshall therefore intertwines both the historical and transhistorical interpretations of anarchism. In *Direct Action: An Ethnography*, David Graeber argues that there are 3 different things that the word 'anarchist' can mean: (1) a person who follows an ideology called 'anarchism' (the historical interpretation); (2) a rebellious person, regardless of time or location, who rejects authority in one form or another (the transhistorical interpretation); or (3) a person who lives in an egalitarian, stateless society.[59]

The historical interpretation, if executed in a clumsy fashion, has the risk of implying that Europeans were the first people to resist hierarchy, which has obviously racist implications. The transhistorical perspective, as long as it does not limit itself to figures like Zeno, Godwin, and Thoreau, has the benefit of emphasizing that non-hierarchical forms of resistance have existed throughout history. Therefore, I think both perspectives on resistance are essential and should be maintained side by side. The problem arises when we use the same word to describe both phenomena because it ends up erasing the distinction. The historical specificity of different forms of resistance in different eras is muddled. Instead, we should see anarchism as nothing more than one of the most recent, and far from the last, examples of anti-authoritarian resistance in a long line of struggle stretching back through time. As the American anarchist Voltairine de Cleyre (1866-1912) wrote, "anarchism … is just the latest reply out of the many the past has given, to that daring, breakaway, volatile, changeful spirit which is never content."[60]

Many of the distinguishing features of anarchism have been historically contingent. As it developed in the 19th century, anarchism was a direct historical response to the decline of feudalism, the advance of the industrial revolution and capitalism, and the development of the modern bureaucratic state. The anarchist concept of revolution developed out of the French Revolution, the tactic of the affinity group grew out of earlier models of Masonic and Carbonari secret brotherhoods,[61] and strategies of mass organization couldn't have existed before innovations in print and communications technology. Using a 19th century European term to label all anti-authoritarian resistance across space and time obscures more than it illuminates.[62] The challenge is to speak about similarities without letting them steamroll differences.

It's true that a number of 19th century anarchists wrote that anarchism had existed throughout history, but one should remember that this was a period when ideas and ideologies, such as nationalism, gained popular legitimacy based on their ties to antiquity. Anarchists had a lot to gain propagandistically by being able to 'demonstrate' that their ideas were 'natural' and as old as time, but that doesn't mean that they were right. As Michael Schmidt and Lucien van der Walt have aptly explained in *Black Flame*, much of the perceived incoherence of the anarchist body of thought stems from the fact that many have erroneously included just about anyone who has ever had an issue with the State without taking other elements of anarchism into consideration.[63] Anarchism simply becomes anti-statism, or resistance in general, without reference to its holistic opposition to all forms of domination.

We should reserve the term 'anarchism' for this specific, though diverse, relatively non-dogmatic, and continually evolving, doctrine connected to specific movements, groups, and individuals as they have emerged and developed in specific times and places over the past century and a half or so, and nothing more. By recognizing the rich, diverse history of resistance across time, and limiting the term 'anarchism' to its context, we can retain the historical specificity of the set of ideas and practices that emerged under the name 'anarchism' in the 19th century without allowing that history or terminology to superimpose itself on all resistance ever. When taken in that light, I agree with Graeber that "all that really changed in the nineteenth century is that some people began to give this [transhistorical] process a name,"[64] however I think that we should allow that name to maintain our understanding of the context from which it emerged.

But we shouldn't go too far in marking the historical borders of anarchism, which have always had blurry regions. As I mentioned earlier, in anarcho-syndicalist unions, for example, many members did not have a 'pure' anarchist philosophy. While it's important to set some guidelines as to the content of the ideology, we should remember that some of the most notable anarchists have behaved in arguably contradictory ways. For example, the famous Catalan anarchist pedagogue Francesc Ferrer i Guàrdia (1859-1909) invested in the stock market to fund anarchist projects,[65] Louise Michel (1830-1905), French anarchist and veteran of the Paris Commune, argued that women should fulfill their domestic roles,[66] the French anarchists Charles Malato and Jean Grave along with the Russian Pyotr Kropotkin were signatories of the "Manifesto of the Sixteen" supporting the Entente Powers in the First World War because they thought it important to preserve the French revolutionary tradition,[67] Mikhail Bakunin made anti-Semitic remarks,[68] and the CNT made some very controversial decisions during the Spanish Civil War including joining the government. Fortunately, anarchists don't name themselves after anyone like Marxists (and Marxist-Leninists, Trotskyists, Maoists, etc.) so we aren't chained to the thoughts or actions of any individual. As David Graeber has pointed out, Marxist tendencies that are closest to anarchism, like Autonomism or Council Communism, don't have figure-heads either.[69]

In trying to pin down a definition of anarchism, some make the mistake of examining it exclusively in terms of its theory or practice in the 1870s or 1930s but, like any other historical phenomenon, it has changed over time. Apart from debatable personal and collective acts, anarchism's holistic perspective on oppression has been constrained by the conditions in which it has existed. This has been evident in issues pertaining to race, sexuality, and gender, for example, but one can also discern the proximity between anarchist thought and mainstream bourgeois thought during the 19th century in an explicit commitment to positivism, aesthetic realism, a Euro-centric conception of the progress of civilization, technological modernization, and biological evolutionary development.[70] Fortunately, anarchism has shed most of that baggage but we can never entirely transcend our historical context. That is why our understanding of anarchism must not be so loose as to be meaningless, but not so rigid as to ignore areas of contradiction and historical transformation.

After this exposition, I hope it has become much clearer that anarchism is not chaos and anarchists are not "gangs of destructive knuckleheads."[71] It is a legitimate political philosophy connected to a vastly popular legacy of struggle expressing anti-authoritarian strains of thought that span millennia of resistance. We should heed the warning of Alexander Berkman (1870-1936), the prominent Lithuanian-American anarchist-communist and sometimes partner of Emma Goldman, "anarchism has many enemies; they won't tell you the truth about it."[72]

Now that we have a better sense of anarchist history and tradition, the next two sections will explore anarchist and Occupy perspectives on economics and democracy, and explain why capitalism and representative government are unjust.

Capitalism

> Capital is directly and indirectly responsible for the violent dehumanization of people. Its violence is political, economic, physical, moral. It is a violence that extracts and steals time from people, robs us of space; it coerces and forces people to produce, consume or die. Capital is the ultimate mechanism for mass dehumanization.
>
> —Alexandre Carvalho, anarchist OWS organizer[73]

A late October headline read "Occupy Wall Street: Not Here to Destroy Capitalism, But to Remind Us Who Saved it."[74] Earlier that month, progressive political commentator Sally Kohn argued that, "most of the Occupy Wall Street protesters aren't opposed to free market capitalism."[75] Kohn was right about the majority of protesters, but 78% of OWS organizers had capital in their crosshairs.

In the context of the turmoil caused by the economic crisis of 2008, the failures of capitalism and the instability of the global economic system were apparent. Occupy pushed economists, commentators, and politicians to reflect on capitalism. In the wake of Occupy, an article in TIME Magazine considered "How to Save Capitalism."[76] In a CNN article Richard Quest asked, "Is Capitalism Outdated in the 21st Century?"[77] Even Republican strategist Frank Luntz said, "I'm so scared of this anti-Wall Street effort. I'm frightened to death...They're having an impact on what the American people think of capitalism." At a strategy session of the Republican Governors Association in Florida in the Fall of 2011 Luntz argued that Republicans shouldn't even use the 'c-word' any more. He said: "I'm trying to get that word removed and we're replacing it with either 'economic freedom' or 'free market'...The public...still prefers capitalism to socialism, but they think that capitalism is immoral."[78] Luntz was right, according to a Pew Research poll from December 2011 50% of those surveyed had a positive view of capitalism (40% negative) while only 31% had a positive view of socialism (60% negative), but this was not the case with the youth. Among those 18-29, 46% were positive about capitalism (47% negative), while 49% were positive about socialism (43% negative).[79] Certainly the crisis inflamed the flaws of capitalism, but whereas liberals and progressives consider rampant unemployment, homelessness, and starvation to be unfortunate blemishes on an otherwise just and efficient economic system, anti-capitalists recognize that capitalism is inherently immoral.

I can't give a full exposition on the evils of capitalism, but I'll briefly touch upon seven of the many problems with capitalism: it's irrational; it's exploitative; it's environmentally catastrophic;

it's racist, sexist, and hetero-normative; and it's anti-democratic.

Capitalism is Irrational. The discipline of economics, like all academic disciplines, consolidates its power by shrouding itself in the cloak of expertise. The uninitiated couldn't possibly have anything worthwhile to contribute besides their consumer preferences. When the economic crisis hit, the media said it was time to turn to the people for a kind of ritualistic, emotive catharsis and time to turn to the policy experts and politicians for solutions. As with representative government as a whole, there was a very clear discursive division of labor. And it's true that within the partially imaginary realm of markets, derivatives, bubbles, and speculation economists have a whole lot more insight than other people, but the professional identity of the economist as the expert of capitalism blinds us to our material reality.

We can see what's happening around us. As a popular Occupy Facebook graphic pointed out, in the United States there are more empty houses than homeless families. Hospitals and other health facilities are being shut down due to lack of funds, medical professionals are unemployed, warehouses of medical supplies are overflowing from the recession, and millions of people around the world are in desperate need of medical care. Schools are closing, teachers are being laid off, and class sizes are rising. Half of the world's food is thrown out everyday at supermarkets and restaurants as people around the world die of starvation.[80] Millions of people who desperately want to participate in meaningful, socially productive labor are sitting at home while there are countless ways that their labor could be utilized in urgent, meaningful ways. As Marxist geographer David Harvey said at the World Social Forum in 2010,

> Surplus capital and surplus labor exist side-by side with seemingly no way to put them back together in the midst of

> immense human suffering and unmet needs. In midsummer of 2009, one third of the capital equipment in the United States stood idle, while some 17 per cent of the workforce were either unemployed, enforced part-timers or "discouraged" workers. What could be more irrational than that![81]

Historically, capitalism has unleashed a wave of unprecedented productivity. Whereas more than 80% of the populations of ancient societies such as Greece or Babylonia had to devote their labor to food production to feed the larger population,[82] today advances in technology and economies of scale have drastically reduced that figure, allowing a much wider range of productive activity. Capitalism has produced the surplus necessary to meet our needs, yet everywhere we see fences, walls, and cops blocking off unused resources from those who need them. We can see this with our own eyes whenever we pass by foreclosed houses, or when we see restaurants tossing industrial-sized trash bags full of food into the dumpster at the end of the day. One of the most successful elements of Occupy Wall Street was its emphasis on the irrationality of this system. Campaigns such as Occupy Our Homes, which focused on foreclosures and housing rights, shed the spotlight on the contrast between the abundance of resources and their separation from those who needed them.

The 'invisible hand of the market' supposedly allocates resources efficiently, but we see that this is far from the case when 23.1% of children in the United States are living in poverty, the second highest figure in the developed world.[83] When I asked Christhian Diaz (25), an artist, OWS organizer, and Colombian immigrant who came to the United States at the age of 11, about political violence, he said it was impossible to speak about any kind of violence without recognizing that "the world produces enough food for the entire world while thousands are starving every day."[84] Although capitalism represented an improvement over feudalism in many ways, we have the resources and the technology to do better than this. We can meet our needs. There's no excuse not to.

Capitalism is Exploitative. Anarchists are heavily indebted to Marx's critique of capitalism. Better than anyone else, Marx dissected the nature of capitalist exploitation to demonstrate how employers only pay workers a fraction of the value they produce while living off of the surplus value they extract. I am not going to rehash Marx's take on exploitation, but you don't have to be familiar with Marx to see that sweatshop conditions prevail around much of the globe. The spread of neo-liberalism, a doctrine that advocates a return to 19th century models of free market capitalism without government restrictions, has meant that global capital has acquired an enhanced ability to search out regions of the world with the lowest labor and safety standards. The market inhibits the ability of governments to improve conditions because doing so prompts capital investment to flow elsewhere. It should be obvious that something is terribly wrong when Apple computers that are being sold for thousands of dollars apiece are being constructed in Chinese factories that are so oppressive that they have installed suicide nets outside their windows[85] to prevent ruthlessly exploited workers from killing themselves.[86] The six wealthiest founders of Wal-mart have a combined wealth of $69.7 billion, equal to that of the bottom 30% of all Americans.[87] Where does all of that money come from? It's blood money squeezed out of millions of disposable workers who have toiled in inhuman conditions such as the 19-hour shifts for $20 a month in one of their factories in Bangladesh.[88]

Defenders of capitalism point to the fact that many developed countries have enacted labor regulations to prohibit such extreme abuses, but (1) the profit incentive will always produce a bottom layer of ultra-exploited labor whether abroad or domestically in the form of undocumented immigrants who are excluded from these protections, and (2) the economic crisis has emphasized how capitalism isn't even working for much of the middle class. When you add up all of the debt incurred from university tuition, medical bills, mortgage payments, and credit card bills in the context of widespread unemployment and underemployment, it's clear that not only Bangladeshi garment workers are being squeezed by this economic system. Yet, most people don't see how their economic plight is a product of the exploitation of labor and not simply a superficial irritation on the otherwise smooth surface of capitalism. Under feudalism the fact that the serf worked part of the year for the master and part of the year for himself was clearly delineated, but the social relationship between the serf and his master was obscured by the myth of hierarchical loyalty. Under capitalism, however, the cold, impersonal, instrumental relationship between employer and worker is crystal clear although the fact that the employer is taking a significant percentage of the worker's labor is obscured.

As anti-capitalists have long pointed out, "the boss needs you, you don't need the boss." Without us, our bosses would be lost, but without the bosses we can manage the economy on our own since we are the real source of all wealth.

Capitalism is Environmentally Catastrophic. It should come as little surprise that an economic system that commodifies all aspects of our social, spiritual, and material world; prevents the development of truly democratic institutions; and prioritizes profit over all other considerations should pose a grave threat to the environment. The environmental impact of capitalism was perhaps the most popular reason given for opposing capitalism in the interviews with OWS organizers. In an era when the traditional left rhetoric of workers and factories has lost some of its luster with young people, the climate crisis has stepped in to remind many why capitalism must be abolished.

I imagine that most readers are all too familiar with the

corporate production of greenhouse gases and their role in the climate crisis. When taken in conjunction with rampant deforestation, toxic dumping, fracking, and oil drilling, it's clear that our environment is in danger. As we have seen with labor regulations, capitalism only respects the environment when it is profitable or it is compelled to do so. As historian Ted Steinberg argued, corporations will "never relinquish the idea that plants, soil, water, forests, other natural resources are anything but forms of capital."[89] To the degree that we allow this anti-social, parasitic economic system to persist, we invite constant attacks on the world around us.

But what about 'green capitalism'? Despite the fact that capitalism is literally driving the planet off a cliff in terms of the rapid rate of climate change, the solution, we are told, is to change our light bulbs, bring our own bags to the supermarket, or buy a hybrid car. We've seen how oil magnates have hampered the development of sustainable energy, and how biofuels are often produced in ways that destroy the biosphere and threaten human rights. This green capitalist 'solution' has extended its arms outwards on a global scale, most evident in the market-oriented Kyoto Protocol. Applauded by economic and political elites across the globe (and even officially endorsed by left-leaning organizations like Greenpeace), the Kyoto Protocol created the world's first international carbon market which allowed governments and industries to trade rights to atmospheric carbon pools thereby forestalling a serious confrontation with the unsustainable nature of modern industry. Policies like the Kyoto Protocol are designed and administered by major industrialists and politicians, so it makes sense that these 'green capitalist' 'solutions' fail to reflect the urgency of an impending environmental catastrophe.[90]

Capitalism is Racist, Sexist, and Hetero-normative. As Malcolm X said, "you can't have capitalism without racism."[91] He was arguing that historically capitalism was built on slavery and white supremacy and today it flourishes by exploiting the cleavages of racial domination that it formed centuries ago. Capitalists frequently wonder why the countries of the 'first world' are so much more prosperous than those of the 'third world' without mentioning the historical legacy of imperialism, colonialism, and slavery. Japan, the only non-Western country to emerge as a world power at the start of the 20th century was, not so coincidentally, also one of the only to avoid colonization.

However, Malcolm X could have made similar arguments about patriarchy and homophobia because capitalism has also utilized hierarchies of gender and sexuality to reinforce its exploitation. It's true that advances in society have been made through the civil rights, women's and gay liberation movements over the past decades. Labor law and real estate standards of conduct now include provisos against discrimination, but those gains are inherently anti-capitalist. They infringe upon the ability of autonomous individuals to contract themselves as they see fit whether such motivations are prompted by racism or not. Capitalism as a system has no problem with women being paid less than men. Capitalism doesn't mind homophobic discrimination in renting apartments. The farther we get from the market the closer we get to justice. These gains were only made through collective struggle that compelled the market to respect their identities. The market feeds off of these power dynamics to divide working people against each other as they focus on their relative status rather than their collective oppression.[92] Historically, the state, capital's bodyguard, has unleashed its harshest oppression upon people of color and queers.[93] It's no coincidence that police kill a black person every 36 hours in the US.[94]

Yet, as economist Michael Albert pointed out, "Capitalism is racist and sexist. This is not intrinsic to the relations of production, but occurs because under the pressure of market competition owners inevitably exploit racial and gender hierarchies produced in other parts of society."[95] The oppressions of race, gender, and sexuality, much like environmental exploitation, will never be eradicated if left to the market.

Capitalism is Anti-Democratic. Although Americans are fanatical about the rhetoric, though rarely the substance, of democracy, they usually don't think about democracy in the workplace. The assumption is that outside of the job we leave class behind as equal citizens with a vote apiece but at work we are subordinate to the boss. The hierarchical class structure of capitalism has perpetuated the myth that democracy is not only unnecessary in the workplace but actually detrimental to its efficiency, while using the veneer of democracy to cloak class rule in the public sphere. As Drew Hornbein (25), a web consultant who worked with the Tech and Internet OWS WGs, pointed out, "the past 500 years or so has been a struggle to create political democracy and now we're butting up against a non-democratic economy. The economy has massive influence in our politics and it doesn't serve people as much as it serves the 1%."[96]

Over the past decades we have been taught that democracy and capitalism are essentially synonymous, but in fact they cannot coexist. In the workplace, private property and the capitalist extraction of surplus value from workers prohibits real, substantive democracy on a mass scale. In societal decision-making, capitalist class relations preclude the possibility that the opinion of a CEO and a domestic worker could carry the same weight. Jillian Buckley (28), an OWS outreach organizer, said capitalism is a "system set up where somebody has to be at the bottom."[97] Throughout much of the 19th century, elites assumed that real democracy would inevitably lead to socialism because workers and peasants would vote to redistribute the wealth in their favor.[98] However, as I will discuss in Chapter 4, they underestimated the power of the market to resist popular infringement.

Anarchist Alternatives to Capitalism

In his CNN article, Richard Quest paraphrased Winston Churchill in saying that "so far there seems to be a view that capitalism may be the worst form of economy—except for all the others."[99] As anti-capitalists, it's essential that we better articulate our alternative to "the worst form of economy." In place of capitalism, anarchists advocate a classless, non-hierarchical, decentralized society where property is held in common and production and consumption are organized in a directly democratic manner. To clarify, opposing private property doesn't mean that someone wouldn't have their own things; it means that the resources and facilities necessary to meet society's needs are subject to popular, directly democratic control. "Anarchists make a distinction between possessions and private property."[100] Political theorists frequently erect a false dichotomy between the free market and monolithic, Soviet-style state planning, but anarchists advocate democratic forms of decentralized planning that take the needs of producers, consumers, and the environment into account.

Jonathan Smucker (34) is an organizer with our Press WG and Occupy Our Homes who had a great deal of previous organizing experience with the global justice movement, School of the Americas Watch, veterans' organizing and other issues. Although he used to identify as an anarchist, he now identifies as a "small 's' socialist" with an "anti-authoritarian bent." Based on his experience working for two years in a collectively run Minneapolis restaurant he told me that,

> I think having democracy in the workplace actually is a really meaningful thing and gives people a greater agency and civic responsibility that even extends beyond the workplace and I think that our resignation on a civic level is tied to our resignation on a workplace level.[101]

A popular historical perspective on building the groundwork for the organization of production 'after the revolution' has been the "embryo hypothesis,"[102] which posits that the democratic, industrial union structure of the anarcho-syndicalist federation could prefigure the organization of a post-capitalist economy. Other anarchists have focused on communities and other alternative institutions as the building blocks of the future society, but either way the goal is to 'build a new world in the shell of the old.' As I discussed with the Bakunin/Marx debate, for anarchists the means should reflect the ends as much as possible. To a great extent, that's exactly what happened in Spain during the Spanish Civil War where workers had already spent decades fine-tuning their collective decision-making practices to the point where they could resume production right after the bourgeoisie fled.

Although Proudhon's mutualism was very popular with early anarchists, federal republicans, and assorted radical artisans, Bakunin played an important role in expounding what he referred to as "collectivism," to distinguish it from state-oriented communist theories, based on the collective ownership of the means of production. At the 1869 Basel Congress of the First International, the supporters of Bakunin and Marx who advocated collective ownership defeated the predominantly French followers of the recently deceased Proudhon (in part because their labor-credit bank collapsed that year), marking the decline of mutualist thought in revolutionary circles.[103] Although anarchist collectivism advocated the collective ownership of property, it involved remuneration based on one's personal production. Since capitalism exploited workers by not paying them the full value of their contribution, collectivists sought to redress that injustice by assuring the individual of the full value of their labor. Greatly appealing to skilled craftsmen, collectivism sanctified "the fruit of one's work realized by the individual."[104]

However, as Alexander Berkman, pointed out,

> But *no one* person has made or can make anything all by himself. It takes many men, of different trades and professions, to create something. The carpenter, for instance, cannot make a simple chair or bench all by himself; not even if he should cut down a tree and prepare the lumber himself. He needs a saw and a hammer, nails and tools, which he cannot make himself. And even if he should make these himself, he would first have to have the raw materials—steel and iron—which other men would have to supply.[105]

Anarchist communism (or anarcho-communism) posits the impossibility, and undesirability, of making exact calculations about individual contributions to a collective process of production. Instead, anarchist communists have advanced Louis Blanc's famous 1839 slogan, "from each according to his abilities, to each according to his needs."[106] All too often critics of this slogan focus on the second half without realizing that the first half requires the participation of those who are able. Essentially they share the same ultimate goal of communism with Marx, but disagree about how to get there.[107] Although historians have not been able to definitively cite the first person to advocate the doctrine of anarchist communism, it developed in the aftermath of Bakunin's death among his followers in the Swiss Jura Federation including the Italians, Errico Malatesta, Andrea Costa, and Carlo Cafiero; the French geographer Élisée Reclus; and the Russian Pyotr Kropotkin.[108] The argument of the anarchist communist is that in a world of abundance we have the tools to create a society where those who work can have their needs met. This is not a utopian vision of the future; it's a realistic assessment of the resources around us.

Anarchist communism has been the dominant anarchist economic vision since the 1880s when it surpassed collectivist concepts of individual remuneration.[109] In the 19th century, many anarcho-communists were opposed to large organizations and unionism, which then had a strong association with collectivism, and had more of an insurrectionary tactical orientation hostile to the gradual construction of a revolutionary movement. Whereas the collectivist position tended to favor skilled workers, the communist position included the needs and interests of women and unskilled workers who came to see collectivism as "the tyranny of unionism over the community."[110] Because of 19th century conflicts between anarcho-communists and collectivist unionists, historians have mistakenly juxtaposed anarcho-communism and anarcho-syndicalism, but since the 20th century most anarcho-syndicalists have also advocated libertarian communism. The communist position gave anarchist unionism a more holistic outlook on the social revolution.

Recently some anarchists have adopted an economic vision called Participatory Economics, or Parecon, developed by Michael Albert, Robin Hahnel and others. Parecon involves the creation of consumer and producer councils grouped into federations to determine production. The main difference with the communist perspective is that Parecon advocates differentiated salaries based on the effort and sacrifice that a given job entails.[111] Either way, anarchists agree that the only just economy is a democratic economy.

I don't have the space here to refute every capitalist objection to the notion of a democratic economy oriented around human need. In short, some of the most common are: the wage system is necessary to compel people to work; the profit incentive is necessary to drive innovation; productive efficiency is inherently hierarchical; and meritocracy is an ethical reflection of differentiated talents and work ethics. Yet, I will take a moment to briefly discuss one key ahistorical fallacy at the heart of these capitalist critiques of socialist alternatives: a timeless understanding of 'human nature.'

Capitalist arguments assume that our present norms of remuneration, incentives, organization and social recognition are timeless manifestations of our underlying dog-eat-dog 'human nature.' In the 19th century, many anarchists attempted to refute such charges by arguing that human nature is fundamentally good but has been corrupted by the state and capitalism. It was basically a mirror image of the argument made against them because many anarchists were constrained by their historical circumstances, characterized by a Victorian biological essentialism.[112] Since the end of the 20th century, though, anarchists have increasingly come to realize that the debate shouldn't be about whether 'human nature' is fundamentally good or bad since in abstraction that doesn't mean anything. Instead, most anarchists argue that people tend to behave poorly when living under oppressive institutions amidst antagonistic social relations, and they tend to behave well when they have been inculcated from birth in a society based on cooperation and meeting needs. As Emma Goldman said, "Poor human nature, what horrible crimes have been committed in thy name! ...how can any one speak of it today, with every soul in a prison, with every heart fettered, wounded, and maimed?"[113]

Any historian could easily point out that our individualistic, materialistic outlook is a very recent, historically contingent product of the underlying capitalist economy. For example, as capitalism was displacing feudalism, it was often very difficult to get workers to work more than was necessary to meet their basic needs. Historian of early modern England Keith Thomas wrote that, "since at least the fourteenth century, observers had complained that journeymen did the minimum amount of work necessary to keep them in food and drink and then devoted themselves to relaxation."[114] The profit incentive had to be taught. Thomas also pointed out that:

> Many inhabitants of rural communities [in England] seem to have been hostile to the maximization of individual gain, preferring a customary allocation of resources and rewards

> which would ensure the perpetuation of the group as a whole. Theirs was a non-accumulative ethic, in which neighborly responsibility, obligations to family members, and contributions to parochial causes ranked higher than the unremitting pursuit of self-interest. Accumulation was disapproved of because it was thought, often rightly, to be at the expense of someone else.[115]

In his 1925 "Essay on the Gift," anthropologist Marcel Mauss demonstrated that pre-modern societies often functioned on 'gift economies' where individuals pursued the well-being of others rather than personal 'profit.'[116] I'm not saying that we should 'go back' to the ways of earlier societies, but that these examples show that if human societies were so drastically different in the past, then it is inevitable that in the future they will be drastically different in ways that we can barely imagine. 'Human nature' is a social construct. As Oscar Wilde said,

> It will, of course, be said that such a scheme as is set forth here is quite unpractical, and goes against human nature. This is perfectly true. It is unpractical, and it goes against human nature. This is why it is worth carrying out, and that is why one proposes it. For what is a practical scheme? A practical scheme is either a scheme that is already in existence, or a scheme that could be carried out under existing conditions. But it is exactly the existing conditions that one objects to; and any scheme that could accept these conditions is wrong and foolish. The conditions will be done away with, and human nature will change. The only thing that one really knows about human nature is that it changes. Change is the one quality we can predicate of it. The systems that fail are those that rely on the permanency of human nature, and not on its growth and development. The error of Louis XIV was that he thought human nature would always be the same. The result

of his error was the French Revolution.[117]

I should also point out that a number of anarchists have made similar arguments about the historical contingency of human nature to critique proposals and theories of a post-capitalist world. Sparrow Ingersoll (30) was one of the familiar anarchist faces of DA who was often seen wearing a black jacket, black knit cap with black sunglasses, and tight black pants. Sparrow identifies as an "insurrectionary anarcho-nihilist" which precludes a positive program for social transformation. As Sparrow told me,

> I don't think that we are qualified to in any way try to construct a new world in the shell of this one or after it ceases to exist because we are diseased by capitalism and so we're not qualified to make those sorts of choices especially now.[118]

Therefore, for Sparrow and others we cannot construct models for a new world because we cannot really think beyond capitalism while we are stuck in it. All we can do is push things in a non-hierarchical direction and future generations will organize things based on their circumstances. Interestingly, Marx made a similar historicist argument about definite theories of the future society because our political thoughts are conditioned by our material conditions. While I agree with the radical historicist angle of such a perspective, I think positive vision is essential. I agree with Yotam Marom (26), a "participatory socialist" involved in organizing some of the major days of action such as October 15, 2011 and November 17, 2011, who said that vision "gives people the drive to fight and understand how to struggle."[119] A positive vision doesn't constrain future generations. As long as it's flexible, it can provide fodder for experimentation. Whatever the future may look like it will have some elements of continuity with the world before it. There's never a clean break.

Nevertheless, regardless of the specificity of OWS visions for the future, an overwhelming number of interviewees emphasized that our post-capitalist economy should be oriented around meeting basic needs. Although most showed no indication of a specific familiarity with anarcho-communist principles, self-identified anarchists carried a strong communist streak when describing their vision, and many who did not identify with a specific ideology listed communism as a contributing factor along with anarchism. Sara Zainab Bokhari (29) was active in People of Color organizing and working to get her Muslim community more involved in the movement. She described herself as "far left," and came to her anti-capitalist perspective through her faith,

> There's a saying that when you have a completely just society it's when a brother who's in need can stick his hand into the pocket of another brother and the second one doesn't flinch. So I guess a society of mutual aid but it's without even needing to ask.[120]

Many seemed to be new to an anti-capitalist orientation, and the fact that capitalism cannot feed, house, and clothe the people of the world despite the wealth it has created appeared to be a popular tipping point. Linnea M. Palmer Paton (23) was one of the most active members of the Press WG. In college she participated in a fair amount of environmental activism, but when I interviewed her on a cold night in late January 2012 she emphasized that her politics were in flux. When I asked about her economic perspective, she hesitated and said that she thought that capitalism on the micro level could have some benefits, since it allows individual choice and personal creativity, but she liked some aspects of anarchism and really wanted an economy where basic needs are met and labor is not based on compulsion.[121] On

September 15, 2012, I was walking around Washington Square Park during one of the weekend events leading up to the one-year anniversary of OWS. The park was packed and various assemblies were convening under signs with letters attached to long poles. I noticed Linnea leading a large environmental assembly and I heard her shout at the top of her lungs with a broad, gleeful smile, "Capitalism doesn't fucking work! It's killing the planet!" The diverse crowd seated around her roared in applause.

The organizers I spoke with affirmed that Occupy had a profoundly radicalizing effect on those who gave their time to it. Lauren Digioia (27) was well known for her blue hair and tattoos. After walking by Zuccotti in late September and hearing the drums, she was pulled into the movement and became the "sanitation queen" scrubbing the park clean in anticipation of the aborted eviction on October 14, 2011. Before she was an "apathetic" musician, but her Occupy experience made her an anarchist. She told me that,

> When I first came to Occupy I thought if we did campaign finance reform and elected [good candidates] then maybe we'd have some hope but you start to see how intertwined it is and you start to see how embedded it is in this corrupt system and that capitalism ultimately only benefits a certain group and that its system is only sustainable on a large body of the planet being oppressed.[122]

As I mentioned earlier, 78% of OWS organizers were opposed to capitalism. Yet it's not always entirely clear what it means to be anti-capitalist. This is not a problem confined to OWS. Socialists of all stripes have long debated whether mutualism, state socialism, Parecon, and a number of other theories are *really* anti-capitalist or not. Considering that the United States has been without a significant Left, not to mention revolutionary Left, for some time, many OWS organizers were not steeped in radical theory. In fact, 30% of organizers had basically no previous political experience at all, and many others had only worked for NGOs or electoral campaigns and were new to radical organizing. While this may have hampered the movement, it also provided space for a more creative sense of experimentation and possibility than if everyone had come in with their pre-packaged outlooks. German organizer Tashy Endres (29) just happened to be in New York in early October 2011 when she stopped by Liberty Square. Although she was scheduled to leave the country on October 4th, she stayed and did non-violent communication trainings. She told me that as opposed to Germany, "here I have the impression that there is a lot less labeling and a lot less categorizing in this movement than in the context that I am used to and I find that very liberating."[123]

Therefore, between the underdeveloped nature of American anti-capitalism and the fact that many people's politics were in transition, I heard a great deal of ambiguity when it came to capitalism. The following quotes demonstrate a theme that I heard from organizers whose politics straddled progressivism and radicalism or those who were recently radicalized: "I'm against this version of capitalism." "Capitalism in its current form isn't working." "I don't like capitalism as it is." "Capitalism as it exists today isn't working." An equitable economy is impossible "within the vision we have of capitalism right now." "I'm not against capitalism entirely, but the way that it is now is only working for very few people."

I think it's important for anti-capitalists to recognize the exciting opportunities implicit in this potentially transitional progressive view of capitalism. I say potentially transitional because the tones of many of these organizers were very hesitant, conflicted, and indeterminate. Sometimes they would express explicitly anti-capitalist perspectives shortly afterward since they were trying make up their minds on the spot. As I will discuss in

Chapter 3, for many anti-capitalists, myself included, the first step in the development of an anti-capitalist perspective is the recognition that 'this' isn't working. Often it takes a while before radicals ascertain the exact contours of what 'this' is, but anarchists shouldn't look down on such a promising first step. We can't expect that everyone's politics will move from A to Z without some intermediary steps. Yet, this phenomena points to a desperate need for anti-capitalist political education to make it clear that the problem is not "capitalism as it exists today," but rather capitalism as it could ever possibly exist.

Similarly, some organizers who identified as anti-capitalists in general explained to me that they were "totally cool with small-scale capitalism at the local level." It's important to emphasize that an economic system predicated on unlimited growth that constantly works toward greater and greater consolidation and economies of scale can never remain small-scale for long. It's an impossibility to consider some hypothetical local capitalism.[124] This tendency was attached to a widespread fetishism of the small and the local in response to the overwhelming size and power of corporations. Many anarchists and non-anarchists envisioned a post-capitalist economy based on small-scale cooperatives and communes. While a good number saw such bodies collaborating at a larger level through regional federations, some either eschewed large-scale collaboration or hadn't thought far enough ahead to mention it. This inclination has not been uncommon throughout the history of anarchism, but the majority perspective has been global in scope and internationalist in outlook. The most significant anarchist groups and theoreticians have consistently advocated the incorporation of small communities and collectives into larger regional federations of production and consumption based on the recognition that resources are not spread equally across the earth. Without coordination there would be no way to redress the global inequality created by capitalism. Extreme localism would merely reproduce it. To me, it's indicative of an excessive tactical emphasis on withdrawal from the state and capital rather than direct attacks upon them, but I'll get into that in Chapter 4.

Democracy

> "Anarchism is founded on the observation that since few men are wise enough to rule themselves, even fewer are wise enough to rule others."[125]
>
> –Edward Abbey (1927-1989), author and anarchist

Anarchists reject all hierarchical social relations even if the top of the hierarchy was elected. No matter the politics of the person or people on top, the very fact that they have been placed into positions of domination invalidates the legitimacy of their actions. Instead, anarchists have advocated forms of direct and participatory democracy that give each participant an equal opportunity to shape the actions of the group. As OWS organizer Shawn Carrié said, "if something affects you, you should have a say in it directly."[126] Examples have included democratic unions, community organizations, workplace cooperatives, collective houses,[127] etc.

Occupy Wall Street made decisions through the consensus process. As opposed to majority voting, which tends to promote the perspective that "I have the greatest idea and I just need to lobby it through,"[128] the goal with consensus is to come up with an outcome that everyone can be satisfied with. It doesn't stifle disagreement; it tries to incorporate diverse opinions. This prevents the alienation of a dissatisfied minority. Consensus decision-making entered the praxis of American radicalism in the 60s through the Student Nonviolent Coordinating Committee (SNCC)[129] and in the 70s and 80s through feminist consciousness-raising circles, the anti-nuclear movement, and Movement for a New Society (MNS) where gay rights activist George Lakey played an important role in bringing the longstanding Quaker use of consensus to activism.[130] Through groups and networks such as ACT UP,[131] Earth First!,[132] and Food Not Bombs[133] the tradition of the consensus process in the context of loosely knit anti-authoritarian politics continued through to the global justice movement of the turn of the 21st century.

When I enrolled at Wesleyan University in September 2001, I witnessed the continuation of those forms of organizing. For several years, I had been eager to get involved with the global justice movement and I was very active in the planning to mobilize students to go down to the IMF/World Bank protest on September 29th. Yet September 11th marked a crucial turning point where the global justice movement segued into the anti-war movement. This was symbolized by the decision to turn the IMF/World Bank protest into perhaps the first sizable anti-war demonstration of the "war on terror" era when the financial meetings were cancelled. Nevertheless, regardless of whether we were organizing against the war or the World Economic Forum, our resistance was steeped in the political culture of the global justice movement. This involved consensus-style decision-making, direct action, affinity groups, and a non-ideological orientation. My experience was similar to a number of other OWS organizers in their late 20s/early 30s who had familiarity with consensus before Occupy, but often in a less formal sense. As OWS organizer Zak Solomon (28) said of his years of experience in the Bay Area "we kind of arrived at decisions through informal consensus. It wasn't as explicit or intentional."[134] It just made sense that if a handful of people in the group were upset that we would try to work things out so we wouldn't lose them.

It wasn't really until I got involved in the reformation of the 1960s group Students for a Democratic Society (SDS) in 2006 in Providence, RI that I started to see a more formal decision-making process being used. At the second SDS National

Convention in Detroit in 2007, I witnessed a masterful example of facilitating a large assembly from Lisa Fithian. Dubbed "Professor Occupy" by *Mother Jones,* Lisa (50) has a wealth of organizing experience ranging from her participation in the labor movement to the WTO protest of 1999 and the Common Ground Collective in New Orleans.[135] In New York, Lisa was involved in the planning for a May 12, 2011 Wall Street protest that drew thousands despite a lack of media coverage. She conducted a wide variety of trainings, helped plan actions, and was one of the main sources of inter-generational knowledge in Occupy. For Lisa, consensus is "the most human form of decision-making."[136]

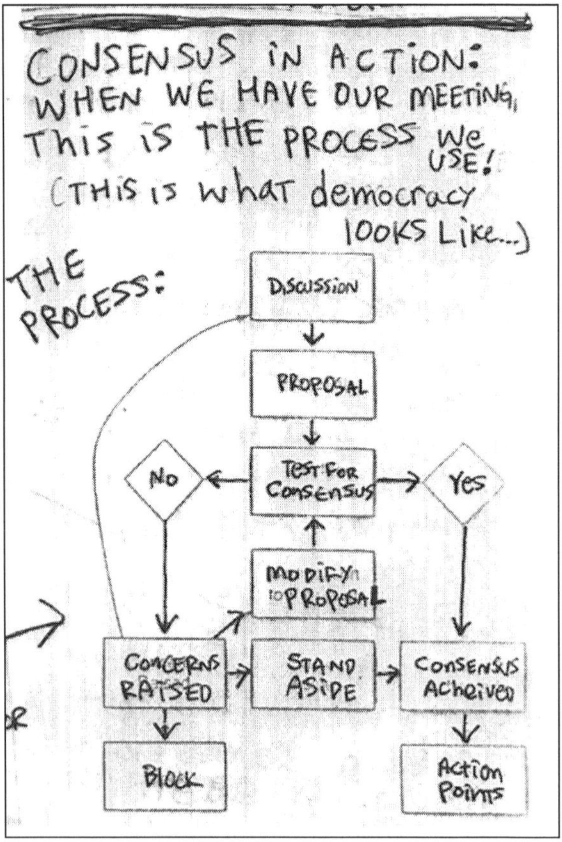

Consensus chart from an OWS handout.

How did consensus work in Occupy? Essentially, after a proposal is brought forth, the presenter takes "clarifying questions" (not listed in the diagram). Clarifying questions are not objections; they are factual questions about unclear aspects of the proposal. After clarifying questions, people can raise "concerns." Next, there is usually a space for "friendly amendments" if it seems that the proposal is contentious. The presenter can decide whether to accept the amendments or not. Then there is a test for consensus. People can either vote in favor, stand aside (meaning that they don't like it but aren't so antagonistic to the proposal that they will stand in the way), or they can block. I've heard different interpretations of the block. Some say it should only be used when one has serious safety or security concerns with the proposal. Others say it means that if the proposal were passed then the individual would no longer feel comfortable continuing with the group because it violated the group's points of unity. True consensus implies that a single block can derail a proposal, but OWS generally used modified consensus, which operated on 90% approval. But it's important to emphasize that consensus is as much about promoting discussion and fostering compromise as it is about the outcome. It's a method of collective action that forces people to take the concerns of the minority seriously. As the influential Italian anarchist Errico Malatesta (1853-1932) argued, "we do not recognize the right of the majority to impose the law on the minority ... it is necessary that majority and minority should succeed in living together peacefully and profitably by mutual agreement and compromise."[137]

Yet historically anarchists *have* made decisions based on majority voting. Bakunin's "International Brotherhood" voted that way (sometimes based on two thirds for important matters),[138] the major anarcho-syndicalist unions such as the CNT vote(d) that way, large international anarchist congresses voted that way, and current "class struggle" anarchist and libertarian socialist groups such as Common Struggle Libertarian

Communist Federation (formerly known as the North Eastern Federation of Anarchist Communists, NEFAC) and the Workers Solidarity Alliance (WSA) vote by majority. The point of Malatesta's quote, though, is not that there cannot be a majority, but that this majority cannot "impose the law." In my interview with David Graeber he highlighted the central role of illegitimate coercion in evaluating forms of decision-making,

> My position on consensus is this: if you do not have the means to compel a minority to go along with a majority decision, whatever you do, it's a form of consensus. Even if you're doing majority vote, you have consensus that everyone's going to go along with majority vote. So you are using consensus if you can't force people to do things.[139]

Therefore, the point is that anarchists are fine with both majority and consensus forms of decision-making as long as they're based on voluntary association.

The most visible example of the consensus process was the general assembly (GA). This was the main decision-making body of the Occupation and anyone could attend and participate fully. Initially they were held twice a day before being scaled back to once a day and then a couple times a week. For many, the GA was their introduction to the movement. During its peak, the GA was frequently an astounding site to behold as over a thousand people crammed into a tiny park in lower Manhattan to practice direct democracy. Looking around, it was clear that the booming echo of waves of the People's Mic (a system where groups repeat someone's speech to amplify the volume in the absence of microphones) awakened a dormant democratic spirit for many participants. After his first GA, soon-to-be OWS organizer Brett G. (29) tweeted "this is the most democratic thing I've seen in my life."[140]

However, there were a number of serious limitations in the OWS general assembly model that emerged as the movement

The People's Mic in action at an OWS General Assembly on Sept. 30, 2011. Photo by David Shankbone.

took off. Part of the problem stemmed from the circumstances of the birth of Occupy Wall Street. Lorenzo Serna (31), a Chicano anarchist from Texas involved in facilitation, outreach, media and live-streaming, recounted his experience of attending planning meetings over the summer of 2011. He went to the meeting of New Yorkers Against Budget Cuts (NYABC), the group that planned the May 12, 2011 Wall Street demonstration, where they decided not to work on the *Adbusters* call to Occupy Wall Street in September because it was a call to action without any organizing behind it. Yet, out of that meeting another was scheduled at the office of the DC37 labor union where it was decided to hold a general assembly (GA) on August 2nd at Bowling Green. On August 2nd members of the Workers World Party (WWP) were giving speeches when Georgia Sagri (32), a Greek anarchist experienced in the ways of popular assemblies, shouted at them that it wasn't really a general assembly.[141] Shortly thereafter a group of "horizontals"[142] organized their own GA, which spawned the infrastructure behind the Occupation. This instance of disruption is often cited as a founding moment, but Isham Christie (27), one of the organizers of the event who would later participate in Outreach and student organizing, clarified that actually the idea was to have a typical rally during the first half to satisfy the WWP, and then have a legitimate GA during the second half to satisfy the anti-authoritarians. Unfortunately, the MC of the event wasn't clear on this, which caused the conflict, but in fact half of the event's organizers also wanted to hold a GA.[143] Nevertheless, Lorenzo explained to me that,

> we went about it kinda wrong. We were planning for September 17th, this day that was put on us, in a way, and we're supposed to be a general assembly to talk about what we should do but we had already made a decision to do something without talking about it. So instantly instead of talking about what a general assembly even was we were trying to plan for this day using the general assembly model without realizing what it was.[144]

Jackie Disalvo (69), a longtime organizer and retired professor involved in the original SDS, the Mississippi Freedom Summer, and labor organizing, concurred when she said that "I don't think we understood what a general assembly was."[145] Before organizers could have time to fine-tune their methods and practices, OWS became an international media sensation and hundreds of people were flooding the GAs. Over time, fewer and fewer organizers attended the GAs because they had dozens of other meetings and tasks they had to deal with throughout the week, the GAs were increasingly populated with people who had little to no investment in the movement (some were quite literally tourists), and they were getting bogged down in allocating money rather than dealing with political issues.

OWS organizer Max Berger (26) said that the "GA stopped being a meaningful place to create collective decisions after about the second week."[146] Jonathan Smucker astutely noted that, "in some ways to me that stuff [GA] was political theater, and really good political theater, but I don't think that majority rules is the enemy."[147] José Whelan (29), a Buddhist anarchist involved in Facilitation and the Structure WG, said that the GA was "a great outreach tool but very difficult medium for day to day logistical work." He was right in saying that organizing ended up happening through personal connections in ways that, at times, were "not transparent."[148] Brittany Robinson (22), an outreach organizer who also helped start the CUNY-wide GA in response to a 34% tuition hike, said that organizing was characterized by "backroom deals," and "the GAs were kind of like a front."[149] Part of the reason for this was that Occupy had an organizing model designed for smaller groups of relatively like-minded people cemented by personal relationships. So with the avalanche of hype, responsibility, and new, inexperienced people, a tension developed between inclusivity and efficiency. The most extreme manifestation of that was the contrast between the declining importance of the GA and increasing role of affinity groups, which I will go into in Chapter 4. The GA was so massive and unwieldy that it wasn't clear for many new people how they could get plugged into organizing. Michael Premo (30), an organizer with the anti-foreclosure group Organizing for Occupation (O4O) who was active with Press and DA, said the GA was "an obtuse fuckin' organism that was sometimes impossible to penetrate."[150]

When the media hype subsided after the eviction of Liberty Square on November 15, 2011, the decline in 'tourist' attendance left the GAs to a small group that didn't represent the movement. At an organizing meeting for May Day on February 4, 2012 someone proposed that we bring our May Day resolution to the GA for approval, and asked if there was anyone in the room who regularly attends GAs who could present the proposal. The room burst into laughter, and Chris Longenecker (24), an anarchist active with DA and May Day planning, smiled and said, "you won't find those people [who attend GAs] here, these are organizers!" Eventually we did present the May Day proposal to the GA for a rubber stamp, but those who worked on the proposal were more representative of OWS than those who were regularly attending GAs. As Brett G., who facilitated some of the final GAs, said, "those who came weren't representative of the community and ... facilitation didn't feel comfortable acknowledging it as a representative body."[151] Marisa Holmes (25), one of the most passionate and dedicated anarchists of Occupy, said by this time "the only people left in the assembly were con artists, informants, and the mentally unstable."[152] By early April, facilitation had disowned the GA and they were cancelled on the official OWS site, nycga.net.

Once organizers started to realize that the GA was ill-prepared for dealing with logistical issues, a series of proposals in late October 2011 led to the approval of a spokescouncil which started running in early November. In a spokescouncil, each group represented appoints a delegate to present their collective decision to the lager body. The delegate is not a representative because they merely communicate the will of the smaller group. The spokescouncil model was used by the Clamshell Alliance in New Hampshire in their struggle against the Seabrook Nuclear Plant[153] and it came to be a fixture of the global justice movement as a way for affinity groups to coordinate before big mobilizations. Most famously, it has been used by the Zapatistas in Chiapas, Mexico. The OWS spokescouncil dealt with logistical issues and only the designated spokes from each WG could present the views of their group (who were sitting with them in the circle) to the larger body. Outside people could come to watch, but it was designed as a space for organizers. Marisa Holmes, a key force behind the organizing of the spokescouncil, explained the frustration with the GA:

> It did not make sense for all those most committed to the movement, who were doing most of the work, to be absent from the decision-making process. It seemed they should be central to it since they were most invested and affected by the outcomes.[154]

The hope was that the GA could return to being an outward-facing tool for recruitment and larger political decisions and discussions while the more tedious issues that bored new people could be moved to the spokescouncil. Occupy managed to pull in

OWS Spokescouncil, Nov. 30, 2011.
Photo by Minister Erik McGregor.

people without previous organizing experience in ways few of us had ever witnessed, but incorporating them into the movement wasn't always a smooth process. Our model of consensus decision-making (not consensus in general) implicitly assumed adherence to a certain set of social norms that many were familiar with but a good number were not. Anthony (29), one of the most active DA organizers, described this dynamic in the following way,

> The GA as it was modeled initially was trying to uphold anarchistic principles ... but folks came in and as more and more 'normalized' folks came in and got engaged they brought all of their social norms with them from the 'me and mine' position and the norms of politics and all of that started to come into the group dynamic. So what started happening is that people were lobbying for a specific idea or really gung-ho for their position and the 'us and ours' part of that would get lost and things would break down into a screaming match ... when I showed up in the beginning, and this is part of what engaged me, it felt like from the first GA there was a clear set of social norms that was being upheld, and when folks were speaking out of turn or getting frustrated with process there were folks around them who were willing to talk to them.[155]

Ari Cowan (22), an anarchist organizer with DA, agreed that our larger decision-making bodies were often ineffective because many of the people participating had no investment in the group and no "shared sense of what the goal is." Ari said, "general assemblies and spokescouncils are containers, and containers can hold things, but it's all about what you put into them."[156] For some, putting inexperienced people into directly democratic structures could be perilous. Beth Bogart (56) had many years of experience in the anti-nuclear, anti-war, and women's rights movements and she was the press secretary for Nelson Mandela after his release from prison. In the fall 2011, she was a mainstay of our Press WG before a cop hit her in the head with his baton as she was holding up the court order allowing us to re-enter Liberty after the eviction on November 15, 2011. Growing up in a Quaker environment, Beth pointed out that "in a Quaker meeting you know these people ... at least you have a commitment to a common set of goals."[157] William Haywood Carey (29), an organizer with the info, finance, and legal WGs named after the famous IWW organizer Big Bill Haywood said, "the thing about Quakers is that they've known each other for 15 years. They're not gonna block for fun."[158] Certainly serious participation in any new form of behavior involves a learning curve. Michael Premo noted that we were unable to "really fully grasp that [direct democracy] is a new muscle that needs to be learned,"[159] and Tashy Endres said, "it works only by the measure that we build a culture around it and we haven't done that yet."[160]

Liberal Libertarianism

But I think the main problem with our attempts at direct democracy was not that we brought in so many new people or that they hadn't yet developed the 'proper' cultural orientation. The problem was not *their* culture; it was *our* culture. Or rather it was a highly problematic cultural element in the Occupy milieu that I have come to refer to as *liberal libertarianism*.[161] *Liberal libertarianism* rejects anything that smacks of coercion even when directed toward those who are actively working against the interests of the group. Let me give you an example. In late November I was in touch with Nick Parker from CNN about filming one of the spokescouncils. After checking with a few facilitators, I was told that it was fine for the media to be there since they were open meetings. I thought that it would be a good opportunity to show the public what our direct democracy looked like since the media so rarely covered the actual movement-building aspect of OWS. The spokescouncil was packed and ready to start when one of the two most nefarious disrupters, who I will refer to as A., stood up and started screaming about the lack of gluten-free food at the OWS kitchen. Despite repeated attempts by Bre (22), the facilitator, to get him to bring up his grievance with the Kitchen group directly or during the allotted time in the meeting, he would not be quiet. Groans, sighs, and facepalms resounded and a few people walked up to A. to try to kindly talk him down from his tirade.

But A. wasn't the real problem because you have to expect that such people will pop up. The problem was the people who responded to Bre's attempts to quiet him by shouting, "Let him speak!" Without the enablers, disrupters wouldn't have had any leverage. Later in the meeting the other notorious disrupter, who I will refer to as B., unleashed one of her many outbursts upon the assembly about the inadequacy of the Kitchen group. Once again, a legitimate concern, but the entire meeting grinded to a halt in front of an international news outlet because of one opinion in a room packed with hundreds. But next to B., as she was shouting, several people were nodding in agreement and approving of her actions. Any attempt to silence anyone in any context was anathema. Doing so, in their eyes, would be replicating 'the system.'

Justin Strekal (23), involved with the SIS (shipping and inventory), Accounting, and Facilitation WGs, said, "the amount of times that A. or B. or assholes were able to bring things to a complete standstill with no repercussions, with no mechanism for exclusion; overall that's harmful."[162] It took a long, tedious series of meetings to finally be able to exclude B. from OWS meetings (with the proviso that she could take steps in good faith to work toward re-admission) because there was a vocal minority that was opposed to excluding anyone for any reason. Priscilla Grim recounted a conversation with an early ACT UP organizer who told Priscilla, "the craziest thing I ever heard about Occupy Wall Street is that you guys were letting anybody show up to these GA things…" if there were people causing problems "at ACT UP we would kick them out."[163]

We had plenty of 'normal' people come to meetings but they "were driven away in droves by disrupters."[164] In this context, the problem wasn't 'normal' people who would generally understand process and exclusion. The problem was the people who had dabbled enough in counterculture and diffusely radical politics to understand the potentially oppressive nature of coercion and authority, but hadn't rid themselves of a lingering liberal individualism that prioritized unconstrained individual 'free speech' over any concept of the collectivity. This outlook considered any speech act to be an 'opinion' as important as any other regardless of who it came from or how or when it was expressed. Everything was reduced an opinion, to which everyone is entitled, including politics. It wasn't uncommon to speak with an anti-capitalist whose ideal future included both socialist and capitalist societies side by side because they didn't want to 'impose' their anti-capitalist vision on anyone else. Yet, if you seriously believe that capitalism is a criminal scheme that crushes the vast majority of humanity under its boot to lavish benefits on a few, how could you say that allowing it to exist anywhere would promote an anti-coercive outlook?

Liberal libertarianism fails to recognize that there are times when the way to end coercion is to coerce. After all, a revolution is the most coercive thing there is,[165] but to most anarchists it's silly to decry militant action against the state and capital as "coercive" given the context of exploitation. William Haywood Carey observed this tendency during his time working with the conflict resolution team:

> we had this, in my opinion, almost religious fanaticism toward anti-authority anything. We would run into instances where it was this constant battle where I would have to take a kid that I know for a fact tried to rape someone out of the park and people would be like 'you can't do that! You can't do that![166]

But even Bakunin wrote that "an anarchist society must also include a measure of legitimate coercive power exercised against those who commit harmful acts against the commonwealth..."[167] I'm not trying to say that disrupting a meeting is on par with rape or other destructive behavior, but I think there is a direct theoretical connection between both instances of liberal libertarianism insofar as both reflect a skewed libertarian tendency to 'let be' and a liberal tendency to emphasize the 'coercion' of the individual (whether the disrupter or the capitalist) while ignoring the coercion of the collective (whether the rest of the meeting or the exploited of society as a whole).

This was apparent in the fact that it was more important for *liberal libertarians* to have a space where anyone could do or say whatever they wanted than it was to organize a collective struggle. That's because for many *liberal libertarians* OWS wasn't really about struggle and coordinated action; it was about an experience of personal growth and emotional expression. Their hazy vision of social transformation is about changing individual hearts and minds through personal interactions without any reference to engaging larger structures of power.

The Racial Dynamics of Inclusion and Exclusion

But there was more going on than a simple inability to deal with disruptors. Since B. was black, the issue had a lot to do with the movement's unresolved internal racial issues. This was evident in a number of the frustrated comments from OWS organizers. Jackie Disalvo said that the spokescouncil and GA were, "destroyed by police agents. There were three women. They used race baiting to defend themselves. I remember one guy in the spokescouncil used to refer to one of the women as 'the woman from the NYPD working group.'"[168] Atiq Zabinski (44), involved with media and an OWS public access TV show, said there was "so much misplaced white guilt that one black person was able to completely derail meeting after meeting after meeting."[169] Marisa Holmes wrote that, "Individuals would come with the stated purpose of disrupting meetings and dissolving Spokescouncil. They held the room hostage by couching their criticisms in anti-oppressive language. This was a disservice to the caucuses, which were effectively silenced as a result."[170] Justine Tunney added, "white liberal guilt killed the GA."[171]

Kanene (32), a performance artist from Brooklyn involved with the Press WG, put her finger on the issue:

> If you kicked somebody out of the GA and they were of color, were you kicking them out because you didn't understand that their tone of voice was a typical tone of voice for a person of color and not to be intimidated by that tone of voice, or could it be that that person really truly did deserve to get kicked out ... or were people afraid to kick the person out because the person was of color even though they were doing something that deserved to get kicked out but you didn't want to be that person to kick them out because then you would be the one who was called a racist.[172]

In many people's eyes the standards of conduct in our democratic structures were catered to the educated white middle class. Negesti said,

> I think people who don't express themselves in the socially acceptable way that upper middle class people or even just regular middle class people [speak], they have a harder time functioning in this movement and they're considered aggressive and I think a lot of their behavior *is* aggressive, however there are the same people who are middle class and they have very violent behaviors but not in the same manner. They have violent body language. The words that they use are violent towards each other and oppressive, but we don't recognize it because the way they do it isn't as jarring to people's experiences.[173]

Unfortunately, many white organizers and participants were extremely hostile to addressing race in any serious way. Overall, 71% of organizers interviewed were white, 11% were of African descent, 8% were non-white Latinos, 6% were South Asian or East Asian, and 4% other. Sonny Singh (33), a Sikh organizer and musician involved in the POC Caucus and Facilitation, told me that the "overall vibe was pretty resistant to really digging in deeply into issues of race in particular or anti-oppression issues in general and there was this real desire to say we're all united."[174] This issue came to the fore in a late September, 2011 GA discussion about whether to include a line in the "Declaration of Occupy Wall Street" that said "As one people, formerly divided by the color of our skin, gender, sexual orientation, religion, or lack thereof, political party and cultural background..." In response to this statement, which "ignored people from countries that have been colonized, communities right here in New York where democratic participation is anything but a given, as well as countless histories of oppression and inequality," Sonny Singh, Hena Ashraf, and Manissa Maharawal (29), one of the founders of the POC Caucus, took the brave step to block that language.[175] It was an important step against the dominant whitewashing ideology that pervaded Occupy. Nicole Carty (24) of Facilitation described a lot of OWS organizers as "post-racial slightly in being like 'and now we can live together' and like, sure, that's beautiful but no we can't and actually you'll see how much we can't and it's really important to carve out these spaces and respect them so we can learn from each other."[176] When Terry (36), an artist involved with Occupy Comix, and other POC organizers went around to different WGs to talk to them about how their voices weren't being heard in the movement, "people would automatically have almost these prepared answers like 'Oh? Did you speak up in a meeting? Oh? Well we're diverse, we're democratic, so there's no reason for that."[177] It was essentially what Joel Olson called "left colorblindness."[178]

I remember standing around with a white progressive OWS organizer in Liberty when the subject of the POC caucus came up. He decried its existence and said that if their notion of "exclusion" had prevailed in the 60s, then black and white people could never have worked together in the Civil Rights Movement. Although it was naïve of me, I was surprised by his comment because I had subconsciously assumed we were beyond that narrow outlook. I pointed out that a number of prominent African American groups such as the Black Panthers had exclusively black membership to assert black autonomy in response to a long history of white supremacy but they still worked in coalition with groups of other races. I don't think I convinced him.

During a spokescouncil discussion about banning people, Sonny Singh raised the question of how we define 'violence' on behalf of the POC Caucus. As he raised important questions about the slipperiness of the term, many people in the room rolled their eyes and 'down-twinkled' his comments.[179] The first time Sara Zainab Bokhari attended a spokescouncil a white person held up a sign that said "Aryan Brotherhood" as a "joke." In response, the POC Caucus tried to stop the proceedings, which they had the right to do under the community agreement. When they did so, they were accused of being "reverse racists" and "overreacting." The spokescouncil process was allowed to turn to mush when the same individuals repeatedly and blatantly halted the proceedings out of process over and over again, but when there was a legitimate grievance raised by the POC Caucus they were met with hostility and an extremely inflexible procedural interpretation.

Many people spoke about OWS process being too lax or too rigid; it was both. When it should have been tighter, a mix of *liberal libertarianism* and a lack of a clear racial justice lens allowed things to fall apart, but when we should have taken a step back to evaluate how our structures were functioning, we were too rigid. On the one hand, a group of predominantly white organizers would sit back and let a single individual shut down everything out of process, while on the other hand they would make it extremely difficult for the POC Caucus to speak when it was their turn in order to carry out their agreed upon role of acting as a safeguard against white supremacy. I think a lot of the hostility that white organizers had against disrupters was unleashed on the POC Caucus as a group which sheds light on the underlying racial dynamics of the situation to begin with.

Part of the problem stemmed from the fact that many new white organizers hadn't had any experience with anti-oppression issues. S. (32) is a longtime anarchist environmental activist involved in Earth First! and the Cascadia Forest Alliance during her time in the Pacific Northwest who participated in the Press WG. She pointed out that she

> had the privilege of going to college and in college there's always that moment in the college activist group where everyone realizes that its rampant with sexism and racism and we're losing people and there are all these heart-to-hearts and trainings and you sort of try to get through it and we all sort of leave with this different understanding of how those dynamics work and we were working a bunch of folks that hadn't gone through those ... We did actually have a bunch of trainings around gender and race stuff but the thing is that everyone goes to nine million meetings so who's gonna go to those meetings? It's gonna be the people who are already invested in those.[180]

Ultimately we couldn't really take steps towards addressing these issues because we couldn't even get on the same page about what the issues were or whether they even really existed. Moving forward, it's clear that we need to design an anti-oppressive meeting structure that can respond to disruptors when necessary while retaining enough flexibility to evolve. As Sonny wrote, "if we can make it through this together and adopt radical, transformative justice approaches to accountability, violence, and harm in our community, perhaps we will in turn be well on our way to creating viable alternatives to this system we all abhor."[181]

The Limits of Consensus

Unfortunately, our consensus process was not up to the challenge of disruptions, potential infiltration, and their enabling *liberal libertarianism* in a context fraught with white supremacy and "left colorblindness." If we had a clearer protocol for excluding disruptive people grounded in a solid anti-oppressive framework, it could have worked much better, but that still would not have dealt with infiltrators who followed process. As OWS organizer Sumumba Sobukwe said, NYPD police commissioner "Ray Kelly can send 5 of his police into a GA and we can have something very progressive as a proposal and it can get blocked."[182] The openness of our meetings was great for recruitment, but it gave our enemies an opportunity to influence our methods of combating them. Historically, anarchists have made many decisions through general assemblies but they have often been general assemblies of members. Allowing anyone and everyone to participate on an equal footing right off the street was useful for propaganda but that practice is not appropriate for all decision-making bodies. This dynamic was exacerbated by the uniform implementation of consensus when it seems that it's most effective when participants share some sense of purpose. As Yotam Marom phrased it, "Occupy did a lot to assert that it's possible to govern ourselves, but also people get carried away and form new orthodoxies like consensus ... consensus is really good sometimes and its really backwards sometimes."[183]

Many people didn't seem to realize that when you vote 'no' to a proposal you are implicitly voting 'yes' to its inverse. So, for example, if someone proposes a new guideline for personal conduct in the group in response to some hateful behavior and it's rejected (perhaps because those who it is aimed at vote it down), then implicitly people have voted in favor of retaining the status quo, at least for the time being. The distinction between 'doing something' and 'not doing something' is misleading because any outcome of a vote will mean that the group will 'do something' either actively or passively. Once you understand this, it becomes clear that in some groups 11% determine the outcome to the detriment of the other 89%. When you get to the point where the minority is obstructing the majority, you have strayed far away from the thoughtfulness and inclusivity of consensus, which is not intended for power struggles. Reflecting upon the use of consensus in MNS George Lakey said that "consensus can be a conservative influence, stifling the prospects of organizational change."[184]

Another problem with our direct democracy was that it wasn't clear how it could scale up to facilitate the self-management of larger groups of people. Many I spoke with, including anarchists, were skeptical or hesitant to speak about the potential for a directly democratic system at a larger regional or global level because our use of consensus at a large level wasn't easily scalable. I think we were on the right track with the spokescouncil's use of delegates, which were conduits for WG decisions rather than autonomous representatives. That provided a hint at what scalable direct democracy could look like. In the future, we must not shy away from creating more large-scale decision-making bodies that operate through mandates carried by recallable delegates. Such mechanisms would retain a concrete, transparent collectivity that new people could engage with rather than a nebulous network based on personal relations. In the spokescouncil we had "a war over membership, which left many casualties."[185] We didn't have clear-cut criteria for determining which OWS groups were 'important' enough to participate. Originally, we started a vetting process for each group, but the lack of clear-cut criteria combined with the *liberal libertarian* aversion to the exclusion of any group bogged down the process until it ground to a halt and the floodgates opened. This meant that organizers increasingly turned to personal relations with each other rather than the body as a formally constituted organism. When combined with our inability to exclude disrupters it turned into the most popular OWS phrase for a disaster: a "shit show."

I think a lot of people learned the wrong lessons from our failures. Many walked away thinking that direct democracy was impossible beyond small groups of people and either concluded that direct democracy was unrealistic or organizing large groups was problematic. If anarchists are serious about building a just, democratic society, we need to reflect that world in our practice. That means that while it's fine to have small collectives and groups, we also need big formations that project our vision of global mutual aid and democratic coordination. Since consensus was so heavily associated with anarchism, anarchism reaped the benefits of its successes and suffered the stigma of its failures when in fact the historical range of anarchist organizing models is far more flexible than OWS reflected.

"We don't have demands; we are the demand"

Understanding the political composition of OWS sheds light on why we never came up with a short list of demands. I found that out of the 192 interviews I conducted, only four organizers wanted a short list of demands to start, although 18 said that in retrospect we should have developed some as we went along. From the start, Cecily McMillan (23) was one of the strongest internal voices for demands. She told me that she was in touch with representatives from sympathetic labor unions and political organizations that were concerned that the movement lacked direction so she helped put together the Demands WG. Eventually they came up with the following demands strategy: a short-term demand that there be no cuts for public sector workers, an intermediate demand for a moratorium on student debt at all New York state institutions, and a long-term demand to end corporate personhood. However, from the start she said that she received a lot of hostility from other organizers who accused her of trying to co-opt OWS on behalf of the Democratic Socialists of America (DSA). She said "horizontalism was being used not to hear everybody's voice but more so being used to make sure that there wouldn't be a unified voice; it was being used as a tool of anarchy rather than a tool for organization…"[186] In the course of my interviews, I never came across another organizer who had participated in the Demands WG and I never knew who any of them were during the fall of 2011. Given the overwhelming hostility to selecting a short list of demands, it's not surprising that the Demands WG got nowhere.

So why was there so much hostility against a short list of demands? First, I'll start with the reasons that we emphasized with the media. As Colby Hopkins (33) argued, "we profess to be a movement of the 99% but the people that are actively participating aren't the 99%"[187] so we can't come up with a finite list of demands until we get more popular involvement. I used this argument a lot with journalists. Early on, *CNN Money* published an article called "Why Occupy Wall Street isn't about a list of demands" which quoted me saying that "making a list of three or four demands would have ended the conversation before it started." Liberals were very receptive to the idea of Occupy Wall Street as a conversation because it implied their brand of non-confrontational political pluralism. I went on to argue that,

> We don't want New York to form its own political agenda and drive the conversation in other cities. I would be unhappy if

> people in LA or Chicago were waiting on us to do something. That would be politics as usual ... To tell everyone that we have the solution to their specific problems, that would be what the political parties are already doing. That isn't working. And that's the whole point.[188]

By leaving the door open to the hypothetical possibility of demands emerging we could maintain the support of the pro-demand camp. Sometimes I'd even state the obvious by pointing out that 'we could end up with a set of demands any day now if the GA approved them.' This made it sound like a tangible reality but we all knew such a list would never pass. Some members of the Press WG, like Beth Bogart and Jeff Smith (41), liked to argue that it really wasn't our job to come up with specific policy solutions because the role of the social movement is to wake up the population. I wasn't fond of that argument because it implied that the government was capable of solving the problem, whereas in fact they *were* the problem. In contrast I really liked Swedish anarchist, People's Kitchen organizer, and fellow Rutgers PhD student Stina Soderling's (28) point that "we don't have demands; we *are* the demand."[189] In other words, OWS was embodying the world it desired.

William Jesse (31) of the Press WG made a good tactical observation that if we had chosen several overarching demands it would have given the media fodder to discredit us.[190] Pundits would have dissected the demands, concluded that they were unrealistic and moved on. Leaving it open-ended allowed us to remain slippery enough to escape any delegitimizing classification. Amin Husain argued against demands saying that,

> basically when you speak of demands you have already reached an advanced stage of the problem and solution. So, problem, solution, demand. That's not where we're at. Many people have different analyses of what the problem is and

what the solution is...[191]

Amin's emphasis on the variety of analyses in OWS points toward one of the most common and sensible arguments against demands: there are too many problems to settle on only a few. If OWS aspired to be an inclusive transformative social justice movement, then how could it eschew a wide variety of urgent political problems that are actually interrelated with Wall Street, the professed focus of the movement? Timothy Eastman (30) of the Media WG came up with a funny analogy to explain why it wouldn't make sense for OWS to have a finite set of ten demands: "I kinda think of it like: Batman doesn't have a list of demands. You know what Batman's about. He doesn't just say 'I'll get these ten criminals then I'm done.'"[192] The benefit of allowing a wide variety of issues to relate to OWS was that it allowed for the creation of inclusive "broad movement space."[193] As David Korn (25) of Comhub (a WG for internal communication) phrased it, "not having demands allowed everybody to come and become part of this, everybody who wanted to, every body who's frustrated, angry or had any kind of issues that they wanted to address felt like this could be their movement."[194]

Tim Fitzgerald (28) was happy with the lack of demands because he was concerned that any short set that would have been agreed upon would have been excessively reformist.[195] This was my first reason for opposing demands. I figured that if a concerted effort were made to narrow down a short list of demands then socialists and progressives would put all of their energy into pushing some sort of nebulous "jobs for all" or "money out of politics" demand that would deflate the revolutionary energy of the encampment. Another interesting take on the issue came from Brett G. who said that OWS was "an umbrella where different issues can coexist and different groups can make demands but the umbrella itself can't make a demand."[196] Occupy wasn't an organization so it couldn't make demands, it could only unite various groups and campaigns that would each formulate their own issue-specific demands.

Perhaps the most common anti-demand argument that I heard was that demanding something from the government or a corporation legitimates their authority. Therefore, the truly revolutionary position to take is to eschew demands entirely. I was really surprised by the prevalence of this argument. Not only is it untrue, it ignores a long history of revolutionary organizing oriented around demands. The CNT, the most successful anarcho-syndicalist union in history, has regularly organized campaigns around specific demands since its inception. On February 15, 2013 the CNT started a campaign around the slogan "*¡Que el paro, no te pare!*" or "Don't let unemployment stop you!" Among the campaign's demands were a 30-hour workweek without reduced salary and a retirement age of 55. Labor organizing is essentially impossible without issuing demands because it leaves workers with the dichotomy of servility or revolution without having the power to accomplish the latter.

This prevalent confusion about the potential role of demands in the revolutionary process stems from a fundamental misunderstanding about who the audience is when demands are issued. Many Occupy organizers seemed to imagine a simple interaction where the protest group issues demands directly to an elite and then waits with fingers crossed for that elite to respond. In other words, many organizers thought of the demands issue in the same way as the media, in terms of *communication with the elite,* and concluded that the only way to avoid a mainstream outlook is the flip the script and never demand anything. But what this perspective misses is that most people *do* believe that elites possess legitimate authority, something that can't be forgotten. It is the role of the revolutionary to disrupt that mindset, but it rarely works to just tell people that they're wrong based on abstract arguments without an example.

Therefore the revolutionary demand often plays the role of testing the popular notion that elites have legitimate authority by saying 'Oh, you say you can provide for the people? Well prove it.'

A classic example can be found in The Ten-Point Program of the Black Panther Party. Their second demand was "We Want Full Employment For Our People." In their description of the demand the Panthers said, "We believe that the federal government is responsible and obligated to give every man employment or a guaranteed income." They knew very well that the government would never fulfill that obligation, so the next sentence said "We believe that if the White American businessmen will not give full employment, then the means of production should be taken from the businessmen and placed in the community..." Essentially the Panthers made the demand of full employment knowing that it could not be met because it would give the people an insight into the inadequacies of the government and lead them to conclude that in the absence of full employment the collective expropriation of the means of production would be the only alternative. The demand functions as a revolutionary intervention in the normal channels of communication between the people and the government.

A related misconception that I heard occasionally was that if your group makes demands, and those demands are met, then you're screwed because you can't continue beyond your originally stated goals. This also seems to come from a lack of experience organizing actual campaigns. A related comment was that issuing demands is weird because it sounds like "we're somehow holding something bizarrely hostage." Some had so little experience that they had only heard the language of demands in the context Hollywood hostage dramas. In some cases, it was a prime example of the worst excesses of Occupy arrogance and bravado that some people could ignore hundreds of years of revolutionary struggle oriented around specific campaigns and essentially say 'demands are dumb, *duh*! How come it took everyone so long to figure that out?'

What those organizers didn't understand is that if you get what you demand, in the case of a labor dispute for example, that doesn't stop your progress, it accelerates it (provided you maintain a revolutionary political orientation). In the early 20th century, the IWW gained tens of thousands of members and scared the federal government so much that it conducted a coordinated campaign of repression to stomp out the union because it won improvements in the daily lives of workers. Errico Malatesta pointed out that if revolutionary demands are met "and if the government does give way, then the people gain confidence in themselves and make ever increasing demands, until such time as the incompatibility between freedom and authority becomes clear and the violent struggle is engaged."[197] Having demands met through struggle is how popular power is built and revolutions are made. Historically, the only sector of the revolutionary left to deny this argument were the insurrectionary anarchists who thought that any improvement in the quality of life of the oppressed made them complacent.[198] Not surprisingly, this minority outlook gained very few adherents. The vast majority of anarchists have always understood that organizing paves the road to victory.

So while I agreed that demands didn't make sense in the Occupy context for many of the reasons explained above, they are often essential tools for revolutionary organizing.

Hidden in Plain Sight: Occupy, Anarchism, and the Media

Was the media entirely oblivious to the anarchist influence in Occupy? Not entirely, but pretty close. One of the main reasons for this is that they didn't know what to look for. In their eyes, anarchists were punk kids in black breaking stuff, and while we had our fair share of punk kids in black, they didn't break things and there were tons of other people who didn't look the part. One afternoon in early October my partner, Senia Barragan (25), was sitting at the press table in Liberty fielding questions from journalists as a member of the Press WG and found herself in a conversation with a reporter from *The Atlantic*. Half way through the conversation the journalist took a moment to scan the throngs of people in the park and said to Senia, "you know, I thought there would be a lot of anarchists here but I don't see any." Senia is an anarchist, but that never occurred to the journalist because all he saw was a young Latina woman who wasn't dressed like a punk. She paused for a second considering what to say, and, smirking, she said "well I *am* an anarchist." "Oh..." he responded.

Very rarely did reporters put the pieces together to realize that our general assemblies, consensus decision-making process, lack of hierarchy, resistance to electoral politics, and emphasis on direct action had anarchism written all over them. Of course you had to know what to look for, and, for reasons discussed in Chapter 1, they didn't. David Graeber wrote a number of pieces about the anarchist influence in Occupy,[199] and the press took note of his participation as an anarchist,[200] to the point of referring to him as "the Anti-Leader of Occupy Wall Street,"[201] but he was seen as just one individual and the issue of anarchism was usually regarded as more of a sideshow, curiosity,[202] or kind of 'did you know' about Occupy rather than an issue of central importance.

Especially early on, the liberal media had no interest in exploring the influence of anarchism because liberals still hoped OWS would become the liberal tea party. A humorous *New York Magazine* article from October 4, 2011 had the headline "Obama's Unlikely Anarchist Friends," and argued that a radical protest movement was good for liberals because it would scare the right into compromising with the Democrats.[203] This article merely used the term "anarchist" facetiously to draw in readers.

Interestingly, I think conservatives were initially less likely than usual to ascribe influence to anarchists because OWS was so big and popular. Instead, they focused on proving that OWS was not organic and grassroots because it was really being organized behind the scenes by George Soros,[204] Moveon.org, and major unions.[205]

By the end of October into early November, however, both liberal and conservative coverage of the 'radical' element of the movement started to converge onto the theme that Occupy was being 'infiltrated' by 'extremists' and anarchists. The liberals were starting to understand that we weren't their Tea Party, and so, with the conservatives, they were increasingly eager to mythologize the recent historical memory of the first month of the movement in order to contrast it and to distance it from a supposedly encroaching radicalism. On November 7, 2011 Michael Gerson, former speechwriter for George Bush, wrote an article in the *Washington Post* with the headline: "As radicalism creeps in, credibility retreats from OWS." In it he gleefully pointed out that, "The emergence of Occupy Wall Street raised Democratic hopes for the emergence of a leftist equivalent of the Tea Party movement. The comparison is now laughable." He went on to argue that we actually have some "ideological coherence" around our "collectivist people's councils" which were inspired by "Marxist socialism" and "anarchism." One for two isn't bad. He concluded by rightly pointing out that despite the hopes of liberals "OWS is not a seminar on income inequality—not the Center for American Progress on a camping trip. It is a leftist movement with a militant wing."[206] He just didn't realize that it was much more than a wing.

On October 25, 2011 James Miller asked in his *New York Times* Op-Ed, "Will Extremists Hijack Occupy Wall Street?"[207] In his October 27, 2011 *CNN* article "Occupy Wall Street is going nowhere without leadership," Marty Linsky argued that it was essential for OWS to "begin to make hard choices, create priorities, allocate human and financial resources, and keep the anarchistic outliers from undermining the potential outcomes."[208] But we weren't outliers, we *were* the potential outcomes.

Over time, as OWS was being portrayed as less and less mainstream and various black bloc actions were carried out on the West Coast, the mainstream media began to focus more and more on the radicalism of OWS. Often extremely conservative media, like Fox News or Glenn Beck, were far ahead on this topic. This was not really because they were initially more observant. Instead, it was because their kneejerk reaction to any demonstration or action to the left of Mitt Romney is always to try to portray it as socialist. It just so happens that this time they were right. As Stefan Fink (23) an anarchist OWS organizer pointed out,

> I listened to Glenn Beck talk recently about anarchism and Occupy and ... he was actually pretty accurate about how Occupy actually does have all these anarchists and does anarchist things and maybe the right should be concerned about that. I think democrats tried to whitewash away the radicalism and say 'actually that's not what they want at all' but the right I think is aware of this radical side.[209]

Buck Sexton, a former CIA agent now working for Glenn Beck's *The Blaze* who wrote an e-book called *Occupy: American Spring, The Making of a Revolution,* claimed that the "core element of a few hundred" OWS organizers were about 1/3 reformist, 1/3 Marxist, and 1/3 anarchist.[210] My findings put the reformist element at a little over 20%, but his estimate shows how many conservatives succeeded in detecting the revolutionary element in Occupy but lacked the knowledge to be able to discern Marxist from anarchist influences. Nevertheless, in an interview with Glenn Beck, he made an all too perceptive observation about the underlying nature of the inner politics of OWS in relation to our outward facing rhetoric:

> Most people, because the way the media's covered it, they tend to think of it as this movement about 'inequality' and trying to address issues of inequality and they use other terms too like 'social justice,' but when you spend a fair amount of time with and around them talking about what they believe, they're pretty steeped actually in hardcore Marxist rhetoric. A lot of them are anarchists. They will say that openly. Sometimes they refer to themselves as anarcho-socialist. They are on occasion surprisingly well read, with people like Mikhail Bakunin, a Russian anarchist, sort of a contemporary of Marx, but they can get into that stuff *because they believe it*. Because they actually want that to happen and they think they're at a particular time in history right now in America where they can push for that. Now they don't say that when MSNBC shows up and they say 'Oh what are you guys here for?' they say 'Wall Street got bailed out and we got sold out.'[211]

Chapter Three

Translating Anarchy

> "Early on, before what I call 'The Great Anarchist Conspiracy of 2011' got revealed, which was Occupy Wall Street, I would say that I wanted horizontal direct democracy, and anyone with a mild understanding of radical politics knows what I'm talking about, but that was a way of jumping around the a-word."
>
> —Guy Steward, anarchist OWS organizer[1]

"Do you identify as a democrat or a republican…" As the reporter from *CNN Money* asked me about my political affiliation, I went into a mini-panic. It was the early morning of October 4, 2011, my first full-fledged day of OWS press work, and as I balanced on the edge of a Zuccotti flowerbed with a Chinese camera-crew patiently waiting for me off to my left and hordes of people shifting by me, I realized that I hadn't fully thought out how I would articulate my politics in relation to Occupy. There was no way that I was going to lie and say I was a democrat. That would completely defeat the purpose. But I hadn't made a conscious decision about whether I would wear the circle-A on my sleeve or not. As the reporter paused, I made a series of frantic political calculations in my mind, but before I could finish she made the decision easy: "…or are you an independent?" "Yes!" I blurted out, "I'm *very* independent!"[2]

The most exciting aspect of OWS for me was the opening it provided for the mass dissemination of anarchist(ic) politics. Unlike some younger organizers who literally thought this could be *the* revolution, everyday I was shocked anew that the occupation continued and people kept showing up. I kept wondering when everyone would wake up and realize that they were engaging in anarchist practices ultimately designed to smash the state. I was sure that they would realize on October 15, 2011 after we carried out direct action against the banks, but they didn't. As the arrest totals mounted, I thought it would fizzle, but it didn't. That's because our message of economic justice and participatory democracy was striking a chord with most Americans. So I tried to squeeze as much juice as possible out of every single opportunity to communicate an essentially anti-authoritarian, anti-capitalist message to the wider public as accessibly as possible before our window of opportunity closed. If I had started off using the word "anarchism," many people would have tuned out right away. Therefore, in a very literal sense, I was "translating anarchy" to people who were receptive to its contents but exceedingly wary of its usual linguistic packaging and popular rhetorical baggage.

And I wasn't alone. I found that 65% of self-identified anarchists among the OWS organizers interviewed decided not to use the terms "anarchism" or "anarchist" when describing their politics to the media or the average person on the street. Moreover, those anarchists who were explicit about their anarchist politics were much less frequently involved in Occupy projects designed to communicate with the broader public. In fact, many of them had to answer my question in hypothetical terms since they had barely done any interviews (or were hostile to speaking with the media) and spent their time organizing. When taken in tandem with the 33% of all organizers who had anarchistic politics but wouldn't identify with anarchism explicitly under any circumstance, it's clear that there was a widespread, largely unspoken commitment to the dissemination of anti-capitalist, anti-hierarchical, anti-oppressive politics in a digestible form. Occupy Wall Street was a mechanism for translating anarchy.

Zombies and "Anonymous Fan-Boys"

I hadn't always considered Occupy to be such a fantastic opportunity to promote anarchist politics. At first I thought it was a joke. During the week leading up to the first day of OWS, September 17, 2011, my partner, Senia, mentioned something about a Wall Street protest she found on Facebook and suggested that we take her 14-year-old sister Karina since the forecast looked good and it would be a nice excuse to go into the city on a Saturday afternoon. Karina's a badass radical-in-training who had her photo in *Punk Planet* leading a large anti-war march holding a large cardboard dove over her head at the age of 9, had her photo in *The New York Times* when she braved a cold winter day to stand on an IWW Starbucks picket line when she was 10, and routinely speaks out against racism and homophobia at her school. When we got to Wall Street in the afternoon, it was blocked off by the police, so we walked down Broadway to Bowling Green. We came upon the satirical, anti-consumerist performance artist Reverend Billy shouting and singing from the stairs of the American Indian Museum, and milled around chatting with the few people we recognized. I didn't even realize that the idea was to sleep in a public space, and when I heard about the idea to occupy, I thought it was a shallow imitation of the tactics used in Tahrir Square in Egypt and Puerta del Sol in Madrid. It seemed like just another self-marginalizing protest.

I wasn't alone in thinking that. Jen Waller (25), a paralegal with the Legal WG, was working for a lawyer down the street from Zuccotti and came down on September 17, but she didn't have a great first impression: "I was like who are all of these out-of-towners? We protest Wall St. all the time. We always have protests in front of the stock exchange. It never does anything."[3] Sam Corbin (28) is a long-time professional organizer with Greenpeace and the Ruckus Society who helped organize the earlier May 12, 2011 Wall Street protest. When she heard about

Occupy Wall Street she thought, "we just did this! What's going on?"[4] Likewise, Michael Premo, a long-time New York organizer, saw a lot of new people and was "slightly suspicious of that."[5] Sparrow Ingersoll didn't recognize many people and characterized it as "a weird meeting of the stand-around-club with a bunch of Anonymous fan-boys."[6] As it turned out, 23% of the organizers I interviewed came from out of the New York area for Occupy Wall Street.

Nevertheless, Senia, Karina, and I went on the march up Broadway to Zuccotti and participated in the first breakout groups, which discussed what the "one demand" might be. I didn't know about the *Adbusters* poster and it seemed absurd to me that anyone there would think they could generate enough leverage to demand anything of anyone. The faces in our small circle were mostly young and their ideas for a single demand focused on things like repealing Citizens United and ending Corporate Personhood. One after another as the megaphone was passed around the circle (before the police banned amplified sound and the now famous People's Mic took over), people decried Corporate Personhood as if it were the source of original sin. After a while I took a turn and basically said that it doesn't matter whether the law recognizes corporations as people, cats, or dogs because it's not about cracking down on 'bad' corporations; it's about the fundamental nature of capitalism. After registering my protest comment, we went to get some dumplings in Chinatown and went home. When I got home I wrote this on Facebook:

> I enjoyed #occupywallstreet today, but it was depressing to see how many young people speaking in the General Assembly clearly have had such limited political education, have only the vaguest structural understanding of capitalism and its relationship with electoral politics, and are desperately searching in the dark to understand what to do.

> If we don't get on that (in a serious way) our youth will think that the solution is to increase the corporate tax rate by 1% and elect more democrats...

Senia and I both thought it was a liberal mess. She said it was,

> Mostly young white folks who I immediately dismissed because I was kind of sick of working with those people. They were saying get money out of politics, end corporate personhood which was kind of really reformist shit which I thought was just kind of weak.[7]

Malcolm Nokizaru (22), an "insurrectionary anarchist nihilist" from Brooklyn who worked with DA, the POC Caucus, and Safer Spaces, thought that "this is gonna be a shitshow and it's not gonna be a global revolution and it's gonna be a bunch of liberals hanging out in public."[8] As we would discover, it *was* a bunch of liberals hanging out, but the essential presence of a core group of anarchist and anarchistic organizers coupled with non-hierarchical organizing models propelled OWS in a much more radical direction.

However, it only occurred to me later that if I had been 18 I would have been bursting with excitement at the prospect of joining a sleep-in near Wall Street, even if it was detached and naïve. But after more than 10 years of experience I thought I had grown wiser (and, as I realized, more jaded). Aaron Bornstein (31), a PhD student in cognitive neuroscience and organizer with the OWS Think Tank and May Day planning, spent years in the global justice and anti-war movements before becoming "sort of disillusioned for a while." He told me,

> I saw the pictures [of OWS] and I watched the livestream and I'm like OK this looks exactly like the college radicals that I knew dressing up putting bandanas on their faces. That's cool,

> I totally get why that's empowering. It's not gonna mean a damn thing…I feel kind of old for thinking that. God I should be excited about this. If I were twenty I would totally be down there right away, what the fuck is going on?[9]

In my experience the naïveté and/or boldness of the early organizers who defied the odds to sleep out on a slab of concrete near Wall Street seemed to have something to do with youth and a lack of political experience (or perhaps fewer soul-crushing political defeats).

That was definitely my qualitative impression, but I decided to test that perception based on the interview data. I divided the 192 organizers I interviewed (plus myself) into 3 groups based on when they started actively organizing with Occupy (not necessarily when they first showed up). Group 1, which had 33 people, was active prior to September 17 planning over the summer of 2011; Group 2, which had 76 people, got involved in September after the occupation started but before it became a media sensation;[10] and Group 3, which had 84 people, got involved from October onward. My hypothesis based on my observations was that Group 2 would be younger and less politically experienced than Group 1, which had the commitment to put things together over the summer, or Group 3, which wasn't convinced about OWS until the momentum got going.

Overall, I didn't find vast differences in age or previous political experience. The average age of the entire group of 192 interviewees was 31,[11] and for each group the figure was nearly identical, although Group 2 was slightly younger (Group 1: 32; Group 2: 30; Group 3: 31). As I suspected, a large percentage of organizers were under 30 (Group 1: 70%; Group 2: 59%; Group 3: 50%), but when I distinguished between those under 25 and those 25-29, I found a noticeable contrast. Among those under 30, 26% were under 25 in Group 1; 57% were under 25 in Group 2; and 31% were under 25 in Group 3. This gives us some quantitative evidence to support my sense that while all three groups were young, the youth of those who took a chance on occupation in late September, often leaving home and traveling across the country, were younger. The percentage of organizers without previous political experience demonstrates a startling shift over time (Group 1: 9%; Group 2: 28%; Group 3: 36%), as OWS brought many into activism for the first time once it became a big deal. Group 3 had a strong dichotomy between experienced organizers and youthful newcomers. Or, as Winnie Wong (38), an anarchist filmmaker and permaculture designer who formed the Sustainability WG said, "it was seasoned activists working with 18-year-olds."[12]

Despite my skepticism, I kept an eye on what was going on through Facebook as I spent my afternoons preparing a guest lecture on 1960s and 70s European radicalism that I was going to give to Rutgers Professor Melissa Feinberg's 20th Century Europe course that I was a Teaching Assistant for. As I read about the Red Brigades[13] and the Provos,[14] I took breaks to read updates about OWS on the internet. Several incidents caught my attention. First, I was happy to see that OWS marched in solidarity with Troy Davis, an African American man murdered by the state of Georgia on September 21st despite appeals from human rights organizations. It reflected a wider understanding of economic justice than I thought the occupation might have. Next, I was really upset to see the video that went viral of the pepper spraying of Chelsea Elliot and Jeanne Mansfield on September 24th, but I was especially taken aback when the video was picked up Lawrence O'Donnell of MSNBC who used it to not only critique police actions but talk about police brutality in general. As much as I may have had critiques of OWS, I respected the fact that people were taking to the streets and at least doing *something* in the prevailing context of apathy. But at the time I thought the video was more significant for the opportunity it gave O'Donnell to speak about the police state than it was for anything having to do with OWS.

Finally, I read on September 29th that the Transit Workers Union (TWU) endorsed OWS.[15] It was clear that something was brewing and my curiosity peaked. So the next day, September 30th, Senia, Karina and I went down to Zuccotti once again and found the park packed with people expecting to see Radiohead. Apparently someone had hoaxed some Occupy organizers claiming to be Radiohead's manager and it was somewhat plausible since they were playing in New York that night.[16] Once the Radiohead fans left in frustration, we had an awesome march over to 1 Police Plaza and held a GA right in their courtyard. There was a large crowd, great enthusiasm and a pleasant lack of the usual authoritarian socialist groups peddling their papers and cramming their outdated slogans into every political orifice. More than anything it just felt good, and I decided I'd come back to every Occupy event I could make it to.

It just so happened that the next event was the infamous march across the Brooklyn Bridge on October 1st. When Senia and I arrived at Zuccotti, people were unloading the first issue of the *Occupied Wall Street Journal*. I was so impressed with the professional layout and presentation of the paper[17] and it's accessible but radical language that I grabbed a stack and started handing them out to spectators as we marched north up Broadway. Usually trying to hand out information to spectators is a challenge and they walk away when they see you coming, but that day people were coming up to *me* to get a paper. People sensed that there was something unusual going on. As we marched, I didn't know that this was going to be 'The Brooklyn Bridge March' since I didn't know where we were heading, so Senia and I ended up on the pedestrian walkway of the bridge because we were handing out papers and that's where the people were. The police didn't seem too concerned that people were flooding the roadway and we were already about halfway across before I noticed them slowly marching with zip-ties in their direction. Of course, if they had just let us get to the other side of the bridge, the roadway would have been blocked for a relatively short time, but arresting more than 700 people and putting them on MTA buses one-by-one ground the bridge to a halt for hours (and made it the media sensation that propelled the movement).

But what really grabbed my attention was the response of the group on the roadway to police encirclement. Instead of widespread panic, someone shouted "Mic-check! Mic-check!" the signal to initiate the People's Mic system of call and response communication, to get people to sit down. After many sat, there was an attempt to hold essentially an impromptu GA right there in the middle to calm the situation and act as a group. It didn't last long as people stood up with the start of arrests, but that moment of group solidarity and collective action in a moment of chaos really spoke to me. It seemed to say that this wasn't just another march ending in arrests, and this wasn't just another group of protesters. In retrospect, I realized that it poked a small hole in the layers of frustration that had been gradually obscuring my optimism over the years.

On Monday October 3rd I felt a deep sense of crisis. As someone who is generally pretty decisive, it was strange to be so torn between the unknown promise of Occupy and my mountain of academic obligations. After some discussion with Senia, I decided to drop everything for a week to spend every day in Zuccotti and see how I felt about things at the end. That week turned into months. At first I just wanted to participate and inject more of an explicitly anti-capitalist orientation into the rhetoric. To that end, before I came down on the 3rd I hurriedly put together a large white sign that said, "THE CRISIS *IS* CAPITALISM."[18] When I got to the park, I laid the sign down among the many lining the pavement along the northwest corner.

A little while later on that day, Senia and I got our faces painted like zombies to go on the zombie march down Wall Street eating fake money. I was pleased to see that some random person was carrying my capitalism sign on the march. When we got back to Zuccotti after the zombie march, NBC *Nightly News* was setting up for a live shot across the street from the south end of the park. Protesters were gathered behind the camera crew in the park watching, and when I walked over (still in full zombie) someone suggested that I start groaning and flailing behind the reporter once the live broadcast was underway. I said, "sure, what the hell," and once the reporter started talking I staggered toward her with fake money falling out of my mouth. Steve the NBC producer, a nice guy sympathetic to OWS who I would soon come to work with on a daily basis, was none too pleased and pushed me back onto the curb. I wasn't sure if it was really live, but a second later I got a call from my mother who was shocked to see me barge into her regular evening news.

At that point, I was really just trying to inject some radicalism and disruption into Occupy, but I gradually began to realize that this was a serious political 'happening' that I wanted to do more to push forward. Reflecting upon the skill set and experience that I brought to the table from organizing a number of press campaigns and drafting press releases for various groups, I decided that I wanted to contribute to the effort to push back against the media's attempt to discredit Occupy. The presence of international news media and flocks of new people every single day provided an amazing opportunity for political expression and I wanted to play a part in preventing OWS from sliding into a voter registration campaign for the Democratic Party. That Monday, I saw Tyler Combelic of the Press WG speaking to reporters while wearing a suit, and so I went up to him and told him I wanted to help out with press work. The following day, Tuesday October 4th, I showed up with a buttoned shirt and khakis and went to find Tyler. When I found him, he was chatting with Mara Schiavocampo of NBC who was working on a piece for *The Today Show*. I said hello and right away he replied, "Hey! Wanna talk to NBC?"

There were so many journalists swarming the park at every moment that the Press WG was eagerly searching for as many dedicated, competent people as possible to handle incoming inquiries in the wake of the Brooklyn Bridge march. Beth Bogart told me that the high point of the Occupy media frenzy was even more intense than when she was the press secretary for Nelson Mandella on his first visit to the United States after being released from prison.[19] Although my impression of OWS had drastically improved over the past week, I was still not convinced that it would last very long or even that the occupation in itself was all that important politically. In late September, I posted an article from *Jacobin* magazine by Malcolm Harris called "Occupied Wall Street: Some Tactical Thoughts" on Facebook.[20] In the article, Harris argued that the occupation of Zuccotti Park wasn't in itself a victory since it did not directly interfere with the operations of the financial sector and that those who thought simply being there was a success in itself were diluted. Generally, I shared Harris's perspective. I didn't think that OWS was really directly contesting power or that it was entrenched in everyday struggles to a degree necessary for longevity. But it was pulling in journalists like mosquitoes to a bug zapper in the summer, so it presented a highly rare opportunity to broadcast radical politics across the world. In other words, I didn't think that OWS would turn into a movement capable of confronting state and capital, or even capable of including a large sector of the New York working class, but, for whatever reason, it managed to capitalize on a bizarre confluence of circumstances to present an opportunity to plant a few anti-authoritarian seeds for the future.

The A-Word

Yet, in order for the seeds to grow, they had to be planted so that the soil would accept them, so to speak. For the majority of OWS anarchists, this meant emphasizing the ideas behind anarchism rather than their misunderstood label. Axle (23), an anarchist organizer from Manhattan with the Outreach and DA WGs, said that the word 'anarchist' is commonly "used for teenagers in all black clothing and Crass patches."[21] Likewise, Bootz (21), an anarchist active with DA who got politicized through Students for a Democratic Society (SDS) in college, said that journalists "think that [the anarchist is] the middle class white liberal college student who dresses in black and runs around the streets at night and breaks property with no political analysis and no understanding and just likes to create chaos."[22] Instead, the "point is to be approachable and relatable," explained S.[23] For Jo Robin (30), an anarchist involved in Occupy New Orleans before coming up to New York to work with OWS Puppetry Guild and Facilitation, it's "more important to walk away from a conversation with someone feeling comfortable with my ideals whether or not they're using the same language that I use."[24]

Instead of explicitly addressing 'anarchism,' organizers like Sergio Jimenez (26), an anarchist from Texas who quit his job to come to New York and work with the Kitchen, Sanitation, and Translation WGs, would speak about the values of autonomy, horizontalism, egalitarianism, and mutual aid.[25] Maria "Sarge" Porto (23), an anarchist EMT from Brooklyn and OWS medic, emphasized sustainable communities and self-sufficiency.[26] The same applied for Mark Adams (32) who was born in Pakistan, grew up in Dubai before spending time in Switzerland and Thailand, and then moved to the United States at 19.[27] He came to OWS in November, and was one of our most active organizers despite being imprisoned on Rikers Island for 45 days over the summer of 2012 for his involvement in the December 17, 2011 occupation of a vacant lot owned by Trinity Church. Although he identifies as an anarchist communist, Mark is concerned about the negative connotations of both terms and instead tends to focus on direct democracy and consensus when communicating with the general public. Andrew (27), an organizer with DA from

Massachusetts, tries to "steer clear of 'anarchist' and 'anarchism' as labels because of how eroded they've been in popular culture and politics in this country."[28] Instead he emphasizes being anti-state, believing in collective organizing, and strong interpersonal relationships.[29]

Patrick Bruner (23) essentially was the Press WG by himself during the first days of the occupation of Liberty Square. Patrick's slick, all-black attire and shaved head led me to suspect his anarchism before it ever came up, but he told me that in the first week he wrote up a list of polarizing political terms to avoid using with the press including "capitalism, anarchism, communism, [and] free market." Patrick added that, "when we talk about this movement we talk about a post-political, directly democratic, people-powered, egalitarian movement. When you put all those words together it means anarchism."[30]

It may seem strange for anarchists to build a group or movement without specifically anarchist politics, or to use strategic language to present their ideas to society, but it's nothing new. For example, Bakunin was adamant that it was important for the First International to remain non-ideological so it could unite the entire working class. He said that if the founders of the International had given it a "socialist, philosophical, definite and positive political doctrine, they would have been in error."[31] Instead of making the entire association explicitly anarchist, Bakunin favored the creation of an anarchist political group that could spread anarchist ideas among the workers as they joined. In 1908, the prominent German anarchist Gustav Landauer organized an anarchist group called the "Socialist Bund" whose newspaper was called *Der Sozialist*. In Landauer's opinion, "Anarchy is just another—due to its negativity and frequent misinterpretation, less useful—name for socialism."[32]

Likewise early syndicalist unions such as the French *Confédération generale du travail* (CGT) or the Industrial Workers of the World (IWW) had anti-authoritarian, anti-capitalist politics and had many anarchist organizers but they did not give their unions overarching political labels. Malatesta was at times critical of anarcho-syndicalism because he thought that unions shouldn't have an explicitly ideological character. I think the track record of the Spanish CNT, for example, provided a more than adequate response to Malatesta's concerns that an anarcho-syndicalist union would "wait for all the workers to become anarchists before inviting them to organize," since it merged considerations of inclusivity with political education.[33] Yet Malatesta's perspective represents another voice in favor of inserting anarchist ideas into a more broadly non-ideological mass organization.

One of the best examples of strategically articulating anarchist politics to appeal to the broader society was the *Partido Liberal Mexicano* (PLM) founded by the Mexican anarchist Ricardo Flores Magón in 1906. Although the PLM was an anarchist group, Magón knew that he would get more popular support for the very same ideas under the 'liberal' banner. Explaining his rationale in a letter to fellow anarchists in the PLM, Magón wrote in 1908:

> In order to obtain great benefits for the people, effective benefits, to work as anarchists would easily crush us ... all is reduced to a conception of mere tactics. If from the first we had called ourselves anarchists no one, or not but a few would have listened to us. Without calling ourselves anarchists we have gone on planting in mind ideas of hatred against the possessing class and against the government caste ... this has been achieved without saying that we are anarchists ... all, then, is a question of tactics.
>
> We must give land to the people in the course of the revolution; so that the poor will not be deceived ... in order not to turn the entire nation against us, we must follow the

> same tactics that we have practiced with such success: we will continue calling ourselves liberals in the course of the revolution but in reality we will be propagating anarchy and executing anarchistic acts.[34]

In another letter he added:

> Only the anarchists will know that we are anarchists. And we will advise them not to call us anarchists in order not to scare such imbeciles that in the depths of their consciousness harbor ideas like ours, but without knowing that they are anarchist ideals, therefore they are accustomed to hear talk about the anarchists in unfavorable terms.[35]

More recently, the Common Ground Collective in New Orleans formed in the aftermath of Hurricane Katrina didn't explicitly identify with anarchism in order to get more people involved.[36] To reiterate, I'm not arguing that anarchists should never use the anarchist label. I'm simply pointing out that there are situations where the non-hierarchical, anti-oppressive, anti-capitalist ideas of anarchism might be better communicated without the label, at least to start. It worked in Mexico and, to a far lesser but still notable extent, it worked with Occupy Wall Street.

Rage, Zapatistas, and Anarcho-Punks with Ham Sandwiches

When I thought about constructing an accessible message that could radicalize a mainstream audience back in the fall of 2011, I reflected upon how I came to reject the oppressive values of the world around me. I was born in New York City in 1982 and grew up in River Vale, New Jersey, a small New York suburb about 15 miles northwest of the Bronx. My parents were public school educators in New Jersey and New York and I had a typically middle class experience.[37] Both of my parents grew up in working class immigrant families (my father's family came from Ireland and my mother's family were Jews from the Russian Empire), and they promoted the values of justice and freethinking. Though they weren't activists during my childhood, my father, Joseph Bray, had participated in the Civil Rights movement in Washington, DC and my mother, Karen Melin, used to attend demonstrations against the Vietnam War and was active in feminist politics.

Given my comfortable suburban upbringing, the interest that I developed in leftist politics in high school did not stem from personal experience of privation or hardship. Instead, it came from a recognition that the affluence of suburban New Jersey came at the expense of much of the rest of the country and much of the rest of the world. Many conservative suburbanites in River Vale and towns like it across the United States hated Occupy and argued that unless you are the poorest of the poor, you are spoiled and ungrateful to protest. In their eyes, it's fabulous for middle class people to work to improve conditions for 'those less well off' through apolitical charity projects, but if someone from my socioeconomic background articulates a broad critique of society striking at the heart of class hierarchy, they are inevitably written off as ungrateful. Moreover, it becomes a slippery slope argument where ultimately the only people who can complain about injustice in the world are those with absolutely nothing. Instead of resigning myself to my privilege, I've tried to work toward challenging it. In that regard, I've joined a long tradition of anarchists and other radicals who have come from middle class or educated backgrounds to support what has historically been a movement of predominantly working class and peasant resistance.[38]

As cliché as it may sound, the most important influence in my exposure to radical politics and my awareness of exploitation around the world was the band Rage Against the Machine. Their seething anger and complete impatience with a world of exploitation was a mirror image of the frustration that I felt as I started to contrast the injustices that I was learning about with the comfort and apathy around me. In addition to their lyrics, I was intrigued by the suggested reading list of radical books that accompanied their 1996 album, *Evil Empire*. Among others on the list, I picked up *Rules for Radicals* by Saul Alinsky, *The Black Panthers Speak*, *Guerrilla Warfare* by Che Guevara, and books by Noam Chomsky such as *Manufacturing Consent*. The band's advocacy on behalf of political prisoners Leonard Peltier of the American Indian Movement and Mumia Abu-Jamal of the Black Panthers led me to read their books *Prison Writings: My Life is a Sundance* and *Live from Death Row*. Their website also had a newsfeed and links where I learned about Indymedia, FAIR (Fairness and Accuracy in Reporting), Counterpunch, and so forth. Every new story I read about political prisoners, toxic dumping, or genetically modified food instilled me with an urgency to change things right then, at that moment. In retrospect it was the same kind of urgency that I saw among many young people at Liberty; the same urgency that had gradually withered away within me as my hopes for short-term change had faded.

Rage also introduced me to the Zapatistas. As someone groping in the dark toward some kind of tangible model of what a truly democratic socialism could look like, the autonomous, directly democratic Zapatista communities of southern Mexico were truly astounding. In high school, I resisted the temptation to label my politics. I knew that corporations were exploitative and I had an inkling of the fact that capitalism as a whole was part of the problem, but I was determined to avoid joining some sort of weird communist sect that I would be embarrassed about later. I wanted to move slowly and intentionally to the left without losing my grounding in my personal ethical and rational perspectives. And while I was wary of the fact that my history teachers were probably biased against the Soviet Bloc when we learned about the Cold War, I knew that if people were willing to risk getting shot or imprisoned to escape their country, then something was dreadfully wrong with the Soviet experiment. So the Zapatistas were an important example of a way out of the false binary of capitalism and Soviet domination. I remember watching an episode of *Total Request Live* (TRL) on MTV after school that had Rage Against the Machine live in the studio in promotion of their third album, *The Battle of Los Angeles*. In addition to their interview, the band had MTV play a 5-minute piece on the Zapatistas. I really admired the fact that they used their media opportunities to promote a radical message to a broad mainstream audience. It all seemed to come full circle for me when I had the opportunity to organize Rage guitarist Tom Morello's performance at Liberty Square in October, 2011.

Yet, it wasn't always clear what to do after learning about what was going on. For me, the most obvious way that I could make a difference was to address the hypocritical dichotomy of liberal yuppies-in-training and the sweatshop labor behind their fashionable labels. In a society that so thoroughly excludes people from managing their own lives and communities while reinforcing the individual consumer identity, it's no surprise that as an alienated New Jersey teenager I felt like consumer politics was my only outlet for action.

I went to little anti-sweatshop demonstrations outside of the GAP in Westwood and Ridgewood organized by kids I knew in the Bergen County punk scene.[39] Even at the time it was clear to me that a half dozen smelly punks outside of a GAP would do more to encourage than dissuade the average GAP customer. For most of them, it was more about reveling in the harassment of passers-by and reinforcing their outsider countercultural status by juxtaposing their patched-up bondage pants and Elmer's glued mohawks to the chic mannequins in the window than it was about organizing a campaign. Nevertheless, at least they were disruptions of materialist monotony. For my senior project in high school, I wrote a novella about sweatshop workers in Honduras and had copies bound to sell at $5 apiece to raise money for the Workers' Rights Consortium which monitors labor conditions at garment factories. In the back, I included a "short" list of corporations that people should boycott because they used sweatshop labor. The thing was that the list included like 50 companies and collectively represented most of the retail economy. After a while it dawned on me that listing 50 companies would overwhelm people, making them less likely to consider boycotting even one clothing line. But the more I learned about labor abuses in different companies, I started to realize that almost the entire economy rests on extreme exploitation and consumer politics offers no way out. Even the supposedly benevolent American Apparel has a strongly anti-union track record.[40] I came to understand that it's really missing the point for middle class activists to use their economic status to buy more expensive 'fair trade' products while condemning working class people for buying cheap products at Wal-mart. It creates "a sense of elitism based on consumer choice"[41] because poor people have to buy cheap things, and capitalism dictates that brutal exploitation will always yield the cheapest product available. When I put all the pieces together, I saw that capitalism cannot be reformed. Yet, consumer politics, such as anti-sweatshop boycotts, were essential to my personal anti-capitalist development because they provided the empirical evidence to support the political argument.

I knew I wasn't down with what happened in the Soviet Union, but the little I learned of anarchism from the anarcho-punks turned me off as well. While it might be excessively charitable to even consider them anarchists in any substantive sense, the kids I knew who threw around the label were driven primarily by a desire to distinguish themselves culturally from the preppy/jock malaise. The most obvious signifier in this process was their patched up jackets and pants and spiked/greasy hair and most of their activities revolved around substance abuse. The goal was to broadcast the loudest 'fuck you' possible through style and action without much consideration beyond that. To me, it seemed like anarchism was entirely about negation without any element of a positive vision for a better world. I didn't want to fall into the stereotype of the angsty youth who shits on everything without having something better in mind. I also preferred to look like a 'normal' person so that I could get more people to agree with my radical ideas. I don't mean to discount the importance of pushing the bounds of acceptable self-presentation, but it's obvious that challenging social norms can impede one's ability to communicate with more socially mainstream people. You have to decide what your goal is and act accordingly. At the time, the following words of Saul Alinsky resonated with me: "If I were organizing in an orthodox Jewish community I would not walk in there eating a ham sandwich, unless I wanted to be rejected so I could have an excuse to cop out."[42] I realized early on that it was important to avoid what Betsy Leondar-Wright of Movement for a New Society called "inessential weirdness" in relating to those I sought to organize with.[43] Also, I've just always personally hated fashion whether mainstream or counter-cultural.

A few crusty punks I knew got into some variant of primitivism and stopped showering entirely. One of them supposedly boiled some of his urine and poured it on his face to get rid of the acne he developed from his filth. I remember standing in the gym locker room listening to one guy explain to me how hunter-gatherers didn't shower frequently and how this reflected the superiority of their lifestyle. Today he's a right-wing Republican in the Army. At the time, I knew that most of these kids didn't really have a substantive political critique, but over the past 10+ years it's been shocking how many of them became ultra-conservatives in the military. At least 6 anarcho-punks I knew in high school joined the military *enthusiastically*. Another one of them spent a few years as an activist before becoming an apathetic petty entrepreneur who travels around the world snowboarding off of the revenue from some coin laundries he owns. Even most of those who didn't join the military have shed any connection to the politics of the bands they listened to and have wholeheartedly embraced the mainstream football-watching, beer-guzzling, consumerist culture that they were supposedly rebelling against in the first place. I chuckle when I see Facebook photos of some of them hanging out with some of the same jocks they loathed 15 years prior. But my point isn't that the anarcho-punk scene breeds reactionaries. There are plenty of committed activists and revolutionaries, including some from Occupy, that were radicalized by bands like Crass, Conflict, and Aus Rotten. Rather, I'm pointing out that we haven't yet created a robust, broad, and inclusive anti-authoritarian counter-culture than can help people transition from an incipient 'fuck the system' to a lifelong involvement in communities of resistance. When most rebellious teenage anarcho-punks reach the limits of playing in bands and shaping Mohawks, there's nothing waiting for them except the mediocrity they were escaping from or a detour to the opposite extreme of armed violence and misogyny in the name of the state. The few I knew who retained a political consciousness gravitated toward institutional, left-liberal, NGO politics in an effort to adapt 'pragmatically' to the 'real world.'

While those kids were sewing on their circle-A patches, I was searching for tangible ways to change society. As the 2000 election approached, it was my first opportunity to vote. During the Democratic Primary, I learned that Al Gore and his wife Tipper were behind the Parents Music Resource Center (PMRC), which promoted artistic censorship and was responsible for the 'Parental Advisory' Stickers on CDs. Many artists lashed out against the PMRC including Rage Against the Machine who walked out on stage naked, with only duct tape covering their mouths and the letters 'PMRC' on their chests, to protest Tipper

Gore's organization in 1993. I was determined to avoid simply falling in line with the Democratic Candidate because he was supposedly better than the Republican, so I gravitated to Ralph Nader and the Green Party. I read one of Nader's books, familiarized myself with the Party platform, and attended one of the Nader super-rallies at Madison Square Garden featuring celebrities like Eddie Vedder, Susan Sarandon, and Michael Moore. I even convinced teachers at Pascack Valley High School to let me play Nader in the mock presidential debate they had organized. Once they gave me the green light (no pun intended), I spent weeks mastering Nader's talking points and reading *Al Gore: A User's Manual* by Alexander Cockburn and Jeffrey St. Clair to dig up dirt on Gore. When the day came, the kid who played Gore (now a corporate lawyer defending one of the major financial firms in a crisis-related suit) only prepared a few days in advance, and the kid who played Bush hadn't prepared at all (which actually made his answers true to his role), so Nader won the school election.

But in the real election Nader got less than 3%; far short of his goal of 5%, which would automatically list him on the ballot next time. As time passed and I got more involved with campus activism, my electoral optimism faded. I came to see that Democrats were right to argue that there was no chance for a third party in the current American system.[44] However, they have always been wrong to imagine that their party, or any other, has a better chance of building a just society.

It wasn't until I took a Spanish Civil War seminar with Nathanael Greene at Wesleyan University that I realized that I was an anarchist. I had to see some living model of what another world could look like, even if it was rough and imperfect, before I could pick up the red and black flag. I devoured classic texts on the Spanish Revolution and wrote my seminar paper about the anarchist collectives.[45] I learned how the people took over their workplaces and communities and ran them better *without* bosses.

This anarchism was very different from suburban punk-rock rebellion. The struggles and sacrifices of workers and peasants to collectively shed generations of oppression and forge a truly equitable society were so beautiful that I knew I had to continue their struggle. Their example was so moving that it could not be for naught.

There are several strategic conclusions that I have drawn from my experiences that greatly influenced how I articulated my anarchist politics to the media. First, I learned the value of presenting my revolutionary ideas in an accessible format. How I dress, the words I choose, and how I articulate them affect how I am received, so if my primary goal is to convince people of what I am saying, then it's often useful to shed my "inessential weirdness." Second, I realized the usefulness of letting tangible examples sketch the outline of my ideas without encumbering them with explicit ideological baggage. Finally, I concluded that the importance that Americans place on the electoral system dictates that any systematic critique should start with the corporate nature of both political parties. Like it or not, that's where most people are at in terms of their political framework, so if you skip past the candidates to alternative institutions, for example, without convincing them of the bankrupt nature of the electoral system, you'll lose them. Yet, once you've made that point, it's important to quickly transition from a factual description of the two-party system to an analysis of the relationship between capitalism and the electoral system to avoid getting bogged down in a campaign finance mindset. In the next section, I will describe the role of the Press WG and how these lessons influenced how I articulated my politics in the context of OWS. To clarify, I am not saying that everyone will respond to the same arguments or rhetorical strategies in the same way, but I hope that my reflections on how I utilized my personal experience of radicalization to shape my arguments might influence others to undergo the same process of self-reflection.

Layers of Occupy Media

Although OWS managed to disseminate a wide variety of amazing alternative media, from cable access television programs to websites, newspapers, theoretical journals, pamphlets and more, most people learned about the movement from the mainstream media. As much as we would love to be able to circumvent their prominence, OWS became an international phenomenon because of the corporate media. When it was just a small group of people in the park, the media inflated OWS beyond proportion. Yet, when CNN and *The New York Times* got bored with us, they popped the bubble they had created leaving us with a relatively small but resolute core of organizers. It was clearly a double-edged sword, but without it we wouldn't have had any weapons at all. Any astute observer could tell that the hype would eventually subside, so for us in the Press WG it was crucial to make the most of the opportunity to speak on such a large platform while it lasted since such opportunities come by perhaps once in a generation.

The Press WG performed several functions. First, it fielded media inquiries and transmitted them to the OWS organizers who were either organizing a specific action or were focusing on a specific issue. We gathered a long list of spokespeople to reflect the movement's diversity in terms of race, gender, age, education, occupation, and religion. We used this list and the Liberty Square networks that developed to counteract the media tendency to gravitate toward white men when they wanted an 'authoritative' statement or search for the most countercultural, inarticulate person they could find when they wanted to make us look like inebriated hippies. Unfortunately, the face of Occupy Wall Street in the press was predominantly white and that certainly didn't accurately reflect the demographics of those most affected by the crisis. In part this was because OWS was disproportionately white (71% of interviewees were white).

Beyond that, though, we should have done a better job from the outset of counteracting the tendency of white men to step in front of the mic. Yet, even when we presented reporters with a diverse set of interviews, they often chose to feature white people instead of the people of color they spoke with.

I think part of the reason that the corporate media featured white faces was that they had a racist tendency to try to create a narrative that 'times are so tough that even middle class white college kids from the suburbs are hurting.' It was true that the economic crisis expanded the devastation of capitalism to affect many who previously considered themselves immune, but when journalists tried to pursue that angle, we used the opportunity to go deeper. For example, I would often start by agreeing with the reporter about the havoc wrought on the middle class. Then, I would cite the havoc as evidence that the economic system only really works for the 1% (an oversimplification, of course, but a useful mechanism to communicate the vast inequities of capitalism). But then I would emphasize that working class people, who are disproportionately people of color, have been suffering under this unjust economic system for much longer than a couple years.

Every day at Liberty, we would say hello to the journalists in the morning as they arrived to check in and let them know we were there if they needed assistance or fill them in on the logistical details of what was going on that day. My partner Senia, a young Latina woman, found that many journalists would ignore her when she introduced herself as part of the Press WG, but when one of the white men in our group stopped by shortly thereafter, the same reporter would give them a warm greeting and ask them questions. Our ability to sculpt the image that the media presented was certainly constrained by the implicit and explicit racism of many journalists. Nevertheless, the Press WG tried to make a concerted effort to recruit people of color and women to counteract the racist tendencies evident in the media and even in the way that the demographics of Liberty developed. After all, the vast majority of the people who could afford to spend a lot of time in the park during the day (when the media came) were either privileged people with flexible schedules or enough of an economic cushion to quit their job, or unemployed and/or homeless. The first group tended to be disproportionately white and university educated, while the latter included more people of color and people who hadn't attended college and therefore tended to have less experience with public speaking. Though we eventually organized media trainings, we failed to get them going on a regular basis during the peak media frenzy. In that chaotic context, the park's demographics produced a situation where those who stepped forward to do press work were predominantly white and university educated, such as myself. Certainly, I recognize that my confidence and experience in public speaking stem from the vast amount of privilege I have enjoyed as an educated white male from a middle class background, and I'm still working on how best to use the skills that my privilege has afforded me to challenge the social structures that initially gave birth to such disparities. My hope is that I can encourage readers with similar backgrounds to undergo a similar process of self-reflection.

In addition to fielding media inquiries, the Press WG also crafted messaging concerning specific actions and general political issues. For example, we had a press release about a potential eviction of Liberty Square prepared in advance of the fateful day on Nov. 15, 2011 including the now famous wording "You Can't Evict an Idea Whose Time Has Come." Most action planning groups came to us for help writing a press release and framing talking points to sharpen their message. Like the rest of OWS, the composition of the Press WG was politically mixed but with a strong anarchist(ic) bent. Of the approximately 25 people who were active with Press for a sustained period at one point or another, nine identified as anarchists (Senia Barragan, Patrick

Bruner, Rebecca Manski, Audrea Lim, S., Rowland Miller, Cari Machet, Jason Ahmadi, and myself). In addition, several others were anti-capitalist anti-authoritarians (including Michael Premo, Jonathan Smucker, Kanene, Aaron Bornstein and Linnea M. Palmer Paton). The rest of the group included several progressives, liberals and social democrats (such as Ed Needham, Jeff Smith, Bill Dobbs, and William Jesse) a socialist (Karanja Wa Gaçuça), an anti-authoritarian Marxist (Shane Gill), a "Marxist leaning" anti-capitalist with a "dose of anarchism" (Beka Economopoulos) and several other non-aligned radicals (like Dana Balicki, Liesbeth Rapp and Beth Bogart). More than half of the working group responsible for transmitting Occupy to the mainstream media had anarchist or anarchistic politics.

However, our political diversity did not inhibit our ability to frame messaging. When disagreements emerged they were rarely, if ever, along ideological lines because Occupy created a pervasive anti-authoritarian climate that smoothed over the rough edges in relations between reformists and revolutionaries. The anarchists in the group were all committed to strategic messaging for the general public, and the progressives saw Occupy as an opportunity to emphasize a structural critique of the electoral and economic systems. Because there was no OWS 'party line' about what the future society should look like or exactly how we should work toward it, everyone in our group, regardless of their politics, could agree on a few overarching points that guided our language with the press: (1) the current economic system is oppressive and only works for the 1%; (2) both political parties are beholden to the 1%; therefore (3) the solution can only come from people-power.[46]

When I spoke to the press, I tried to turn my sound-bites into condensed stories encompassing some variation of all three of these points regardless of what line of questioning I was presented with. One of the beautiful things about Occupy was that a broad range of anarchists and anti-authoritarians could frame their ideas in many different ways. In short, there were many ways that people were translating anarchy, but here I will take a moment to explain how I contributed to this project. The following is a recreation of the kind of medium-length sound-bite I grew accustomed to giving dozens of times a day while sitting at the press table in Liberty:

> Occupy is a response to the mass economic injustice perpetrated by Wall Street and the 1% on the American people. Since 2008, we've seen the banks illegally evict thousands of families while Wall Street executives get Christmas bonuses for destroying lives. But we've had enough! We need an economy based on human need rather than Wall Street profits that provides working people with food, housing, healthcare and education. But we've seen that both Bush and Obama bailed out the banks, not the people. Both parties rely on banks and corporations and prioritize the 1% over the 99%. We've been told to turn to the politicians for answers, but after Obama we've seen that movie, and we know how it ends. If we want a true democracy, we have to make it ourselves. That's why we're in the streets.

In this example, and others like it, I tried to direct relatable talking points in an anarchist(ic) direction. To give a better sense of how I did that I'm going to break down each section starting with the first:

> (1) Occupy is a response to the mass economic injustice perpetrated by Wall Street and the 1% on the American people. Since 2008, we've seen the banks illegally evict thousands of families while Wall Street executives get Christmas bonuses for destroying lives.

I started with the oppressive nature of the economy, which in my mind was 'the problem' in my larger narrative sequence of 'the problem,' followed by its 'false solution,' and finally its 'real solution.' I often spoke about foreclosures because the reality of entire families being kicked out of their homes, often illegally, is one of the most brutal examples of the havoc wrought by the crisis. In addition, this example partially bypasses capitalist meritocratic notions by implying that even if adults are supposedly 'negligent' in their economic affairs, their children are harmed also. Emphasizing the illegality of evictions was a complicated issue in my mind. On the one hand, it implied that legal evictions were less heinous and that the solution was a proper enforcement of the law. On the other hand, labeling evictions 'illegal' was the most effective way to immediately discredit them to the public. I decided that it was useful to start my critique with a reference to illegality because it signaled those listening to the presence of malfeasance and grabbed their attention for a more sustained critique of the economic and political system. In addition, I think it's useful for people to realize that financial institutions will routinely break the law and hurt people in the pursuit of profit. Such associations contribute

Me sitting at the Press table in Oct. 2011.

to a more structural association between capitalism and 'criminality.'

The challenge in my eyes was to forge a structural critique out of personalized tales of hardship because that is how people have been trained to think. The unfortunate reality was that to achieve maximum impact we had to dance with the popular portrayal of the crisis as an aberration in order to be able to segue into a (partially veiled) critique of capitalism. That's why I usually made specific reference to the crisis and 2008 and portrayed our collective mindset as a group of people who suddenly woke up to the injustices around us rather than longtime political activists who had been saying the same things for many years (though I was always transparent about being a longtime activist myself). That narrative appealed to the American love affair with 'non-ideological' politics and civic participation grounded in immediate personal experiences rather than structural analyses. Moreover, new people who actually *did* just become politicized could feel like their experience was part of a new phenomenon.

By emphasizing the disparity between evicted families and Wall Street bonuses, I could allude to capitalism's gross mismanagement of resources and the fact that the market doesn't accurately reward socially productive labor. In essence, I was destabilizing the popular standard of "A fair day's wage for a fair day's work," which the IWW rightly derides as a "conservative motto."[47] I pointed out that this accepted perspective on remuneration had been warped to the point that those who destroyed the economy were getting rich while those who made the economy run were being ruined.

> (2) We need an economy based on human need rather than Wall Street profits that provides working people with food, housing, healthcare and education.

On the surface, my argument that working people should have food, housing, healthcare, and education drew strength from the popular logic that wages should reflect work done, but, by paring that with an argument for the prioritization of need, I was actually arguing that remuneration should be based on the communist motto "from each according to their ability, to each according to their need."[48] If you are able to work, and contribute your abilities to the collectivity, you should receive what you need from the resources of society.

The media filtered the entire movement through the prism of 'inequality,' but ironically, perhaps, I used this anarcho-communist framework to refute reporters who implied that we wanted absolute equality for everyone in everything to redbait us. I would deny that claim and argue that it isn't fundamentally about inequality; it's about working people having what they need for a fulfilling life. I wasn't satisfied with phrasing the issue in terms of 'inequality' because that angle didn't directly confront a capitalist ideology that praises inequality. Capitalist ideologues welcome inequality because they think that over time it will contribute to an economic system that improves the material conditions of those at the bottom. As the liberal philosopher John Rawls argued in his influential essay "A Theory of Justice," it's acceptable to increase inequality as long as it coincides with improvements for the poor. Therefore, statistics about inequality talk past these arguments. Instead, I tried to emphasize that the immediate material conditions for the working class in the United States are insufferable. Vast capitalist inequality has not accomplished its goal of better conditions at the bottom. That phrasing rang true for those who held onto "a fair day's wage for a fair day's work" though it stemmed from the fact that "to each according to their need" is not about absolute equality because different people have different needs. I used the language of the "conservative motto" to pivot toward the "revolutionary watchword."[49]

Certainly, liberal audiences interpreted my references to 'need' in terms of reinforcing social programs. My economic arguments were intentionally rooted in the 'common sense' meritocratic perspective that people should get what they work for. I intentionally allowed space for a mainstream interpretation, and that interpretation greatly contributed to Occupy's popularity. I didn't explicitly deride 'capitalism,' because avoiding the term brought in people who associate 'capitalism' with rewarding hard work and personal initiative. I tried to champion the ideas of hard work and personal and collective initiative while destabilizing the supposedly natural capitalist relationship between work and reward. The second layer of the rhetorical strategy, however, was to give people revolutionary criteria to evaluate the financial system. The emphasis on need as the most important gauge of an economy (along with environmental sustainability) provided many people with a 'common sense' litmus test to evaluate capitalism. It's futile to try to convince people of the evils of capitalism without having first instilled the importance of human need and sustainability as the only possible guiding principles for a just economy. Therefore, at the front line of Occupy public discourse in the media, I tried to push as many people as possible toward that first step of recalibrating their economic criteria.

I did my best to convince people that a just economy is one oriented around human need and that currently our economy subsumes the needs of the 99% under the profit incentive of the 1%. Once someone has taken that first step toward need, all that blocks them from crossing the anti-capitalist finish line is (a) to realize that the market, by its very nature, obstructs the fulfillment of human need on a global scale, and (b) to believe that another world is truly possible. Through my work with the Press WG, I made some contributions toward demonstrating the incompatibility of the market system and the fulfillment of human needs. Meanwhile, the media produced by Occupy (the second layer of OWS communication) honed in on the inherently brutal nature of capitalism and the movement and occupation itself (the third layer of OWS communication) pointed the way toward another world.

> (3) But we've seen that both Bush and Obama bailed out the banks, not the people. Both parties rely on banks and corporations and prioritize the 1% over the 99%. We've been told to turn to the politicians for answers, but after Obama we've seen that movie, and we know how it ends.

The second part of my sound-bite narrative was to refute the 'false solution' to 'the problem.' As I often phrased it in lengthier interviews, 'Occupy Wall Street was an experimental reaction to a crisis situation when the normal paths of political action were closed off. Normally,' I would continue, 'people turn to their elected representatives to improve their situations but we've seen over the past years that both parties care more about their rich donors than working people. If writing letters to congress would fix the problem we'd be doing that, but it's become plainly obvious that it won't. We've been left with no option but to organize ourselves.' Thinking back to my process of radicalization, it was essential for me to fully comprehend the bankrupt nature of the (or indeed any) electoral system before I could move toward the development of a revolutionary stance. I pointed to the bank bailouts as one of the most recent and unpopular examples of how both Bush and Obama acted the same in bailing out the banks rather than the people.

Obama was the ultimate example of the fact that no matter how charismatic or progressive a candidate might seem during their campaign, once in office the constraints of the market and the political system would necessarily keep them in line with the status quo of the upper class. It was very instructive that both Bush and Obama (seemingly opposite presidents) essentially enacted the same kinds of bailouts in response to the economic crisis. That's because they weren't really in any position to be deciding anything. They were just following the internal logic of the global financial system. When I was asked what I, or we, thought about capitalism or socialism, I would specify that the perspectives of Occupy participants ranged from anarchists and communists to liberals to right wing libertarians[50] and then try to disrupt the premises of the question. To do this, I would point out that the rules of the free market weren't applied to banks and financial institutions when they failed but they were ruthlessly enforced on homeowners, students, and workers. I would say that it's "socialism for the rich and capitalism for everyone else." I think I first heard this kind of phrasing from Noam Chomsky, but recently I learned that the same basic phrase was used by Martin Luther King Jr. and others over the decades.[51] That phrasing sapped capitalism of its associations with fairness and free competition.

> (4) If we want a true democracy, we have to make it ourselves. That's why we're in the streets.

The final part was to put forward the 'real solution' to 'the problem,' which was people-power. As I explained in Chapter 1, journalists often could not understand exactly how we thought we could change anything with protests and marches especially if we were not simply pandering to the politicians. What I realized in the process of doing OWS Press work was that both reformists and revolutionaries within the movement could generally agree that the best way to make change in the short and long term was through popular mobilization rather than electoral campaigning. Frequently, when I speak with people who are unfamiliar with the history and theory of revolutionary politics, they will argue that it's all well and good to want to change the structure of society some day in the future, but in the short term people are suffering and in need of immediate action. Many have the mistaken impression that we can only either work to improve things now or improve things later without understanding that many of the most profound transformations in the immediate conditions of everyday people have come as the result of popular social pressure often geared toward building a new society. I would constantly explain to confused/ distracted/disinterested journalists that although mainstream history has ascribed credit for advances such as civil rights, women's suffrage, and labor rights to benevolent politicians, these developments wouldn't have happened without the movements behind them. Presidents and other politicians don't operate in a social vacuum; they respond to pressure. As Voltairine de Cleyre phrased it, "it would be very stupid to say that no good results are ever brought about by political action; sometimes good things do come about that way. But never until individual rebellion, followed by mass rebellion, has forced it."[52] In fact, going through mainstream political channels to achieve an immediate goal is often counterproductive. By ceding the primary source of agency to the politician or political institution, you chain your campaign to their whims. You might win at first only to see the politician reverse course six months later. I'll go into anarchist perspectives on electoral politics in more depth in Chapter 4, but for now I'll just emphasize that an understanding of the central role of social pressure in shaping public policy can be used quite effectively to redirect political energy from planting lawn signs to occupying bank lobbies.

As we'll see later in the chapter, many people latched onto this kind of open, accessible messaging and pursued its anarchist(ic) currents toward adopting an anti-authoritarian outlook themselves. Like many others, I saw my role in this process as encouraging people to step onto the Occupy path with an implicitly anarchist road map. From there they could see for themselves where they ended up.

Other forms of Occupy media contributed to this project as well. *The Occupied Wall Street Journal* carried a rather similar tone despite a wide variety of contributors. Although the first issue of the paper[53] refers to OWS as a "revolution"[54] and Nathan Schneider mentions that the notion of the General Assembly has "roots in anarchist thought," it had a notable absence of references to (anti-)capitalism or explicitly radical politics. Likewise, the second issue[55] included an article by Naomi Klein that mentioned "taking on capitalism" in 1999, and an article by Chris Hedges that argued against working within the system, called electoral politics a "farce," and advocated the end of the "corporate state," but it maintained a 'non-ideological' radical tone. This pattern continued throughout the first six issues of the paper despite featuring pieces from known anarchist/anti-authoritarian writers such as Derrick Jensen, Rebecca Solnit,

THE OCCUPIED WALL STREET JOURNAL

NEW YORK UNITES! WEDNESDAY OCT. 5

THE REVOLUTION BEGINS AT HOME

Wall Street Protests Enter Third Week

Learning from the World

Cover of the first issue of *The Occupied Wall Street Journal*.

Simon Critchley, Maia Ramnath, socialists and Marxists such as Cornel West and Slavoj Žižek, and OWS anarchists and anti-authoritarians such as Manissa Maharawal, Rebecca Manski, and Yotam Marom.

The three main people behind the paper were Jed Brandt, a Maoist, Priscilla Grim, an anti-capitalist who described her politics as "common sense,"[56] and Michael Levitin (36) a journalist who would have called himself a "liberal" before OWS but no longer identifies with that label. Despite their radicalism, Priscilla told me that they "didn't want to make a paper for people who were already there." Instead the intended audience was "people who were watching the action but were apolitical and weren't involved." The idea was for the *OWSJ* to avoid being "*that* radical" or "too political one way or another." It was so important to her that she communicate with a mainstream audience that she would "frequently go [to Zuccotti] in my work clothes because I wanted people to identify, like you should be here too ... I would be in my interview suit and people would look at me in a whole different light. Their whole face would change."[57]

The first and primary OWS website was occupywallst.org (sometimes referred to as 'storg') which was run by a collective primarily composed of anarchist transwomen. Amelia (21) said that "we all have a similar political ideology, in that we consider ourselves anti-authoritarians, anti-statists, anti-capitalists as well as maintaining a very heavy focus on anti-oppression ... we see ourselves as running propaganda for the movement."[58] But most of the site's content was either factual or logistical, or it reflected kind of an open, populist, anti-corporate message. There were certainly occasional exceptions such as a September 17, 2011 statement that included calls for "workers not only to strike, but to seize their workplaces collectively and organize them democratically," but they were infrequent enough to stop short of scaring away a mainstream audience. The most fury I observed came when they posted the statement of solidarity from Mumia Abu-Jamal in December 2011. In the comments section one person wrote "the forum admins have been INFILTRATED by right-wing elements, who are probably behind this extremely DIVISIVE Mumia post." Another wrote, "Let us all keep in mind that this website has somehow strayed from the original purpose of bringing the lawbreakers of Wall Street and the Banks (Not all of Wall Street and all Banks, lets be definitive here) to justice and to effectively clear the way to get their influences out of our political system." The fact that regular visitors to a site run by anarchists thought that the message was about prosecuting *some* bankers shows how they managed to make the tone strident, passionate, and inclusive. As site founder Justine Tunney phrased it, "we wanted to make it as radical as we could get away with."[59]

The Occupy theory journal *Tidal* was a bit more explicitly radical. This made sense considering the fact that reading longer, more complex articles is more time-consuming, so presumably most people who would spend that time would already have a heightened interest in Occupy. I thought of the Press WG, the newspaper, and the website as the first layer of OWS communication with the broader public, more in-depth publications like *Tidal* as the second layer of communication. I would imagine that most *Tidal* readers had already heard something about OWS from the mainstream media and/or come across the newspaper or website in advance of reading the theory journal. I'd say that speaking with actual organizers and attending meetings would be the third level of communication. It was very common in OWS meetings for people to speak freely about how capitalism was the enemy and we needed to build a new world based on egalitarian principles. Once someone was sufficiently enticed by the first two layers of radicalization they could get the full dose of anarchist(ic) politics in person.

The first issue of *Tidal*, released in December 2011, started off

Cover of the second issue of *Tidal*, the Occupy Theory Journal. The image is from the Dec. 17, 2011 (D17) attempted occupation of a vacant lot in lower Manhattan.

Mural of D17 painted on the outside of the Madrid squatted social center *Casa Blanca*. This space was a key hub for the 15M movement before police bricked it up and painted over the mural. Photo by Mark Bray.

with a Situationist[60] style communiqué about cultural alienation and "a vague spiritual nausea." In the last paragraph it asked, "What do we want from Wall Street? Nothing, because it has nothing to offer us." Yet, the communiqué also utilizes the prevalent motif of the newly radicalized protester when it says that, "we sense something is wrong only through the odd clue." This phrasing invites the apolitical reader to think of the clues about alienation in their own lives, but it certainly doesn't reflect the anti-capitalist, anti-authoritarian orientation of *Tidal*'s editorial staff which, over the course of its first 3 editions, included Isham Christie, a "direct-action, psycho-analytic, Hegelian, anarcho-communist;"[61] someone who adopted the pseudonym of the famous left communist "Rosa Luxemburg"; Amin Husain, an anti-authoritarian anti-capitalist;[62] and Laura Gottesdiener (25) and Yates McKee (32) who were greatly radicalized in an anti-authoritarian direction by their participation in Occupy.[63] These were not people who were just patching things together on the fly based on "the odd clue."

Likewise, anarchist organizer Suzahn Ebrahimian (23) wrote an article advocating mutual aid, horizontality, solidarity, and autonomy as strategies to confront the state and the police but only mentioned 'anarchism' when describing Voltairine de Cleyre as "a great anarchist thinker." Suzahn was a great example of an anarchist who was wary of using the term 'anarchism' with the general public but became increasingly excited about using it to bring new people into the anarchist movement. Suzahn explained that,

> now that there's this awareness of horizontality it's actually very useful for me to talk about anarchism [within Occupy] because people aren't as scared of it for some reason now … it's pushed people forward … people are starting to open up a little [to anarchism] … what's changed for me is that I'm more militant about using the word all the time without fear

> of alienating anybody because obviously I can just show through the movement that these principles are great.[64]

Over time, *Tidal*'s rhetoric became more explicitly radical and included more explicitly anti-capitalist references.[65] By the third edition, dated September 2012, there was an article called "Beyond Climate, Beyond Capitalism," a statement from the editors spoke about OWS resisting "a dying capitalist system," right after an article from radical historian Jeremy Brecher, and Christopher Key argued in "Mutual Aid in the Face of the Storm" that "capitalism has warped and colonized our human relationships."

This growth in references to (anti-)capitalism reflected an enhanced radicalization in the explicit presentation of OWS politics throughout the year starting, I would argue, in December 2011 when the 'golden age' of OWS was ending. Though some have dated the end of the popular phase of Occupy Wall Street at the eviction from Zuccotti on November 15, 2011, we managed to carry a lot of momentum throughout the next month (though it would be accurate to describe it as the beginning of the end of that phase). The eviction actually gave us a temporary dose of adrenaline in a context where momentum had already been declining in early November. In the long run, however, our mass popularity inevitably declined. Yet, November 17, 2011 (N17) was arguably our most successful day of action, we managed to get very impressive crowds out to our day of action against foreclosures in East New York on December 6, 2011 (D6, arguably our best day of press coverage), and our day of action against Goldman Sachs on December 12, 2011 (D12) was very successful.

Although it was clearly the poor step-sister to the more highly touted mobilizations of D6 and D17, D12 ended up being a very lively march on Goldman Sachs headquarters on a freezing-cold week-day morning despite only having a little over a week's time to plan it.[66] I was the stage manager and MC of the day's finale: a

Kanene as the Goldman Sachs Vampire Squid on Dec. 12, 2011 (D12). Photo by Jessica Lehrman.

mock press conference featuring Kanene, a multi-talented performance artist, dressed up as the Goldman Sachs vampire-squid fielding questions from fake reporters.[67] I was very pessimistic about the potential turnout, but we managed to get several hundred people to turn up generating the same enthusiasm that we had come to expect. D12 was interesting, though, because it was the first time that I heard the "*anticapitalista*" chant that would become an OWS hallmark by the spring. As we were marching around the Goldman Sachs building before the press conference some marchers started chanting "a-anti-anticapitalista!" which is a common left chant in Spain and other Spanish speaking countries. By the time DA was organizing our weekly "spring training" marches on Wall Street leading up to May Day 2012, it was widely understood that the marches would all culminate with a celebratory, dancing chant of "a-anti-anticapitalista!" even including some who I know for a fact do not identify as anti-capitalists. Over time, early OWS chants like

"*Anticapitalista*" chant and celebration after "The People's Gong" outside of the Stock Exchange to conclude an OWS "Spring Training" march, April 20, 2012. Photo by Minister Erik McGregor.

"Banks got Bailed Out, We Got Sold Out" and "We are the 99%" gave way to ones like "The System Has Got to Die, Hella Hella Occupy!" (showing the influence of organizers from California).

I first started to see the air seeping out of the Occupy balloon on December 17, 2011 (D17) when we launched an action against Trinity Church (one of the largest real estate owners in New York City) to pressure them to make a long vacant lot they owned next to Duarte Square public for another encampment. I'll get into the merits and flaws of that action in Chapter 4, but for now I'll just mention that I noticed that the usual throngs of demonstrators didn't mobilize despite the hype that we tried to generate for the three month anniversary of OWS and a supposed 're-occupation.' Sure, there were maybe a thousand or 1,500 people there, but I could tell that we could no longer count on a constant stream of bodies and energy no matter what we did. My sense proved to be correct since the only other time, as of this writing in March 2013, that we had truly sizeable crowds was May Day 2012. But with that decline in mass attendance came a noticeable increase in the level of rhetorical and symbolic radicalism in our marches and secondary layers of public communication.[68]

Are We the 99%?

Probably the most influential example of presenting anarchist concepts in a digestible form was the slogan "we are the 99%." Hailed as "arguably the most successful slogan since 'Hell no, we won't go,'" by Paul Taylor of the Pew Research Center,[69] the concept of the 99% transcended Occupy to become an iconic political symbol around the world. It became so omnipresent that it even made its way into mainstream electoral politics, sitcoms, and advertising.[70] Around the one-year anniversary of OWS in September 2012, many considered the concept of "the 99%" to be the most lasting achievement of the movement. John Carney of CNBC tweeted "I reckon #OWS was so successful that the accomplishments have turned invisible. 99% is everyone's term now."[71] As I told *Metro* in New York, "the language of the 99 percent and the 1 percent has now almost become cliché because it's so popular."[72] The slogan capitalized on the increasing public visibility of economic inequality statistics over the past decade showing that the top 1% of the United States controlled about 35.6% of the country's private wealth, more than the bottom 90% combined.[73] I can't remember when I first heard "we are the 99%" chanted at an Occupy event because it didn't strike me as an original slogan. The left had been so thoroughly saturated with that inequality statistic that it seemed very obvious. It was only a little later that it occurred to me that it was an innovative slogan.

Like Occupy Wall Street itself, the concept of the 99% was so successful because it reclaimed a sense of class conflict under a seemingly apolitical guise. It pointed to irrefutable economic statistics about economic inequality that allowed people to feel 'non-partisan' in their rage. In a country where any political rhetoric about the plight of the working class and the avarice of the rich is painted as 'class warfare,' though it rarely is unfortunately, "we are the 99%" was a popular shield against such portrayals. As I discussed in Chapter 2, it put capitalists and capitalism on the defensive and provided space for substantive critiques of our undemocratic economy. Moreover, the notion of "the 99%" was exceptionally inclusive and thereby allowed middle class (and even some upper class) people to feel like they were just as much "The People" as anyone else. As I will soon discuss, the expansive nature of the slogan helped get massive numbers of people on the streets, but often at the expense of political clarity.

So what does the slogan have to do with anarchism? The first person to propose that OWS use the language of "99%" was the anarchist anthropologist David Graeber who suggested that we speak of ourselves as "a 99% Movement." The first public use of "99%" in Occupy was for a flier for the second GA at the Potato Famine Memorial on August 9, 2012 created by two Spanish organizers from the 15M movement using Graeber's suggestion. It said "WE, THE 99% CALL FOR AN OPEN GENERAL ASSEMBLY." The final piece in the process was when Chris from the Kitchen WG created the "We are the 99%" Tumblr, featuring photos of people holding signs describing their economic plight, which spawned the complete phrase.[74] Like Graeber, Chris is an anarchist striving to forge a classless, non-hierarchical society.

It's instructive, however, that both David and Chris were among those Occupy anarchists who were transparent about their politics to the public while also promoting a more accessible message that could appeal to the majority of Americans. Graeber has been known as an anarchist public intellectual for a while and he used his role in the movement to advocate for anarchism. But even Chris, who had a less public role in Occupy, thought it was important to be entirely forthcoming with his politics in relation to Occupy to present himself as an "ambassador of anarchy":

> I feel that it's important to show that I'm not a scary person as an anarchist. Yes, I do believe that the state and the capitalist economic system are vicious, evil, and monstrous institutions that must be shut down, burned down, pulled down and taken down wall by wall by any non-violent means necessary. But that doesn't necessarily mean that I'm out to be frightening. No! Personally I think I'm quite friendly. I'm quite affable ... I want to surprise people. I want people to think after they get to talk to me that this person is an anarchist but he's not the kind of anarchist I thought he would be. This isn't what I imagined in my mind when I thought of anarchists.[75]

This demonstrates the fact that there is no neat binary between being explicit or implicit with one's anarchist politics in a mass movement. Instead it's about assessing one's audience in a specific context and the best language to achieve one's goal. Occupy Wall Street worked because it had various rhetorical layers of radicalism that could nudge people in a revolutionary direction while still meeting them where they were at politically. This meant that while there were many OWS organizers who shifted their tone for a mainstream audience, there were also many who spoke openly about anarchism and radical politics. One might call it a "diversity of rhetoric." As a result, we could use more accessible, and at times over-simplified, rhetoric for a mainstream audience in order to pull people in and sharpen the content of the message. This is what happened with "the 99%."

The beauty of "the 99%" is that it opens seemingly non-ideological space where de-politicized Americans can engage in dialogue and action around class. The ugliness of "the 99%" is that it obscures vastly unequal power dynamics between upper, middle, working class and poor people. For example, the minimum household income of the 1% in the United States in 2010 was $516,633, down from a peak of $646,195 in 2007. In contrast, the most a household could earn to be in the bottom 40% was $33,870, and the maximum for the bottom 20% was $16,961 in 2010.[76] It's clearly a perversion of the spirit of "the 99%" for someone making a half million dollars a year to feel included, but they would mathematically belong as much as anyone else. Apart from the obvious flattening of class dynamics, this outlook has at times precluded an open collective interrogation of class privilege within Occupy.

Moreover, although the statistical emphasis of "the 99%" has provided it with a 'non-ideological' veneer, its complete focus on income differentials as the proper gauge of class oppression obscures the fundamental role of ownership of the means of production, access to productive resources, and labor hierarchy within capitalism. One of the most effective propagandistic feats of the American elite has been to convince working people that class is about income and that we all work, just with drastically different budgets. But that narrow understanding of class simply encourages the pursuit of higher salaries without delving into the structures of labor discipline. It's well suited to a liberal band-aid remedy of graduated taxation and an adjusted minimum wage.

Another related problem was the liberal line "the police are the 99%." No doubt statistically that's true as much as it is for someone who makes $500,000 a year, but this argument fails to distinguish between the 99% as a normative claim as opposed to a factual description. As a description it's accurate to point out that the police are working class, but as a normative claim the 99% is intended to describe class resistance. Therefore, it's essential to understand that, regardless of their class origins, the police are the army of capital historically born out of southern slave patrols and industrial labor disputes. CSI or Law and Order may tell us that they exist to catch serial murderers, but their primary structural role is to protect private property and enforce the social hierarchies that grease the wheels of capitalism. As Morrigan Phillips argued, "The 99% analysis needs to acknowledge that for the bottom 10% to 20%, the police, prison guards and other agents of the criminal justice system are not allies and are certainly not 'in it together' with poor communities of color."[77] At times it was truly absurd to see Occupy demonstrators being beaten and shoved by the cops while holding onto the propaganda that they exist to "protect and serve." One organizer who was beaten up and imprisoned on the night of the raid of Liberty Square told me:

> I don't blame the police for setting the policy. They're scared too, they have families, they get paychecks. If they stop getting those paychecks they can't feed their family. While that night during my time in jail my anger was directed toward the police, on reflection it's really not justified.

I would have hoped we could have gotten beyond the 'they were only following orders' excuse. Of course, they're people with families—all structures of oppression are operated by people with families—but we can't use the structure to excuse the individuals who collectively compose the structure. Overall, however, police violence had a very radicalizing effect on a number of OWS organizers. For example, Olivia (31) is a freelance stage manager who considered herself a "liberal and a democrat" before getting involved with the Kitchen and May Day planning groups of OWS. Previously she "thought cops are good and the police are there for the good of the community." But the night of the raid she saw that the "cops were targeting me and my friends who weren't doing anything illegal." It "was an eye-opener" that made her realize how tenuous her rights were and instilled "a distrust of the police." As a result her "life has been completely changed by Occupy Wall Street" and she's an anti-capitalist anti-authoritarian though she "didn't' really have knowledge of what that was until about six months ago."[78] Similarly Brett G. came to OWS as a "self-identified liberal" who had campaigned for Obama. After getting arrested several times, he radicalized:

> Ethically, and this is something I've evolved on, I'm less and less feeling like police are people. At the beginning when I first became involved my view was well the police are part of the 99%, they're facing a lot of the same economic issues but ... if they have a uniform on or continue to be a police officer there are levels of disengagement that they have to go through so that they're no longer people, they're just the brutal arm of the state.[79]

Nevertheless, although "the 99%" was a nebulous term open to a variety of interpretations, it was also a highly effective slogan despite its flaws because it managed to spark a nascent class-consciousness and mobilize thousands of people across the country. Moreover, there was a widespread commitment among OWS organizers to use it merely as an initial point of engagement on a longer educational path of revolutionary class politics.

"You Attract More Flies with Honey": Picking Up the Red and Black Flag

Although it was useful to present the ideas behind anarchism without its rhetorical baggage, the presence of OWS organizers who spoke openly about 'anarchism' and the prevalence of anarchist literature provided by the In Our Hearts anarchist collective led many to take the final step toward the rejection of all forms of oppression. However, the interesting relationship that I noticed in my interviews was that a large percentage of the anarchist organizers who were comfortable speaking openly about 'anarchism' to the press or people on the street did so because they felt like OWS had opened a space for the legitimate use of the label. But that space for an explicit discussion of 'anarchism' was opened by the mass popularity and success of OWS horizontalism, which developed, in part, because many of us refrained from labeling ourselves or the movement as 'anarchist.' Leading with the ideas allowed the label to follow for many anarchist organizers.

For example, Elizabeth Arce (24), a livestreamer and OWS musician who had worked with In Our Hearts previously, said that,

> Occupy has brought out a lot of what anarchism really is and I think the public view has changed a lot, which is really interesting to see. I think I used to shy away from saying 'I am an anarchist' because of those negative ideas but now I feel like I should really say it. Even though I don't want to be too attached to a word, I also want to redefine words, and that's a word I want to redefine and I think it's already being redefined and I want to help that along.[80]

Ben Reynoso (29), an organizer active with Info and DA, told me that he "wouldn't use 'anarchist' early on." Instead he would focus on direct democracy and cooperative enterprises. But by the time we spoke in June, 2012 he was "tending to [speak openly about 'anarchism'] more now." He added that "At first I thought it would scare people away, but now I think it's important to bring that into the conversation so it doesn't scare people away and to show people that normal people are anarchists."[81]

Sitting around a big table in the front office of WBAI public radio in New York, Luke Richardson (26), an organizer involved with Media and the Occupy radio show, explained to me that,

> In the beginning I was very much focused on Occupy as an action and broadening its appeal and not giving them

> anything to really pigeonhole about … For, I would say, the first three weeks I didn't say 'anarchy' once. Not once … you attract more flies with honey and it worked. We brought a whole lot of people in. Then the anarchist literature table came up. And all of a sudden you saw that people were actually interested in anarchism … and then we all started to come out of the closet a little bit.[82]

Madeline Nelson (56), a longtime anarchist organizer involved in the anti-nuclear, environmental, and women's rights movements in the 80s, used the same metaphor as Luke. As we spoke sitting on the hot sidewalk outside of Trinity Church on Broadway during a demonstration against the imprisonment of OWS organizer Mark Adams in late June 2012, Madeline reflected on the changes she had observed in popular perspectives on anarchism,

> It's almost like this coming out for anarchists. It was almost like when Gay people couldn't say 'Hey, I'm Queer. Get used to it.' It's like, 'Hey, I'm an Anarchist. Get used to it.' But for years we would say 'life beyond capitalism' 'alternatives' we would say 'non-hierarchical' 'horizontal' 'leaderless' which really are code words for an anarchist … Now I would [say that I'm an anarchist] and that's really liberating for me.[83]

A confluence of factors including the widespread practice of horizontalism and collective action, anarchist literature from In Our Hearts and the People's Library, and the influence of anarchist organizers brought many new people into anarchism. Certainly these influences shaped the politics of many who did not come to identify as anarchists, but during the course of my interviews I spoke with 13 organizers who became (or realized that they already were) anarchists through Occupy Wall Street. Let's take a look at some examples.

Ronny Nuñez (24) grew up in the Dominican Republic before moving to New York as a child. He was "a left-leaning independent" who had never been politically involved before coming to Occupy and working with the Outreach and Kitchen WGs and the People of Color Caucus. In college he read some essays by Kropotkin and said, "I really liked it, I really enjoyed it but I didn't think it was possible. And so when Occupy Wall Street happened and I got to see it first hand in practice it really spoke to me." Now Ronny is an anarchist. I asked him to describe how his Occupy experience led him to identify as an anarchist and he said "it's really the people. People coming together willing to hash out their differences or willing to hash out their problems to eventually come to a consensus. It was the true principle of cooperation."[84]

Austin Guest (31) was a Jobs With Justice (JWJ) organizer originally from California who had high hopes for Obama in 2008 and thought that "anarchists [were] deluded and a little scary." At first he came down to Liberty in the evenings after work, often bringing his camera to capture the scene. On October 5th JWJ gave him the opportunity to spend half of his work time on OWS, and he became one of the most active and energetic organizers in DA known for his brightly colored fluorescent hats and gloves. But over time several "radicalizing" experiences led him to quit his job to put all of his time into the movement. After being brutally arrested by the police at the enormous Times Square demonstration on October 15, 2011, he said that "for the first time I really got that the cops are the army of the 1%."[85] Experiencing the anarchist "culture of care" that people showed for each other in the context of state repression showed him a "positive side that the media never sees." He read Graeber's *Direct Action*, AK Thompson's *Black Bloc, White Riot*, some anarcha-feminist essays that OWS anarchist Suzahn Ebrahimian gave him, he checked out the readings from the Occupy-related anarchist discussion group Café de Cleyre (launched by OWS anarchists Matt Presto and Marisa Holmes) and he became "a newly minted social anarchist."[86]

George Machado (21) was "a left-leaning democrat" from Harlem without any previous political experience besides campaigning for Obama in 2008. When he first heard about OWS he thought it would just be "well-intentioned liberal white college kids" and dismissed it. But on October 5th he came down to the massive OWS union march, which proved to be "a life-changing experience." That night George slept in the park and a homeless man tripped over him as he was sleeping, accidentally cutting him in the head with a bottle. George smiled as he described the incident, and as he pointed to the scar from the bottle he gleefully recounted how awesome he thought it was that he could just walk over to the medic tent, get patched up, and go back to sleep. George got involved in doing outreach in Harlem before gravitating to DA. He "was swallowing theory whole." He read the *Communist Manifesto* in a day, devoured anarchist zines, and had immersed himself in a wide variety of political conversations. Eventually he was drawn to anarchism through Murray Bookchin's writings on social ecology. He said "I've never learned so much in such a short period of time … this is the greatest thing to ever happen to me … before this I was incredibly depressed."[87]

On October 8, 2011, Stacey Hessler (39) came up from Florida for Occupy Wall Street. Although she was a little disappointed with the size of the encampment at first, she quickly got involved with a variety of Working Groups including Sanitation, Sustainability, and Housing. She said that she really appreciated the wide variety of issues that OWS protested:

> At first it was like well corporations aren't people, end Citizens United, and put the regulations back on the banks. Those were like the things that I was thinking would make the changes, but then when I started seeing the prison system and

> the court system and the education system and going to these different protests that were about those specific issues ... I started to realize that it's like every system is messed up and every system needs to be completely changed.

So Stacey read a bunch of the anarchist zines from In Our Hearts and shifted toward anarchism:

> When I first came to Occupy Wall Street I was more like 'let's change the system so it works' and so more of like a reformist I guess ... but really since I've been here and I've read different material that I've come across I'm getting more into [anarchism] ... I would rather see the whole system smashed than reform it.[88]

Rowland Miller (29) moved to New York in 2007 to work at various non-profits after growing up in Louisville, Kentucky. Apart from a few anti-war marches, he hadn't been politically involved before gradually getting involved with OWS throughout the course of the fall of 2011. Over time, he made his way into DA, Outreach, and PR and started to learn about anarchism. Previously, he said, "I'd always figured that anarchism was just a matter of people wanting to be violent or say there should be no rules; everyone out for themselves. No governance, no accountability." Upon reflecting on his emergent affinity for anarchism, Rowland cited two main experiences: reading Graeber's *Direct Action* and witnessing Lisa Fithian's "way with people." Her ability as facilitator and organizer to "understand people's desires, articulate them and address them helped keep the movement functional" and showed Roland that direct democracy could work if done right.[89]

Nicholas "OWS Tea" (26) was working in a high end Manhattan restaurant in the fall of 2011 when some of his friends, such as Isham Christie, brought him down to the park.

Though he lacked previous political organizing experience, a month later he quit his job to spend all of his time with the movement. He got the moniker "Tea Guy" for brewing hot tea as the temperature dropped, and he put a lot of time into May Day planning into the spring. He told me that, "OWS really opened up a new lens for me to even understand politics. I guess like a lot of other people pre-OWS I never even gave anarchism much thought...I didn't really think outside the 'republicrat' nonsense box, and so OWS really opened up my understanding of participatory, direct democracy…I didn't really think outside the 'republicrat' nonsense box, and so OWS really opened up my understanding of participatory, direct democracy…" The experiences that he cited as influential in his anarchist development included the experience of the assemblies and democratic meetings, having conversations about direct democracy, and zines from the People's Library and In Our Hearts. He said, "right off the bat the In Our Hearts group really held it down!" As a new anarchist with an interest in expressing anarchist ideas to the public, Nicholas takes a nuanced approach. He explained that "people have been trained to think that anarchy is chaos and danger and anarchists are terrorists, so I try to be cautious about who I open up that dialogue with. But, I do like to approach the idea with just about anybody because it can give strangers an opportunity to start looking at things such as anarchism in a new way." He tries to be broad and undefined about his ideas and then start to associate them with the ideological label. He likes to "wait on it instead of dropping that whole thing up front."[90]

Both Tim Fitzgerald and Louis Jargow (24) had been exposed to anarchist ideas prior to Occupy but needed to see elements of it in action before being fully convinced. Tim was familiar with consensus from his time in the youth movement of the Unitarian Universalists where he learned a little about anarchism, but instead he spent his time helping to run Democratic campaigns in 2006 and 2008. Like many in Occupy, and especially those who moved in a more radical or anarchist direction, Tim and Louis were very disappointed in Obama and the Democrats. Tim said,

> I was nerdy enough to follow almost all the house races of 2006 and 2008 and all the senate races of 2006 and 2008. I had this critique that if we followed the game very closely and made really shrewd decisions about how to interact with it that we would be able to … get the ball in our court and then play the game we want to play. And I don't think that's what happened at all. We got people in there who were supposed to do that. 2006 and 2008 are both really part of that for me. Instead we had the Democrats fumbling the ball repeatedly and almost throwing the game. I can't even think of all of the times that Harry Reed or Nancy Pelosi did the exact opposite of what they should have done. And when Obama came into office I was like 'OK now they have a leader that can keep them focused on undoing all of the damage that Bush had done and tipping the balance of power from this insane oligarchic gang that had been running the government for eight years.' And then they didn't do it.

Likewise, Louis vacillated between more radical and liberal stances following his disillusionment as an Obama canvasser. He said that the failure of Obama was "crucial" in his political development but it took until Occupy for him to identify as an anarchist "since I didn't have an experience of anarchists or anarchism and the sort of pleasant beautiful ways that that can be lived and practiced."[91] Tim had a similar experience since he was familiar with anarchist doctrine, but seeing the ideas in practice through modes of direct action and direct democracy "really made it seem like a tenable thing to me."[92]

* * *

But not all anarchists have been positive about OWS. Mike Andrews (30), one of the three original members of the OWS tactical team over the summer of 2011 who helped make the decision to occupy Zuccotti on the first day, told me about some of the anarchists who had written OWS off as "just a bunch of fucking liberals." Sitting in a diner near Washington Square Park after a February May Day Planning meeting Mike said,

> I have some friends who have identified as anarchists for much longer than I've been interested in anarchism and who have been very active in anarchism in New York for as long as they've been here ... and I'm just consistently astonished at how all they can do is shit on Occupy Wall Street. And it's been interesting for me. I counter that by saying you can't judge OWS by media coverage or the Facebook page. You have to come down ... I try to tell them, 'look anarchists have been involved in this from the start ... anarchists are still very active in this. The entire framework is built on anarchist principles. This is a mass movement that has anarchism at its core. You will *NEVER, EVER* encounter this ever again.'

Ultimately, Mike summed up an important part of the problem when he added that, "some anarchists are so attached to this outsider status where they don't have to engage with people outside their affinity group."[93] Or, as the famous Chinese anarchist Ba Jin wrote in the 1920s, "'Perfection or nothing' is the idea of an individualist, not the idea of a revolutionary who fights for the interests of the people, because such an idea does not reflect the needs of the people."[94]

Something somewhat similar happened with the "Class War Camp" (CWC) of Liberty Square. CWC was a 'neighborhood' in the middle of the park toward the west side primarily composed of anti-capitalist punk and countercultural youth. Though there were maybe 20-30 people who ever belonged to their encampment, they usually had about 8 there at any given time.[95] It included the entire range of anti-capitalist politics from anarchists to Stalinists. One anarchist Class War Camper explained to me that the idea was to focus on anti-capitalism as a group and then work out the other differences later. I'm not sure if he understood what I meant when I replied that we, the anarchists, had tried that a few times before historically, but one way or another we always ended up in front of the firing squads. Once I saw an anarchist flag, a communist flag, a Guy Fawkes mask, and an American flag side by side on their tent (oh, Occupy...). For many, especially themselves, they were *the* revolutionary formation of OWS. Whenever a journalist or writer wanted an insurrectionary quote that's where they'd go. In the collectively written book *Occupying Wall Street* by the "Writers for the 99%," a CWC participant named KV said of the west side of the park: "This side of the camp isn't for reform. This side's for revolution ... It's not liberal college kids. We don't want to fix the system, we want to fucking burn it to the ground."[96]

KV's quote points to some important internal tensions between the east side of the park (where most of the organizing and the General Assemblies happened) and the west side (where the drum circle played and more of the countercultural and homeless people slept). While I think the dichotomy has been overstated somewhat, it was real. And the organizers who spent most of their time on the east side were overwhelmingly college educated, even if they seemed to come from a variety of class backgrounds. But it wasn't a political divide. As I've shown, those that KV dismissed as "liberal college students" were largely anti-capitalist, anti-authoritarians though they may not have always dressed the part.[97] Most of CWC didn't get it because they didn't participate in any of the politics of the encampment. The only CWCer I knew who organized was Zak (22), an anti-authoritarian communist without any prior political experience. Speaking with him in the atrium at 60 Wall St, Zak lamented CWC's inability to spread their anti-capitalist message: "we were very much against involving ourselves in the organization as a whole. Most people in Class War Camp, for example, never ever went to the GA, ever. Most didn't involve themselves in any other working groups ... so after the raid we just spread to the wind."[98]

* * *

And likewise into the wind were scattered many of the Occupy organizers and groups as the unifying coherence of the "Occupy Wall Street" umbrella faded after the mega-project of organizing May Day 2012. Our decentralized structure spiraled out of control to the point that we became a network of projects rather than a unified directly democratic entity. Nevertheless, it is clear that Occupy Wall Street proved to be an effective vehicle for translating anarchy because it could bring in progressives and left-leaning democrats and infuse their politics with anarchist ideas. Some of them left with a more critical stance on electoral politics and a greater appreciation for direct action and direct democracy, and others walked away as anarchists. Both are important, though. The fact that the radical left in the United States has been so thoroughly imbued with anarchist practice, if not always anarchist politics, is an important step toward the long-term creation of a left libertarian mass movement. Though we may be scattered to the wind, I am confident that the dispersal of our anti-authoritarian ideas back across the country will provide the opportunity for them to plant the seeds of future resistance.

Chapter Four

Why We Need a Revolution or: Beyond "Socialism in One Park"

"Never be deceived that the rich will allow you to vote away their wealth."
—Lucy Parsons

The Electoral Question

Tess Cohen (26) was working as a nanny in New York when she stopped by the occupation of Zuccotti Park on September 19, 2011. Though she was "into it almost immediately," she "kept [her] distance at first." Tess had volunteered for the Kerry campaign in 2004 and the Obama campaign in 2008, but hadn't had any experience with activism or organizing before throwing herself into the frantic effort to scrub down Liberty Square in the pouring rain on October 13, 2011 to prevent Mayor Bloomberg's threatened "cleaning." By the end of the month she was livestreaming General Assemblies. When I asked her to describe her politics in late August 2012, she said that although only ten months prior she used to think that representative democracy was working just fine, she was getting more and more influenced by anarchism and its "values and praxis of self-empowerment" (though she refrained from labeling herself). But perhaps the real turning point for Tess, and many others like her, was the first term of the Obama administration. Tess said,

> If you'd asked me four years ago I would have said that my politics are Obama and a lot's happened since then and I've learned a lot since then. I would be lying if I were to say that I don't feel some sort of faith in Obama as a person and in his

politics, however I have absolutely zero at this point in the system as a whole, so I'm pretty reticent to vote.[1]

In many ways, Occupy Wall Street *was* spawned by Obama, but not how Fox News imagined. In 2008, Obama rode a wave of youthful energy into the White House as the most charismatic and dynamic Democratic candidate since JFK. In the eyes of many young people who had only ever been politically conscious during a George W. Bush presidency, Obama was poised to unleash a progressive monsoon. Nicholas "OWS Tea" thought that "this guy's gonna actually be progressive in his approach to our military domination of the planet and maybe he's gonna do something to help out students too ... and that all turned out to be exactly the opposite." He felt "disappointed" and "betrayed" and won't vote anymore because the experience led him to feel like "voting, especially in the system that we're asked to vote in, doesn't give us any real choice and it feels like a big scam."[2] Likewise, Brett G. canvassed for Obama in Ohio and Pennsylvania but walked away considering the Obama presidency to be a "horrible disappointment." He said, "we got our hopes up that one person could make radical change ... but even the most radical person from OWS, if they were president would be boxed in by the structure."[3]

The organizers that I interviewed were critical of a wide variety of Obama's policies and decisions including: his failure to close Guantanamo; his continuation and acceleration of the war in Afghanistan; his intense augmentation of the use of unmanned drones to launch attacks ("an unprecedented move: a foreign government carrying out military strikes on an independent and sovereign state without declaring war") in Pakistan (2,570-3,337 Pakistanis have been killed by American drones including 176 children),[4] Yemen (over 800 deaths from drone strikes during his first term),[5] and Somalia,[6] and his drone attack "kill list";[7] his military involvement in Libya, Mali, and Niger;[8] his waiving of the child soldier ban in Yemen and Congo;[9] his signing of the National Defense Authorization Act (NDAA) known for "codifying indefinite military detention without charge or trial into law for the first time in American history";[10] his extension of George W. Bush's PATRIOT ACT which makes it easier for the government to spy on its citizens;[11] his signing of H.R. 347 which prohibits protests in and around areas where someone is being protected by the secret service;[12] his record-setting deportations of undocumented migrants (1.2 million in his first 3 years alone);[13] his failure to act on behalf of Bradley Manning (lauded for leaking evidence of US military war crimes); his signing of the FAA Reauthorization Act which makes it harder for workers to unionize;[14] his failure to prosecute the Wall Street criminals;[15] his signing of new free trade agreements with Colombia, Panama, and South Korea;[16] his reduction of the period of Pell Grant eligibility for students by 33%;[17] his watered down "healthcare law for corporations";[18] his promotion of "clean coal" and lack of a serious focus on climate change;[19] his cuts to Social Security and Medicare (between $200-380 billion more than the GOP) and the fact that whereas under Bush "65 cents of every dollar of income growth went to the top 1 percent," under Obama "that number is 93 cents out of every dollar."[20]

As Lisa Fithian told me, Obama has been "just as bad as Bush on everything as far as I'm concerned."[21] In 2008, Obama portrayed himself as a progressive but that image had faded for the vast majority of OWS after four years and a trail of broken campaign promises including:

> A higher minimum wage, a ban on the replacement of striking workers, seven days of paid sick leave, a more diverse media ownership structure, renegotiation of NAFTA, letting bankruptcy judges write down mortgage debt, a ban on illegal wiretaps, an end to national security letters, stopping the war on whistle-blowers, passing the Employee Free

> Choice Act, restoring habeas corpus and labor protections in the FAA bill.[22]

Pete Dutro (36), one of the main organizers of the Finance WG who used to run a tattoo shop, said Obama, "talked a good game and then basically took Bush's policies and implemented them even further."[23] Obama's continuation of Bush's policies, especially in terms of foreign policy, has been so thoroughly ignored by Democrats that a Washington Post-ABC News Poll showed that a vast majority of democrats supported Obama's decision to continue the policies they loathed four years earlier including keeping Guantanamo open and launching drone strikes.[24] Edward Needham (44) of the Press WG used to be so involved with the Democratic Party of his home state of Maine that he ran for State Representative on the Democratic ticket twice and became the state director of draftobama.org in 2008. But by the time I sat down to talk with him near the Garibaldi statue in Washington Square Park in June of 2012, he had made the painful decision to join the Green Party although he had been opposed to supporting Ralph Nader in 2000. He said, "I've been very disappointed. It's not that I believe that [Obama's] tried a number of things and hasn't been successful. I just don't think he's tried a number of things ... He's the best republican president we've seen in quite a while."[25] And Obama would actually agree. Safely re-elected to his second term, Obama revealed on Miami's *Noticias Univision 23* on December 12, 2012 that "the truth of the matter is that my policies are so mainstream that if I had set the same policies that I had back in the 1980s, I would be considered a moderate republican."[26] Clearly Goldi (45), organizer of music-related OWS groups including the 'Guitarmy,' was right when he said "I thought [Obama] was more of a closet radical and that he was gonna unleash that once he was in office and to my disappointment he was a closet conservative."[27]

However, Obama's policies do not detract from the enormous historical significance of an African American attaining the highest political office in the United States, and the political-symbolic importance that this achievement has had for people of African descent around the world. In many ways, the jubilation and sense of pride that many felt at Obama's election had much more to do with its relation to centuries of struggle against white supremacy than Obama the politician. Atiq Zabinski recalled the celebration that erupted in his Brooklyn neighborhood in 2008 and said that the "celebration was more important than the thing it was celebrating."[28]

Moreover, from a radical perspective, Obama's victory has been of significant value in counteracting the notion that the problem with society is the individual politician (in terms of their identity, politics, or anything else) rather than the structures of power around them. Obama's failure to live up to his supposedly progressive potential radicalized many young people when OWS emerged.

Sam Corbin also pointed out another key feature of the Obama campaign that set the stage for Occupy. As opposed to Hillary Clinton's more traditional campaign, Obama's campaign:

> Said, 'you have to do it. You have to be in the street. You have to come out. You have to organize.' And he got a huge incredible organizing structure together. People were really motivated. People who had never been involved in politics were working super, super hard, and I was kinda like 'wow, this is great this many people are mobilized because if and when he's disappointing they will know how to organize and they will feel ownership over his decisions and they will be like you told us to hold you accountable, here we are.' That didn't materialize as much as I thought it would a couple of years ago, but I think a big part of why some of the more liberal left is as motivated as it is, is because of that...[29]

When that organizing structure was dismantled and Obama turned back on his campaign promises "we saw the hangover," as Aaron Bornstein phrased it, when "a real, serious despair" settled over the left-liberal universe.[30] Perhaps this "hangover" was one reason why it took a few years for crisis-related protests to develop, but that's pure speculation. What isn't speculation is the fact that the organizers of Occupy Wall Street almost completely lost their hope in electoral politics between 2008 and 2012. My interview data shows that 66% of organizers who were eligible to vote in 2008 voted for Obama, 13% voted for Nader or the Green Party, and the rest abstained or wrote-in. However, only 16% of organizers definitely intended to vote for Obama in 2012, 10% intended to vote for a third party, and 51% intended to abstain or write-in. It's important to clarify that 20% of organizers said they weren't sure what they would do and my guess is that more than half of them cast ballots for Obama by default. Nevertheless, even if you increase the 2012 figure to about 26% it's still a huge drop-off and the uncertainty is indicative of a widespread disenchantment. Even liberal and progressive organizers voted with remorse.

For example, Jake DeGroot (26) spent years advocating for progressive issues like campaign finance reform and phone-banked for Obama in 2008, but before Occupy he said, "I never considered myself an activist." Jake got very involved with OWS, primarily through tech and social media related working groups, but he maintained faith in the possibility of reforming capitalism and America's representative political system. He said that in 2012 he would probably "begrudgingly" vote for Obama "but what I won't do is campaign for him and phone-bank for him and give money to his campaign and I won't be [voting] enthusiastically."[31]

For others, the shift away from Obama and the Democratic Party was more radical. Stan (29) was working in Alabama when he used his vacation to come up to New York to check out OWS on Oct. 20, 2011. Though he hadn't had previous organizing experience apart from participation in the American Atheist Alliance, when he arrived he attended the entirety of a six-hour Think Tank session and fell in love with the movement. After the vacation, he returned to Alabama and quit his job to devote himself to OWS. Since then, he's been involved with Labor Outreach (he now works for a union), Facilitation, Immigrant Workers' Justice and other WGs. Though his friends jokingly refer to him as a "Stanarchist," Stan rejects labels and considers himself "a whatever works person" in favor of "a total direct democracy." Nevertheless, through his Occupy experience he came to the perspective that "we need to stop looking at [Obama] or even these buildings around us as saviors. We need to look to each other." In the 2012 presidential election he said he wouldn't vote for Obama again; instead he would support a third party or write-in Vermin Supreme.[32]

Isham Christie voted for Obama in 2008 but abstained in 2012. As he described to me, Obama's first term was a formative political experience:

> I saw a lot more clearly that the system was more to blame than a specific president. Growing up with George Bush it was easy to demonize George Bush and say he's the specific root of all social evils. But then when someone who I thought was fine and liberal [got elected], I didn't have much hope that he would do anything, but to see how little he actually did actually increased and furthered my systemic analysis that whoever's really in charge, while there might be some differences in social services and maybe a little bit better pro-union, the change I would like to see is not gonna come from a ballot box.[33]

Drew Hornbein came away with a similar perspective on electoral politics after witnessing how the Obama campaign "built a grassroots organizing platform and then dismantled it." He said:

> One of biggest takeaways that I've gotten from being involved with [OWS] is like: do not expect anyone else to do it for you. The bad guys are waking up everyday and working their asses off and if you and yours aren't doing the same you're not going to get what you think is right by voting once every four years.

Drew voted Obama in 2008 and ultimately decided to vote for him again in 2012 after conversations with "women, minorities, and immigrants" who considered the difference between Obama and Romney to be significant.[34]

Likewise Ethan (22) is an activist from Minneapolis who was involved in environmental activism before Occupy. He happened to be in Egypt meeting with activists when OWS started, and was arrested for a short time by soldiers who threatened and intimidated him under accusations of being a spy. Once he made it to New York, he got involved with Facilitation, Interoccupy, and helped design the spokescouncil. Though he emphasized that "ideologies are dangerous and alienating and isolating," he's an anti-capitalist, anti-authoritarian. Ethan had high hopes for Obama in 2008, but said that his disenchantment helped him understand that society's ills are "deeply embedded in the entire system." Like, Drew, however, he voted for Obama in 2012 saying:

> I know that it won't make much of a difference. I mean Obama and Romney are gonna do the same for the economy, pretty much the same on foreign policy; they're gonna do the same destructive shit to the environment. It's gonna be pretty much the same, but if the difference between Obama and Romney is a woman's access to Planned Parenthood then who am I to

> deny someone that right? ... There are at least some differences enough that will have a tangible impact in people's lives that it would be irresponsible of me not to vote.[35]

As Ethan pointed out, there are, of course, differences between the Republican and Democratic candidates for President every four years. In 2012, as in many other elections, one of the most emphasized issues on the left was women's rights. It's true that their policies diverged regarding abortion and funding for Planned Parenthood, but the contrasts were also somewhat overstated. For example, Obama overruled the FDA and many scientists when he insisted that women under 17 shouldn't have access to Plan B birth control because he was "a father of two daughters." In addition his healthcare bill was subject to the Hyde Amendment prohibiting government money from being used for abortions, and one of his supreme court nominations, Sonya Sotomayor, has already ruled to limit access to abortion in her career, while the other, Elena Kagan, doesn't have a clear stance.[36] Moreover, Pakistani women who have had their families incinerated by flying death machines, immigrant women who have been deported, (predominantly) women of color who have themselves been incarcerated or had their loved ones imprisoned for minor drug possession, and working and middle class women who have had their families evicted from their longtime homes because of the crimes of a handful of bankers *might* not see Obama's track record on women's rights the same way. As activist and writer Gina Rodríguez-Drix so eloquently said,

> I cannot vote for someone who will keep abortion rights but support gas drilling, which is a practice known to harm the reproductive system and cause miscarriage, birth defects, and death ... I will not support anyone who wants to lock my people away. I will not support someone who bombs other

women's children. I will not.[37]

Nevertheless, Obama repealed Don't Ask Don't Tell (though most radical queers are quick to point out that the right to fight for empire doesn't equal queer liberation), he super-belatedly supported gay marriage (also far from the goals of radical queers and anarchists who oppose the institution of marriage),[38] and he implemented a policy that allowed many undocumented students to avoid deportation (though it fell short of the DREAM Act and didn't end his record-setting deportations). So it is undeniable that there were some real differences that directly affected people's lives, as imperfect as they were.

Moreover, the election provided a forum for people to battle over America's contentious social and cultural divide between relatively secular liberals and religious conservatives. This was surely evident in Bill Livsey's take on the election. Bill (48) grew up in a staunchly republican family in Florida that threw him out of the house for being gay at the age of 16. He started organizing with ACT UP in Los Angeles in the 80s and shook Reagan's hand with red paint on it in 1983. After getting involved with OWS, Bill became a mainstay of DA. Sitting at a table outside Trinity Church on Broadway, Bill told me that he had "lost faith in the American system of government," but wryly added: "There's not much difference between the democrats and the republicans ... they're both bought and sold by the corporations and it's the same imperialism, it's just that the Obama brand of imperialism doesn't require you to suck off Jesus."[39]

Why Your (Non)Vote Doesn't Matter

However, although we as Americans are taught from a very early age that voting is the pinnacle of citizenship and political action, anarchists, and most OWS organizers, agree that the simple five-minute act of pulling a lever or filling in a bubble for high political office is perhaps the *least* important political act you can take. Why is that? Well, for starters your vote doesn't actually affect the outcome of the election. Let's take the presidential election, supposedly the most important, as an example. The media makes it very clear that unless you live in Ohio, Florida, or some other swing state you might as well stay home because your state's fate has been pre-determined. Moreover, the margins of victory in swing states are so vast that you would have a much better chance of winning the lottery than having your vote affect the outcome of a state's race. Obama's margin of victory in Ohio was more than 100,000 votes in 2012, and in the tight Florida race it was still over 73,000.[40] Even in the once-in-a-lifetime case of the Bush/Gore race in Florida in 2000 the final margin of victory for Bush was 537 votes.[41] And if you have a problem with one of the two main candidates and vote for a third party you are said to have thrown away your vote anyway. Some democracy. Also, by listing the vote tallies in terms of the percentage of those who voted rather than the percentage of eligible voters, the media artificially inflates voter participation and discredits electoral abstention. When I was in San Sebastián, Spain, I noticed that a local newspaper actually listed the percentages of the major parties alongside the percentage of eligible voters who abstained and those who submitted blank ballots (representing the vast majority of potential voters).

The sanctity of the individual voting act also relies on an unacknowledged philosophical premise, something I only started to realize when I took a metaphysics class in college. I remember we were having a discussion about "causation" and when, if ever, it was possible to say that A caused B philosophically. The conclusion the professor came to was that if B would happen whether or not A occurred, then one could not say that A caused B. After class, I asked him if that same logic could be used to argue that it doesn't matter whether or not an individual votes since one vote never determines the outcome and, after a moment of consternation, he agreed before quickly interjecting, "but please go vote!" Of course, if you consider A to be the collective act of people voting as a group, then A certainly causes B, the outcome of the election. In other words, if many people stopped voting, that would have a significant effect. Essentially the individual act of voting only makes sense when performed in accordance with some version of Immanuel Kant's notion of universalizability. For Kant, this meant that, "I ought never to act except in such a way that I can also will that my maxim should become a universal law."[42] When applied to voting, that means that although an individual vote may not be sufficient to cause an outcome, when one votes, one acts so that one's behavior sets a standard of conduct for others that contributes to the collective voting process. (Not to mention the tremendous social gratification that voting confers on the voter in American society, evident in the 'I voted' stickers, but that's another story).

The irony is that although the individual act of voting relies on the principle of universalizability, whenever someone invokes the same principle for the purpose of supporting a third candidate or pursuing an alternative political strategy, they are belittled. When I supported Nader in 2000, people asked my why I'd 'throw away my vote' rather than supporting the 'lesser of two evils,' and I'd respond by asking 'what if *every* disenchanted Democrat voted Green? Then we'd have something going!' I was usually dismissed as being 'impractical' since it was foolish to think of my single act of voting as being expressive of a universalizable pattern of behavior although voting for one of the two major parties relies on the same logic. People told me that I might as well stay home on election day since my vote wouldn't 'matter,' but I could say the same thing to any voter in any major race since the larger impact of voting is entirely dependent on individual choices becoming wider patterns of behavior. So while it's true that if thousands of Democratic voters had stayed home in 2012 Romney would have won, it's also true that if thousands of Democrats had actually embraced the principle of universalizability that they unknowingly abide by and set off on an alternative political path then real change might have actually come.

That rationalization of voting might suffice if politicians were actually acting according to the desires of their constituencies, but they're not. In a capitalist economy, those with large concentrations of wealth necessarily enjoy equivalent political power. This dynamic is exacerbated by the lack of legitimate campaign finance laws, but most importantly it stems from the fundamental nature of the market system. Corporations and financial institutions have become so powerful that they can even bypass the supposed norms of the market to get massive government subsidies and safety nets when they screw up. Sure, campaign advisors scrutinize data from the polls about voter preferences, but it's understood that voter opinions only matter when they're about the narrow strata of politics that is open to contestation. Much like the criteria of *communication with the elite* discussed in Chapter 1, voter opinions gain legitimacy based on their proximity to the already established stances of the candidates. If, for example, you want to use your vote to chastise Obama for signing a bill (NDAA) that broke with the entirety of American legal history by allowing American citizens to be detained without due process, you're out of luck. If you want your vote to 'matter' there is no alternative; Obama and the Democratic Party have a monopoly over the American 'left.' Instead you are encouraged to ignore issues that the candidates agree on (which is almost all of them) and decide based on a set of issues whose outcomes do not threaten the underlying class hierarchy.

But even if American politicians had a more sincere interest in improving the plight of working people, there's only so much that they could possibly accomplish within the capitalist economy. Just look at the recent failures of European social democratic parties. The historical project of pursuing socialism through electoral means started in the late 19th century under the influence of the reformist socialist Eduard Bernstein of the Social Democratic Party of Germany (SPD). As struggles for universal manhood suffrage were gaining traction across Europe, many socialists thought that socialism could be elected into existence since the working class constituted the majority of society and therefore the majority of voters. Over the course of the first third of the twentieth century a number of strong socialist parties emerged, but Sweden was the only country to introduce a modern welfare state prior to World War II. However, the collapse of capitalism after the Great Depression, the dominant examples of Nazi and Soviet state-controlled economics, and the allied experiences of wartime planning propelled mainstream economic thought in a state-socialist direction in the postwar period. Laissez-faire economics was thought to have faded into history. In the 1950s free-market ideologue Milton Friedman "was an academic joke."[43] Free market ideology survived better in Italy and West Germany because of widespread wariness of state planning inherited from the Mussolini and Hitler regimes, but even they maintained mixed economies.[44]

Although very few American politicians have explicitly labeled themselves socialists, Eugene Debs being a notable exception, a number of reforms to the economic system over the past century have followed a watered-down model of European social democracy toward ameliorating the worst excesses of capitalism. In response to the labor movement and massive social unrest, reformist politicians eventually instituted child labor laws, the 8-hour day, health and safety regulations, social security, Medicare and Medicaid, welfare, the minimum wage, environmental regulations, and so forth. It's important to understand that although these laws bolstered the state before the specter of social revolution, all of them are ideologically anti-capitalist insofar as they infringe upon the ability of (supposedly) autonomous individuals to make contracts with each other as they see fit. If a ten-year old 'autonomously' decides that they want to work in a factory, who are you to stop them? If they don't want to work there, no one's putting a gun to their head. If someone wants to sell their labor for $1 an hour that should be their right, no? Of course that individualistic perspective on social relations omits the fact that the working class as a group has had to sell its labor to the employing, capitalist class to avoid starvation since they have a monopoly on life-sustaining resources. As we know from history, capitalism only places value in profits and economic growth. Left to its own devices, it creates utterly inhuman working conditions without even the modest feudal social safety net that it obliterated when it emerged on the world stage.

However, it appears that we are seeing an end to the first chapter in the history of social democracy as the limits of attempts to moderate capitalism have become widely apparent. In part, this is because in an era of capitalist globalization progressive legislation often causes capital flight. In that way, the market puts a glass ceiling on the extent to which the 'democratic' system can modulate the market. In the United States, labor, safety and environmental regulations scared away industry long ago. The global 'free' market encourages a race to the bottom where the cheapest labor and most inhuman working conditions prevail. It's laughable to hear Obama promising to bring back industry to the United States by offering tax incentives while he continues to sign free trade agreements. In Europe, the limitations of working toward socialism through parliamentary politics became fully apparent when the economic crisis forced socialist leaders in countries such as Spain and Greece to enact austerity measures. There is no clearer example of the fact that within a capitalist economy the market reigns supreme. If we truly want to democratize our workplace and collectively control our resources so that people have what they need to live decent lives then we can't dance around the market; we have to smash it. Over the past hundred years the social democrats have played the role of Sisyphus pushing the boulder of gradual social reform up the mountain only to see it start to roll back down in recent years as the market tilted the slope.

Therefore, it's not terribly important whether any given individual votes or not since our individual votes don't matter and our votes as a group have only a very limited potential to change anything systemic. But, as these examples have shown, it is crucially important to avoid falling into the trap of electoral politics as a vision of social transformation. Whether from a liberal or socialist perspective, the notion that social issues can be solved by electing someone else to deal with them is one of the most disempowering and unreliable forms of social struggle. Not only is it impossible to know exactly what a politician will do once in office, the electoral mindset conditions people to look to figures of authority for guidance and aid which circumscribes the horizons of horizontal mutual aid and solidarity.

Overall, 51% of organizers intended to abstain or write-in protest candidates like Emma Goldman, Vermin Supreme or Stephen Colbert in 2012, and among the anarchists of OWS it was 70%. Zu Solanas (19), an "anarchist without adjectives" from Paterson, NJ active in DA, said that she preferred writing-in something ridiculous to abstaining because she liked the "idea of displaying not apathy but frustration."[45] Apart from the reasons cited above, a number of OWS anarchists don't vote because anarchists oppose the principle of representation. It is inherently unjust for someone to make important decisions for someone else without their input and often without their consent. It's a manifestation of the kind of hierarchy that anarchism was born to oppose. Yet, it is crucial to distinguish between representatives and delegates. In order to facilitate large-scale decision-making, anarchists have always used delegates to communicate the perspectives of others, but, as opposed to representatives, delegates don't have independent legislative authority. They exist merely as vessels to convey the perspectives of others. Anarchists aren't opposed to voting as a principle or practice; rather, we oppose voting for people rather than issues, and oppose any political system characterized by disparities in wealth and power.

Although anarchist groups have historically organized campaigns encouraging electoral abstention, in recent years it's become more common in the United States for anarchists to trivialize the discrete voting act, regardless of whether one performs it or not, while reserving their sharpest critiques for the role of electoral politics in maintaining capitalism and the state. A notable example of this trend was a 2004 pamphlet distributed by the anarchist collective/network Crimethinc saying "Don't Just Vote—Get Active."[46] The pamphlet's argument wasn't about promoting abstention; it was about trivializing the voting act while encouraging collective action during the other 364 days of the year. Therefore, as an anarchist political organizer, I often think it's worthwhile to debate the merits of Democratic candidates in order to expose their unethical policies, but I don't exert any energy trying to convince anyone else not to vote. Instead, I push people to organize themselves.

In addition to the small slice of policy differences between Romney and Obama, one of the most common reasons that OWS organizers gave for voting was that they wanted to honor the sacrifices and struggles endured by African Americans and women to get the vote. Certainly I am among many anarchists who recognize the deep significance of those movements and respect those who honor their ancestors with their ballots. For many, Obama's victory represented the fulfillment of generations of struggle, and its historical and political significance should not be dismissed. However, one should bear in mind that the electoral vision of courageous suffragettes and freedom riders did not include Super PACs, billions in campaign contributions, and corporate hegemony in the service of a system that sends more African American men to prison than college. Moreover, many have fought and died for a wide variety of issues including union organizing but we never hear the argument that 'If you're not part of a labor union then you're dishonoring the memory of those who died for the right to unionize.' Many also fought and died for genuine socialism across the world over the past 150 years, and so for many anarchists and anti-authoritarians electoral abstention, direct action, and mutual aid are how we honor the sacrifices of our fallen comrades from Chicago to Buenos Aires, from Oaxaca to Bialystok. For freedom fighters, whether in the American south or the Global South, liberation doesn't start or end at the ballot box.

Fortunately, within Occupy the issue of electoral politics was not very contentious because almost everyone could agree that it was vital to keep social movements and voting separate. The (un)official OWS position on electoral politics was that individuals could do whatever they want, but as a group we would never endorse a candidate or try to persuade anyone about voting. This stance was important not only for its ability to keep the peace between anarchists and Democrats, but also for its ability to bring new people into direct action politics and gradually wean them off of our voting-centric political culture. Because even those organizers who thought that voting was important would agree that the real struggle is in the streets.

Direct Action

As opposed to the 'indirect action' of electoral politics, anarchists advocate 'direct action.' The pivotal difference between the two is that direct action is a manner of addressing political goals that eschews the involvement of politicians or the state. As Voltairine de Cleyre phrased it in her influential essay *Direct Action*, "every person who ever had a plan to do anything, and went and did it, or who laid his plan before others, and won their co-operation to do it with him, without going to external authorities to please do the thing for them, was a direct-actionist."[47]

If a community wants to transform an abandoned lot into a community garden, a strategy of indirect action would involve collecting petitions and trying to pressure a local elected official to make the garden happen. A strategy of direct action might have the people build the garden without permission and then organize a campaign of defense around the already established fact of the garden. Certainly the two strategies are far from mutually exclusive, and it often makes sense to go through the indirect process in order to justify the ultimate necessity of direct action for people who have retained faith in the political system. Moreover, the ability to hang onto the garden after building it would likely rely on its implicit or explicit acceptance by the local government. But direct action isn't about never having anything to do with politicians; it's about building actions and campaigns on an autonomous foundation and using our collective power to push around politicians rather than prostrating ourselves before them. Direct action dictates that political responses follow our collective action rather than the other way around.

Classic examples of direct action focus on workplace struggles where exploited workers strike, commit acts of sabotage, or occupy their factories to ameliorate their conditions rather than turn to the paternalistic benevolence of a 'third-party' political authority. For example, during its heyday, the IWW wouldn't even sign contracts with employers because they didn't want to codify wage exploitation and they didn't want anything standing in between them and their ability to engage in factory floor direct action at a moment's notice to fight the boss; not even a contract they may have signed in the past. Historically, the ideological affinity toward direct action on the part of anarchists and syndicalists distinguished them from social democrats and Marxist-Leninists who emphasized the centrality of the (indirect) political struggle for socialism. In that sense, the direct/indirect action distinction has reflected the debate over electoral politics on the immediate, tactical level.

Direct action plays such a crucial role in anarchist praxis because it's a mindset and method of struggle that simultaneously improves conditions around us while also inculcating a sense of individual and collective power at the expense of the legitimacy of existing authorities. As I discussed in Chapter 3, anarchists are often misrepresented as being solely concerned with the world of the future without recognizing the importance of improving the world around us right now. Through direct action, anarchists merge the two by coercing authorities into key concessions and, in so doing, demonstrating the latent power that we have when we act as an autonomous collectivity. As the Japanese anarchist Kubo Yuzuru wrote in 1928:

> I need not point out that raising wages and improving working conditions are not our goals per se. On the contrary, they are nothing more than a means or rationale, yet by such means we ought to rouse direct action and cultivate a bud of anarchism through daily struggle, which I believe will be the preparation for revolution…[48]

The more that we realize that our self-activity is capable of overriding the interests of bosses and government officials, the closer we get to envisioning a world without them. When successful, direct action provides a glimpse into the egalitarian society of the future since "insofar as one is capable, one proceeds as if the state does not exist",[49] it is the epitome of prefigurative politics since the means encompass the ends.

Probably the best and most concise definition of 'direct action' I've ever heard came from Jason Ahmadi (26) of Press, Facilitation, and DA who described it as "unmediated problem-solving." According to that definition, OWS really actually engaged in very little direct action since a march can rarely solve any problem directly. While I don't think that the exact definition of direct action is all that important, I think it became so diffuse within OWS that actions were often oriented to be ends in themselves without a larger picture of what we were working toward. I even had one organizer tell me that they "voted in the presidential election as a direct action, if that's possible." No, by definition it's not.

Given the strong association between direct action and anarchism, it was no surprise that the Direct Action (DA) WG was the anarchist center of gravity in OWS. To those unacquainted with the history and theoretical importance of direct action, the name of the working group sounded rather innocuous, but for those of us with some context it was obvious that the selection of the name "Direct Action" had heavy ideological undertones. Throughout the first year of OWS, DA remained one of the largest, if not the largest, WG with almost daily meetings, including a four hour Sunday meeting, every week. Jerry Goralnick (57) is an anarcho-pacifist who has been part of The Living Theater, an experimental anti-authoritarian theater group, for over 25 years. Whenever I came down to 60 Wall St. (the atrium of Deutsche Bank where most OWS meeting were held in the winter of 2011-12) for a DA meeting, I could always be sure to see Jerry. When I asked him about the special nature of DA he said,

> Direct Action, as a working group, is pretty highly functional and a lot of working groups are not. We feel, and we say to people, one of the reasons that we think that we do function well is because we are to a large extent anarchist. So we're people who are very interested in horizontal forms and are willing to work on them and are overjoyed in participating in them.[50]

By virtue of being the main action-planning group within an

action-oriented movement, DA accumulated quite a bit of power over the direction of OWS. As DA organizer CJ Holm (30) said,

> We're a clearinghouse for OWS actions and that's tons of power and we drive the movement … [we're in the position to decide] let's all do this particular action but not this other action because the people in this group ideologically don't jive with this action so we're not gonna do it so [as a result] nobody else is gonna do it.[51]

When Sara Zainab Bokhari first got involved with OWS she gravitated toward DA saying "I felt like those were the people who were at the center of the movement … and that if I wanted to have a part in what this ended up being I had to be in [the DA meetings]."[52] In a sense, I made a similar calculation when I started regularly attending DA meetings in late October while the media frenzy temporarily abated. In early October, there was often very limited communication between those organizing actions and those doing the press work. At times we would find out about the day's main action at the same time as the reporters since things were moving so quickly.

By the spring, I was the main Press liaison with DA and played an active role in organizing for May Day 2012. As I got more and more involved with the group, I saw how important DA had become in lending authenticity or legitimacy to an action in the context of the dissipation of Occupy following the eviction from Liberty. Since the spokescouncil and general assembly were unable to hold some sense of center for the movement, the endorsement of DA became an essential precondition for a successful action. After a while, there were so many protests and events listed on the New York City General Assembly site (nycga.org) that many people would limit themselves to DA-related actions since they tended to have more movement buy-in. Therefore, more and more of our meeting time was getting taken up by requests for endorsements for a litany of Occupy/quasi-Occupy actions (if that distinction made any sense anymore) to the point where the group decided to end the practice of endorsing anything since it became a situation where DA organizers became unofficial judges for the actions of others.

Although official endorsements ended after a while, the unofficial process filtering Occupy actions continued. For example, our Thursday evening meetings in 60 Wall St. were designed to allow a big chunk of open time for people to break into groups to discuss and plan for specific actions. Each meeting, about four or five upcoming actions or ongoing campaigns would be proposed and people attending the meeting would decide which breakout group they wanted to join based on their level of interest in the various actions.

In February 2012 a woman from the "Ad Hoc Committee Against the Suppression of the Occupy Movement" came to the meeting with a couple of friends and proposed a breakout group about their upcoming rally on February 28 in Union Square called "STOP the Suppression of the Occupy Movement." The issue was that none of these people had been active in OWS at all and some of them were members of the Revolutionary Communist Party (RCP) known for the classic authoritarian communist ploy of creating front organizations to lure in new members with broad slogans. When they proposed that there be a breakout group for their event, the facilitator, Ray (26), said that would be fine, but that honestly probably not a lot of people were going to participate in their breakout since there were a number of other actions being planned, such as the national day of action against the American Legislative Exchange Council (ALEC) on February 29. The woman from the "Ad Hoc Committee" insisted on having their own breakout group, and, predictably, it ended up consisting of her and her friends since not a single other person chose to participate in their discussion. To a great extent, Occupy actions were filtered through a predominantly anarchist(ic) group of organizers in a context where one's social capital and loose political orientation played an important role in pushing certain proposals forward while pulling others out of consideration.

The Affinity Group

Yet, although many actions were planned through the Direct Action WG, a number of the largest and most significant actions were planned in private by affinity groups before being presented to DA or the GA for a rubber stamp. Before getting into those internal politics, let me briefly discuss the history of the "affinity group." Over the past 15 years, the term has referred to a small group of about 5-15 activists who know each other well enough to collaborate on important projects and trust each other enough to potentially engage in risky or illegal actions knowing that they'll all have each other's back. This form of small group organization received a surge of popularity during the global justice movement of the turn of the 21st century. At large summits, such as meetings of the IMF/World Bank or the G8, different affinity group members were tasked to perform different functions such as being a medic, performing legal aid duties, and so forth. The origins of the affinity group are often ascribed to the *grupos de afinidad* of the Spanish *Federación Anarquista Ibérica* (FAI),[53] an anarchist political organization designed to keep the anarcho-syndicalist *Confederación Nacional del Trabajo* (CNT) on an anarchist path. Brief references to the birth of the affinity group often speak about the FAI using it during the Spanish Civil War, without realizing that the FAI was formed in 1927 during the dictatorship of Miguel Primo de Rivera when the CNT was illegal and forced underground. Therefore, a significant impetus behind the FAI's adoption of the *grupo de afinidad* was the desire to avoid getting arrested and potentially tortured, sent to a penal colony, or executed.

But the term "*grupo de afinidad*" actually predated the FAI, and was used by clandestine anarchist groups in the 19th century, probably ever since Spanish anarchists were first forced underground by the Restoration government of Antonio Cánovas del Castillo in 1874.[54] Moreover, the anarchists didn't invent the tightly knit clandestine political group. Rather, they inherited it from the world of mid-19th century bourgeois republican insurrectionary politics. For example, the Spanish Democratic Party was founded in 1849 and went underground in 1857. While underground, its basic unit of organization was a 10-person clandestine cell called the *choza*. The main difference with the *grupo de afinidad* was the hierarchy of the *choza*, since each Democratic Party group had a leader who was the only person in contact with the leaders of the other regional *chozas* who were organized into a central committee called the Phalanstery.[55] This organizational form was the norm for republican, and later anarchist, resistance to monarchism and was practiced by the Italian Carbonari, Masonic groups, and others from Spain to Russia.

As this historical context demonstrates, the term "affinity group" has undergone some significant mutations over the past century and a half. After Murray Bookchin and others revived the affinity group in the United States while researching the Spanish anarchists, it became a hallmark of the anti-nuclear and radical feminist movements before gaining its current notoriety from its use in the global justice movement. Prior to Occupy, I had always understood an affinity group to be a collection of people who had worked with each other for years and were pretty certain that they could trust each other not to be infiltrators or cops. And while that's still what it is for many people, in Occupy, affinity groups were formed after knowing each other for a few weeks in the park. Certainly the repercussions for accidentally letting in an infiltrator were usually not that serious, since OWS didn't engage in super-risky behavior, but it still represented a watering-down of the concept. For the one-year anniversary of OWS on September 17, 2012, the action plan was to shut down the Wall Street area through a series of coordinated affinity group actions organized in advance through a spokescouncil. At that spokescouncil on the night of the 16th there were hundreds of out-of-towners who had come into for the anniversary and many of them didn't have a group and wanted to plug in. The facilitators of the spokescouncil helped individuals find "affinity groups" to join, but it was clear that the term had lost all meaning and had become activist lingo for "group." In a similar vein, Aaron Black (39), one of the more active liberal OWS organizers who said that "horizontalism is bullshit," said he was part of a 300-person "affinity group" dedicated to some reformist objective like getting money out of politics.[56] The fact that the meaning of the "affinity group" went from a clandestine insurrectionary cell whose precision was a matter of life and death to a random group of protesters who had never previously met each other or a large reformist network says a lot about the stakes of our struggles over time.

Nevertheless, many of the most important OWS actions were planned by small groups of committed organizers using the label "affinity group" (and since they used the term I will use it to refer to them despite shifts in its meaning over time). One example of a major action organized by small group was the two-month anniversary of OWS on November 17, 2011 (N17), two days after the eviction of Liberty. Though it had been in the works for weeks prior to the eviction, symbolically it came to represent the resilience of the movement in the face of state repression. The day was organized into three main parts named breakfast, lunch, and dinner. For "breakfast," people gathered across the street from Liberty by "the red cube" on Broadway at around 7AM. I arrived at Wall St. at about 4:50 AM to do press work because there were rumors that some affinity groups might be planning early morning actions on Wall Street before the security perimeter was established (the rumors proved to be unfounded). It was eerie walking down Wall St. without anyone in sight apart from a few mounted cops preparing for the day's events. By 5:30, police had closed off the entire street to anyone who didn't have a work pass. The police set up a fenced-in press pen by the intersection of Wall and Broadway where a number of camera crews were already doing live broadcasts previewing the showdown that was expected in a matter of hours. After filling in the journalists on what to expect, I walked up Broadway to find that by about 7:30 there were easily 2,000 energetic people ready to march on a chilly Thursday morning in November. The police seemed to expect us to march down Broadway as a single group and try to push our way toward the Stock Exchange so they set up a defensive perimeter around Wall St. and the Stock Exchange to prevent us from coming in, but we did two things that really

A 'medical bloc' on the morning of Nov. 17, 2011 (N17). Note the anarchist circle-A on the left, the "capitalism kills" sign third from the left, and "ACAB" (meaning All Cops Are Bastards) written around the edges of the sign on the right. Photo by Minister Erik McGregor.

threw them off. First, we broke into 3 different marches that wound their way through the small side streets around Wall St. The police divided themselves up between the three, but there were so many people squeezed into such small streets that after a while the marches were indistinguishable and there were just people everywhere clogging up the works. Second, rather than trying to charge past the police to get near the Stock Exchange we held our ground at all of the intersections leading into Wall St. so that the bankers couldn't get through.

Organizers on walkie-talkies called for reinforcements at different intersections if their numbers started to thin out so that for about a half an hour, from maybe 9-9:30, we had every entrance into Wall St. blocked off with masses of unruly demonstrators. After walking around to the various intersections, I stopped at Wall and Broadway. There a group of about 8 Occupy people were linking arms in front of the TD Bank building preventing anyone from getting in or out and masses of people were making it very difficult for the police to check IDs to let people in. After a little while, the police closed off the Wall and Broadway entrance and started telling the angry bankers to go try other entrances into the Stock Exchange area. But the suits angrily responded that they had just tried going to different entrances and the police there had told them to come over here! Wearing my big winter jacket, I just got on line with the Wall St. workers as if I too was waiting my turn to show my ID and go into work just to make the line longer. Once it became apparent that a motley crew of hippies, punks, and tree-huggers was going to make them 30 minutes late to their morning meetings, the bankers started to verbally assault the police for not "doing their jobs."

For a brief window of time we had won. We spend countless hours trying to fight back against the capitalists who are destroying the planet and exploiting millions and for once we reached them, if ever so slightly. But the indignation on their faces at the notion that the 'plebs' had stepped out of line was politically one of the most gratifying things I've ever seen. After a while, the police responded with shoving and arrests. They even set up a checkpoint on Broadway between Wall and Zuccotti only allowing people with press credentials to walk down the street. I was scheduled to do a live interview on Broadway across from the barricades at Wall St. for BBC with Laura Trevelyan, but I couldn't get down the street. She tried to get me through by telling the police that I was her cameraman, but without a press badge they wouldn't let me though so I had to jog around the block behind Trinity Church to be able to make it in time for the live spot.

Not surprisingly, the mainstream media's take was basically 'OWS planned to storm stock exchange and failed' without taking into account the historic feat of stopping traffic into the symbolic hub of world capitalism for 30 minutes during the morning commute with nothing more than our bodies. "Lunch" involved "Occupy the Subways" which was a series of speak-outs by different subway stops around the 5 boroughs before people took the subway to the Brooklyn Bridge for the "dinner" march across the bridge with more than 30,000 people. Without the slightest shred of evidence the media interpreted "Occupy the Subways" to mean that we intended to shut down the entire subway system. As a result, some of the coverage turned a remarkable day of protest into sound bites from confused commuters about how they *really* needed to use the subway that day. At the same time as the subway speak-outs there was a large and raucous student march that took the streets after leaving from Union Square. Overall, I'd say it was the most amazing political day of my life given its combination of mass participation and confrontation.

Despite the massive turnout, however, the bulk of N17 was organized by a group of about 12 people according to N17 organizer Henry "Hambone" Harris (34), an anti-capitalist, anti-authoritarian with experience in Earth First! and the National Lawyers Guild. I attended a couple of the large N17 organizing meetings run by DA, but much of the nitty-gritty detail was worked out by a small group to limit the "wingnut factor." In retrospect, Hambone told me that "some of us really felt like we needed to limit participation or we just weren't going to get anything done, and we were just gonna get screamed at by crazy people which ultimately was really totally misanthropic and misguided on our part."[57]

A similar dynamic was in effect with the affinity groups that organized D6 and D17. On December 6, 2011, the Occupy Our Homes initiative had its first national day of action with more than 50 anti-foreclosure actions in over 20 cities. In New York, Occupy collaborated with a number of local groups, including Picture the Homeless, New York Communities for Change (NYCC), VOCAL-NY and more, to organize a march through East New York in Brooklyn, an area disproportionately affected by the housing crisis. The march passed by a number of foreclosed buildings that were ripe for occupation, before ending at an abandoned house that organizers had occupied to move in a homeless family (once repairs were completed). The march had a good turnout, great energy, and the local people waved to us as we passed and seemed to appreciate the nature of the action in an area that rarely sees high profile demonstrations. The media coverage had never been more positive, and it was exhilarating to be able to make the case in the mainstream media that expropriation was the most effective response to the economic crisis. To me it was a fabulous example of real direct action in practice. Rather than petitioning the government for relief that would never come, organizers could take the resources that were sitting there and put them to use for those who needed them.

There was one major problem, however: the house wasn't owned by the bank; its owner, Wise Ahadzi, had been in foreclosure proceedings with Bank of America but still owned the house. Before we knew it, the *New York Post* was running headlines like "'They took my place!' Single dad trying to take back home occupied by OWS" which made the absentee owner a victim being preyed upon by Occupy's greedy hoards.[58] Part of the confusion surrounding preparations for the action stemmed from the fact that on two separate occasions D6 organizers had already identified a foreclosed house for occupation and broken into it only to see a construction crew show up the next day because the house had been sold.[59] Therefore, since the date for D6 had been established well in advance, organizers were scrambling at the last minute to find a suitable house. Unfortunately one of the community groups "dropped the ball on some of their research" and they were left with a situation where they were considering a house that was in foreclosure but not bank owned yet. They decided that if the owner showed up they would try to work with him.[60] In this chaotic context some, such as Jonathan Smucker, were "arguing that we should pull the plug the night before," but the action proceeded nevertheless.[61] To make matters worse many of the Occupy people who stayed in the house for 'eviction defense,' and were not part of the original organizing group, treated the occupied house like their own space to the point where the man who was supposedly moving in didn't feel comfortable there any more.[62]

D17 was another example of a major OWS action planned in large part by an affinity group. The action was billed as a "re-occupation" to celebrate the three-month anniversary of OWS and bring the movement back into the public spotlight. The target was a lot next to Duarte Square owned by Trinity Church that had been empty for a long time. On the morning of November 15, 2011, immediately following the early morning eviction of Liberty, we converged on Duarte and some people attempted to occupy the lot only to be arrested shortly thereafter. Over the following weeks, however, D17 organizers gained the support of religious leaders from Occupy Faith, including Rev.

Michael Ellick of Judson Memorial Church, Catholic nun Sr. Susan Wilcox, Catholic priest Fr. Paul Mayer, and former Episcopal Bishop George Packard, the National Council of Elders (a group of former civil rights leaders), and they even won over some members of the local community board to the idea of pressuring Trinity to let us use the space while it was empty. Bishop Desmond Tutu came out in support of our request and a concert was being planned involving Lou Reed and possibly Patti Smith.

I remember standing (since there were far more people than chairs) in the DA meeting at 60 Wall St. where the D17 affinity group was making their pitch for DA endorsement of their action. They argued that the occupation of public space was vital to the continuation of OWS and emphasized that the pressure they were building against Trinity with the help of influential allies was close to paying off. Some DA organizers raised the concern that a campaign against a church would play poorly in the media and would turn off a lot of people. Although Trinity Church has been one of the largest real estate holders in Manhattan since Queen Anne gave the church 215 acres of land in 1705,[63] it turned out that we had a very difficult time communicating the message that regarding this piece of land Trinity was more of a real estate company than a church. I was concerned about that challenge from a press perspective, but more than anything I was worried that if Trinity didn't cave, we'd be expending a lot of energy, resources, and public attention on an action that would make us weaker rather than stronger. I went up to a few of the D17 organizers and asked them directly, "Honestly, do you think this is going to work?" And they all unflinchingly said "yes." In retrospect, I was very frustrated with their overconfidence.

So, when it came time to test for consensus on the D17 proposal at the meeting, I figured that these people must have their fingers on the pulse of this process and that if we could get thousands of people to come to that lot then maybe Trinity would cave if, supposedly, they were close already. Ultimately everyone at the meeting gave the proposal up-twinkles (the upward finger wiggles that indicate approval) except for Jordan who stood aside (meaning that he wasn't in favor of the proposal but wouldn't stand in its way) because of the concern that we were over-extending ourselves after having several big actions over the past month.

Although I still had my doubts about the wisdom/efficacy of the plan, I wanted to help make it as successful as possible. But soon it started to become evident that the momentum wasn't going to be as strong as expected. Bishop Desmond Tutu changed his mind about the action (giving the media even more fodder to demonize us), the concert was moved from Duarte itself to the WBAI studio (so people were encouraged to bring radios to the park to listen to it), and Trinity wasn't budging. Patrick Bruner, Karanja Wa Gaçuça, Senia and I met with members of the D17 affinity group to discuss the press strategy for the action and initially they were clear about framing the action as a re-occupation, but later they said that there might not even be an attempt to take the space. Sensing the increased likelihood that we wouldn't end the day in control of the vacant lot, our press release emphasized celebrating three months of Occupy and a festive atmosphere and buried the potential re-occupation at the bottom of the page, despite its prominence in D17 promotional materials, saying "While the event may include a reoccupation the event itself is a broader celebration and expansion of Occupy Wall Street..."

The morning of the 17th, D17 organizers and Press WG members met at a café on Canal St. to touch base. Some members of the Press WG were so aggravated about the negative press that this action was generating (because of its conflict with a church) that they weren't sure they even wanted to do press work that day. I wasn't thrilled either and I didn't think that our claim to the vacant space was strong enough to convince most people, but if we had already committed ourselves to picking a fight with a corporate church, I was ready to spend the day tarnishing their image in the media. But, as I mentioned in Chapter 3, we didn't get the massive turnout that our high-profile actions had been getting over the past month or so. While there were perhaps a couple thousand people there, a good turnout by normal activist standards, we had come to expect a lot more.

The hours passed as people milled around Duarte Square checking out the mobile People's Library, perusing the information tables, holding signs, and chatting while the police maintained a presence between the crowd in the square and the fenced in lot next to it. I was told that an attempt to take the lot was scheduled and that I would be notified like 15 minutes in advance. Given the police and the tall fence I really had no idea how anyone would get on the other side, but when I got the text in the late afternoon saying that it was about to happen, I noticed groups of organizers carrying long ladders covered by banners to disguise them. More and more people started to gather around them as they marched making it difficult to discern what they were carrying from a distance. They made the clever decision to march away from the square and then turn around a side street to come at the lot from the other side of the square. Once we got close the ladders were raised, as if we were storming a fortress, and the iconic moment when former Bishop George Packard raised his fist at the top of the ladder before jumping into the lot was etched into Occupy imagery. The crowd roared and some people lifted up the bottom of the fence for people to come in. But despite the energy and enthusiasm very few people out of the large crowd entered the lot effectively isolating those who had gone over or under the fence.

Over the coming days I wondered how D17 would impact the momentum of OWS. On the one hand, the conflict with the church was highly detrimental to Occupy's public image, but on the other, the photos of clergy going over the fence to illegally occupy the lot were some of the most spectacular American protest images in recent memory. Ultimately, I think that Occupy's mainstream profile was locked into an irreversible downward spiral after the evictions across the country and that OWS would have ended up following a very similar path of growth/decline (depending on your perspective) regardless. That is not to say that messaging is unimportant, but I think that the spectacle of protest has a short shelf life in the absence of real organizing that achieves tangible results.

Looking back, D17 organizer Andrew pointed out that most people in their affinity group were "first time organizers ... [who] took on something that was much larger than [they] were able to do." In his opinion, the action failed "because of inexperience and poor organizing" not because it was necessarily a bad idea to begin with.[64] Katie Davidson (32), a D17 organizer and documentary filmmaker, lamented their lack of legal preparation in light of the 45-day jail sentence that Mark Adams received for his D17 participation.[65] D17 organizer Will Gusakov (28) said that the goal of taking the lot was overly ambitious and "an almost impossible task," but added that, "the folks in that affinity group that felt so strongly that it was really necessary to keep momentum and visibility were probably right considering what's happened."[66] What happened was that, apart from a few brief moments here and there, OWS receded from public view and gradually disintegrated into a diffuse network rather than a coherent entity unto itself.

Many of the organizers that I spoke with mentioned a strong tension between the D6 and D17 groups, although some were involved in both like Will Gusakov. Will said that the general perception was that the D6 people were more experienced and more 'reformist' and focused on messaging and building institutional relationships with established groups while the D17 were more anti-institutional and radically action-oriented. Certainly that distinction is really overstated and I can attest to the fact that both groups placed a strong emphasis on messaging and action and had similarly radical politics. Yet the two actions do represent the two main strategic directions within Occupy: a focus on campaigns, organizing, and alliance building, and a focus on occupying public space and prioritizing the occupation as the main element of OWS. Though I tend to lean more in the organizing direction, in this context the two were actually dependent on each other. Without eventually getting some tangible organizing underway, a second occupation would have devolved into an ineffectual counter-cultural spectacle, and in the absence of an occupation it was very hard to organize under the Occupy umbrella because people understandably thought Occupy Wall Street was over, or at least on the decline.

But for the purposes of this discussion, I am much less concerned with the outcomes of those actions and their internal politics than I am with the fact that they were organized (and at times mismanaged) by small self-appointed groups. This dynamic left many upset about the lack of transparency. Josh Ehrenberg (21), an enthusiastic organizer with DA and Comfort, said,

> We gave a whole lot of power to people to request that we go into a space that we had really little idea of the legal ramifications of … We had like two weeks to decide whether we were gonna sign onto this or not and they did a fucking terrible job of getting people to sign on to it and a fucking terrible job of including people in the decision-making … We're hearing from the same voices over and over again.[67]

Certainly in the early months we lacked a well-designed infrastructure and procedure for designing actions and the media hype accelerated our sense of urgency to "expand or collapse."[68] I understand that pressure and it certainly made the Press WG, for example, much less proactive about bringing in more people to contribute than we might have been otherwise. If those groups of organizers hadn't taken the initiative to plan these actions, it's likely that OWS would have stagnated even earlier since we didn't have a well-formulated action-planning model. It's also true that in a case such as D6, where organizers are breaking into abandoned buildings, you need a certain degree of security culture to reduce the risk of infiltration. In a case like that, it makes sense to have a small (relatively) tightly knit group take care of that aspect of the preparation.

Therefore, I think the early tendency for affinity groups to plan some of the most important actions is understandable in a chaotic, time-sensitive context that lacked a clearly defined action-planning alternative. But it became highly problematic that as a movement we never really stopped to assess the efficacy of what we were doing and where we needed to go, especially considering the power of some affinity groups. Unfortunately, I think many within Occupy thought of the movement more as a series of events than a body working to map out a long-term strategy, so once an action was over it was over and people just moved onto the next big thing.

Ideally, however, we should work to build bridges between organizing groups and the rest of the movement. For example, the May Day subgroup of DA created several committees (based on the initial "kicking ass and taking names" organizing proposal from anarchists Zu Solanas and Ari Cowan) that could focus on their area of preparation while maintaining contact with the rest of the group. Although there were groups of people who were far more involved in the preparation than others, they were part of open groups with a clear mandate. This was easier to accomplish for May Day since we had months rather than weeks to prepare, but it was more organizationally transparent.

A similar issue emerged with the *Occupied Wall Street Journal* and the main website occupywallst.org (aka storg). Although both were widely perceived to be 'official' OWS outlets, they

Flier for OWS May Day mutual aid 2012.

were both run by autonomous affinity groups. This raised the serious question of who could speak for OWS. After a while, some members of the Internet WG called upon the storg organizers to hand over their website. Drew Hornbein was one of the Internet WG members who tried to take control of the autonomous website. Sitting on the lawn of Washington Square Park almost a year later, Drew told me how he would walk through Liberty and have people ask him why his WG posted this or that on the website and Drew would have no idea what they were talking about. His group was frustrated that the storg organizers were "empowered because somebody [Justine Tunney] bought a domain name the first day." But in retrospect

Drew said it was "absurd of us to have asked them to give up the website" so that it could be controlled by the Internet group affiliated with the GA. "Now it seems so quaint, so funny since there is no GA,"[69] yet storg continues to post updates about resistance around the globe.

These tensions point to Occupy's nebulous status as something in between an organization and a network (while the GA and Spokescouncil operated). To the degree that such a group has a legitimate and competent center of gravity, it makes sense democratically for action-planning groups, newspapers, and websites that play an important role in shaping the direction of the movement to be accountable to those that they act/speak for. As it turned out, however, we lacked the logistical capacity to be able to channel so many new, often inexperienced, people into large organizational bodies that could allow such relationships of accountability to develop that would improve Occupy's daily functionality rather than hinder it.

Defining Violence

The issue of autonomy in relation to the larger group was perhaps most vehemently contested when it came to the issue of (non)violence within the movement. Although the various incarnations of the violence/non-violence debate date back to the 19th century if not earlier, it had not taken up a lot of space within OWS until Chris Hedges wrote his article "The Cancer in Occupy" demonizing what he referred to as "the Black Bloc anarchists" in response to Occupy Oakland's use of militant street tactics.[70]

What is a black bloc? In short, it's a street tactic involving a group of people covering their faces (often with bandanas, balaclavas, motorcycle helmets, or gas masks) and concealing their identities by dressing in black (making it difficult to pick out an individual in the larger group) in order to be able to carry out a wide range of militant actions. Sometimes participants bring implements to defend themselves, such as shields or body armor, and sometimes, though much less frequently in the US, they bring slingshots, Molotov cocktails, and paint bombs. Although commentators routinely speak about the black bloc as if it were a discernible entity unto itself, it makes as much sense to speak of the black bloc as a specific group called "the black bloc" as it does to speak of "the petition-signers" or "the sign-holders."

Ironically, although the specter of the black bloc sparked such heated debates, black blocs were never formed in any New York OWS events (though there were a smattering of masked participants). During the OWS heyday in the fall of 2011, the issue didn't come up because we were so busy with immediate, pressing issues and there wasn't significant disagreement about the best tactics to use. As David Graeber explained in his reply to Hedges' "The Cancer in Occupy," the anarchists who started OWS "collectively decided that we would adopt a strategy of Gandhian non-violence and eschew acts of property damage. Many of us had taken part in Black Blocs. We just didn't feel that it was an appropriate tactic for the situation we were in."[71] As he told me, "we have to bear in mind that this is probably the most securitized, militarized 10,000 square feet on the face of the planet."[72] Luke Richardson said, "I was one of the probably two people who showed up on the first day in black bloc with goggles and a mask and I was looking around like 'Oh, where's the party?' I just assumed that that element would be there."[73] But it wasn't.

Throughout the fall we may have linked arms and marched against police lines or put our bodies on the line in acts of nonviolent direct action, but it never occurred to anyone to seriously consider organizing a bloc. The first time the issue came up at all was on October 15, 2011 during the international day of action when Italian demonstrators engaged in widespread property destruction described by the *New York Times* as "the worst rioting in Italy since the Group of 8 summit meeting in Genoa in 2001."[74] Since, for whatever reason, the Italian demonstrations were associated with Occupy internationally, we were asked for our take on the rioting. Given the fact that the sound bite format precludes the kind of nuanced, detailed explanation that would be necessary for sympathetic Occupy organizers to rationalize widespread property destruction, and the fanatical condemnation of any non-state 'violence,' members of the Press WG could never venture into the territory of arguing on behalf of what is widely perceived as 'violence.' If we, as the most outward facing messaging group in Occupy, had taken even a step down that road not only would it alienate a lot of potential supporters, it would thoroughly shift the media focus from our message of economic justice and direct democracy to questions of violence (even when we didn't fall into their trap this often happened anyway). I think it was the role of secondary forms of Occupy expression that were oriented toward those already interested in Occupy to tackle such complex issues.

But our WG also made it a policy not to throw 'violent' protesters under the bus and fall into the 'good protester/bad protester' dichotomy by condemning their actions. Patrick Bruner of the Press WG explained our strategy well when he said that:

> We've said that we endorse non-violent direct actions. A movement that endorses non-violent direct action is a movement where [if something violent] happens we say 'That's not us. We didn't do that. We didn't endorse that action. The action that we endorsed was walking down the street that day.'[75]

Therefore, rather than falling into the media trap of commenting on the actions of others, we tried to limit our responses to descriptions of our own actions and strategies. This certainly doesn't solve the problem, since such comments imply an unfavorable attitude toward 'violent' actions, but it was the best balancing act we could pull off given the American political climate.

The issue of 'violence' gained increased attention in response to the repression and resistance of Occupy Oakland (OO), which faced perhaps the harshest police repression brought down upon the Occupy movement. Although the initial eviction of Oscar Grant Park on October 25, 2011 gained the most attention because the police fractured Iraq War veteran Scott Olsen's skull with a tear gas canister and then threw a flash bang grenade at the medics attending to him,[76] Oakland routinely faced attacks with rubber bullets, beanbag rounds, and tear gas. OO's struggles

Occupy Oakland, Oct. 29, 2011. Photo by Quinn Norton.

against the police flared up on January 28, 2012 when police responded to the attempted occupation of the vacant Kaiser Convention Center, which was to be turned into a community center, with rubber bullets and over 400 arrests. Defending themselves with shields and makeshift barricades, some demonstrators understandably responded to police attacks by throwing rocks, bottles, chairs, and other projectiles. As a gesture of solidarity, Occupies across the country organized a "Solidarity Sunday" the next day.[77] Although our WG didn't put out a press release specifically responding to the events of January 28th, whenever asked we were entirely clear about our solidarity with Oakland and our condemnation of police repression.

Yet, it wasn't until Chris Hedges wrote his article "The Cancer in Occupy" on February 6th that the debate over 'violence' started in earnest. As David Graeber, Don Gato, Peter Gelderloos and others demonstrated in their responses,[78] Hedges' article was littered with factual inaccuracies. Regardless of one's perspective on the black bloc, property destruction or anything else, it was disheartening to see someone as intelligent as Hedges write something so important in such a hasty, careless manner. Some of his most glaring errors included: his description of the black bloc as a "movement" rather than a tactic used by anarchists and non-anarchists alike;[79] his claim that black bloc participants "do not believe in organization" although many participate in political organizations and unions; and his claim that they hate the Zapatistas and love primitivist author John Zerzan and the Unabomber, when in fact most people I've known who have participated in black blocs cite the Zapatistas as one of their main influences and are not primitivists. Perhaps most ridiculous was that Hedges thought it reasonable to describe the black bloc as "criminal," a "cancer" in the movement, and something that "turns human beings into beasts" while also arguing that

> The Black Bloc movement bears the rigidity and dogmatism of all absolutist sects. Its adherents alone possess the truth. They alone understand. They alone arrogate the right, because they are enlightened and we are not, to dismiss and ignore competing points of view as infantile and irrelevant.

They hear only their own voices.[80]

Talk about the pot calling the kettle black (bloc). Subsequently, a number of writers addressed the myriad of flaws in Hedges' argument and emphasized the role that violent arguments against the black bloc can play in inciting violence against anarchists and those who engage in militant tactics. In describing the black bloc as a "cancer," Hedges tapped into a long tradition of dehumanizing rhetoric that has been used to exclude a wide variety of groups from society over the generations. Hedges should have known that fascists have been known for using medical imagery and describing Jews and other undesirables as a "cancer" when discussing their task of revitalizing society.[81] After all, you can't reason or negotiate with cancer. The only option is to physically cut it out of the (social) body. It's especially ironic considering the fact that just two years earlier Hedges wrote an article called "The Greeks Get It" praising the riotous Greek response to austerity. I guess he didn't realize that many of the Greek rioters who "get it" use black bloc tactics.[82] Moreover, as Graeber pointed out, portrayals of militancy as a cancer in the movement have emboldened many avowedly 'pacifist' demonstrators to physically attack those engaging in militant protest tactics or turn them over to the violence of the police. Occupy Oakland organizers Emily Brissette and Mike King witnessed this phenomenon in action and characterized it as, "internal pacification on a power-trip, the morphing of self-avowed 'peaceful protesters' into agents of order, a peoples' militia for the police State."[83]

Needless to say, Hedges' article caused quite a stir in New York as some called for a movement-wide "peace pledge" while others held onto the principle of "diversity of tactics" agreed upon by DA in the early days of the occupation. As Dave Haack (27), a Wobbly and Occupy your Workplace organizer, said, Hedges "took a narrative that wasn't part of the Occupy movement and put it in there."[84] I don't think it was a coincidence that this debate only gripped the movement once it hit a lull over the winter. In the absence of the unifying influence of the occupation and regular doses of immediate action, the uncertainty shrouding the future of occupy was projected onto the 'violence' debate.

Given the divisive nature of the conflict, DA organized an "Open Forum on the Concepts of Solidarity, Tactics & Action Agreements" from 6-10pm on Friday, February 10, 2012. I think a lot of people came to witness the 'shitshow' they expected to unfold, but surprisingly everyone got along and we had some really fantastic discussions (in part thanks to the amazing facilitation of Jason Ahmadi). Although it was a Friday night, several hundred people packed the alternative arts space of 16 Beaver, many of them walking away with a better understanding of the issue.

But that discussion (and a follow-up discussion the following week) couldn't patch up the divisions that had emerged. Christine Crowther (24), a democratic socialist from North Carolina with the Accounting WG, said that the violence "debate was utterly destructive to the movement ... generally speaking I think that having the conversation drew attention away from the fact that by and large overall it was a peaceful protest and made it as if there were two sides of the issue ... [when it] wasn't a big force in the first place."[85] Others described the overall debate as "sophomoric and destructive"[86] and a "derailment ... [that caused us to] let time piss away and lose our chance to discuss the real issues."[87] For a lot of people, however, the relevance of the debate related to the issue of extending solidarity to Occupy Oakland. It was important that we prevented those that wanted to impose their anti-confrontational attitude on the entire movement from standing in the way of OWS supporting OO.

Regardless of whether it was an issue worth addressing or avoiding, and despite the fact that the only notable property destruction that occurred during the first year of OWS was when a cop smashed a medic's head through a window, the issue caused so much commotion that it's important to address. Moreover, the 'violence' question seems to pop up anew with every generation of activists so hopefully these reflections will be useful for some.

Through my interviews, I managed to get a much better sense of what OWS organizers thought about violence. For many interviewees, something is violent when it causes, or intends to cause, harm to a living being. The importance of distinguishing between living beings and property in radical definitions of violence grew following the Seattle WTO protest in 1999 and the controversy surrounding black bloc property destruction. After the demonstration, the ACME Collective issued a communiqué on behalf of some of participants in the Seattle black bloc arguing that, "property destruction is not a violent activity unless it destroys lives or causes pain in the process."[88] Subsequently it has been very common for defenders of property destruction to argue that such tactics fit within a non-violent framework. This tendency was evident in the fact that approximately 59% of interviewees said that property destruction is not violence while only 17% said it is. Others pointed out that we cannot speak of 'property destruction' as having a one-dimensional relationship to definitions of violence. For example, some considered breaking the lock of an abandoned house with the intention of converting it into a social center to be clearly nonviolent, while smashing a window could be violent if it frightened spectators. Overall, 24% said that one could only determine whether property destruction is violent based on the context.

However, most interviewees spent a few moments emphasizing the overwhelmingly violent nature of capitalism and the state before they would even start to address questions of 'violence' in social movements. Shane Gill (32) of the Press WG emphasized that we live in a thoroughly violent society where even "paying my taxes is a violent act."[89] While journalists expend all of their energy decrying a broken window, supposedly the epitome of violence, they ignore, and are therefore complicit in, the constant structural violence of capitalism and the state. This shouldn't be surprising since, as Max Weber famously phrased it, the state is an entity that possesses a "monopoly on the legitimate use of violence." The state maintains its power by disseminating the perspective that non-state violence is illegitimate. In contrast, state violence is legitimate, and by virtue of its legitimacy it gradually recedes from considerations of violence. Reporters won't describe the police as 'violent' even when they shoot someone,[90] but when protesters step out of line in the slightest they are called violent. When ABC World News reported on the Brooklyn Bridge march the anchor said "The demonstrations have been mostly peaceful until yesterday when 700 were arrested..."[91] Similarly, Oakland Mayor Quan called Occupy's port blockade "economic violence."[92] The march and the port blockade deviated from mainstream standards of "peaceful" protest although they were non-violent. Why? Because they disrupted the status quo. To be "peaceful" is to be complacent.

Apart from addressing the statist and capitalist hypocrisy of the media, other organizers emphasized the importance of situating our definitions of violence within specific relationships of domination. As Betsy Catlin (22), a DA organizer from Maine, explained, the violence of the state and the violence that stems from resistance are "different violences" because one must "consider the actor's relation to power within the system."[93] From Betsy's standpoint it's a mistake to speak about violence as a homogenous entity independent from power. Patrick Bruner took a different angle when he argued that "self-defense is not violence." He explained that, "when the oppressed are resisting against the oppressors, like we are, there can be no initiation of violence. It's necessarily an initiation of self-defense because of the act of oppression ... any act of resistance is not violence."[94]

More than any other interpretation, Patrick's definition of violence as an act committed by an oppressor highlights the subjective nature of the concept of violence. As Sam Corbin pointed out, "one of the problems that we've had in this conversation is this linking of 'violence' to judgment calls about what's good or bad; so violence is 'bad' and non-violence is 'good.'"[95] I agree that the debate was muddled by the unaddressed tendency to turn 'violence' into an ethical valuation. Most Occupy people would simply determine the ethical status of various acts and then orient their definitions of violence around their pre-established moral outlooks. This simply collapses the two categories and obscures the subjectivity of ethical perspectives behind the supposed objectivity of the concept of violence. Sparrow Ingersoll took a different approach when they said "I think that property destruction is violence; I just don't care."[96] Rather than trying to argue that property destruction is non-violent in order to justify it, Sparrow and some others embraced ethically justifiable violence.

A 2002 pamphlet called "Against the Corpse Machine" argued against the anarchist tactic of justifying property destruction by denying its violent status:

> Instead of claiming that smashing a window isn't violent—a point that average people reject out of common sense (and therefore makes me wonder about the common sense of some anarchists)—why don't we drop the semantics and admit that, yes, it's very clearly violent and then make a case for it?[97]

The pamphlet goes on to point out that the effort made to categorize property destruction as non-violent implies a rejection of violence which most black bloc participants would disagree with. Anthony echoed this argument when he said that:

> A lot of people like to argue that it's [property destruction's] not violent and therefore it's OK and I actually suggest that that's supporting the argument that violence is inherently bad ... property destruction is *totally* violent. It's different than violence inflicted on a living being, but it's violence. But it's really important to also note that for me that doesn't make it bad or wrong.[98]

Likewise, Axle argued that we should "burn down the banks, burn them all fucking down. Is that violent? *Sure it's violent!* Is it justified? *Sure it's justified!*"[99] It's clear by now that attempts to convince public opinion that property destruction is nonviolent rarely succeed. If you think smashing a window is a worthwhile political act to undertake, then you should be cognizant that, like it or not, it will be considered violence by the vast majority of society. That's why I'm not especially interested in debating definitions of violence. Even if it's possible to define violence, how society views it is a much more important factor in deciding which actions are ethically and tactically worthwhile.

Predictably, OWS perspectives on the tactical usefulness of property destruction ran the gamut. Some, like Goldi, emphasized the direct economic impact of property destruction:

> Huge corporations don't like to lose stuff of value. They don't mind you writing letters to your congressman that are gonna get thrown in the trash. They don't mind you picketing in your little free speech zone in cages outside their offices. They do mind losing money and if you do something that makes them lose money that deeply, deeply affects them.[100]

Similarly, Ingrid Burrington (25) of the Think Tank and May Day Planning said that property destruction can be useful to

> speak to institutions of power that don't really care about

> your little puppet that's outside their building but they care about a broken window and they care about what it says to other people when they see that someone hates this institution enough to break its window.[101]

Others had a different take. Will Gusakov said it was "laughable" to think that smashing a window hurts a corporation.[102] Michael Levitin said, "it's a no brainer. Unless you want to simply get fired upon by the police and turn the public against you ... you don't engage in acts of frustration and anger at authority by lashing out in vandalistic or violent ways."[103] Mariano Muñoz-Elias (32), a Peruvian organizer involved in the Spanish Assembly, emphasized that if you intend to commit acts of property destruction, you

> have to do your homework ... some of the people who will be affected by it are working class people if their workplace is going to be closed for a week...they could become homeless. Property destruction is great if it's really targeted and only hits the 1%.[104]

From Ari Cowan's standpoint, property destruction could potentially make banks think twice about especially heinous actions:

> I think that even though in some ways breaking the window of a bank may not be tactically effective in causing any real damage to that bank, it can send a very clear message and in that way affect the actual ways that these banks function and change their understanding of what they are able to do without folks rising up and fighting back.[105]

Fanshen (44), a communist and longtime organizer involved with Facilitation, entirely disputed the notion that property destruction could be inspirational for anyone saying,

> I haven't heard of anyone who's ever gotten inspired [by property destruction]. I haven't heard a bunch of people saying 'I saw you trash that Chase bank and I just knew I had to get involved.' I've never heard of that. I've never heard anyone say this. It doesn't inspire anyone.[106]

Clearly, Fanshen was orienting his comments around the American context and I agree that such acts do not inspire most people in this country at this time. The political culture of southern Europe or Latin America, for example, is very different given their more confrontational political culture and graver economic recession, but walking around Madrid or Bogotá, for example, and seeing anti-capitalist graffiti all over the ATMs and banks creates a powerful atmosphere of resistance.

In the spring of 2013, Madrid neighborhood assemblies, housing rights groups, and the local branch of the anti-foreclosure PAH movement (*Plataforma de Afectados por la Hipoteca* or literally Movement of those Affected by Mortgages) started organizing protests at the homes of pro-austerity politicians called *escraches* (a term borrowed from Argentina). During their marches, they passed out green and red stickers that marchers stuck on telephone polls, street signs, and bank windows. I was amazed to see hundreds of demonstrators of all ages plastering the windows of major banks with anti-foreclosure stickers as the police stood back and watched. This was an example of what most Americans would consider to be property destruction that had so much popular support that the authorities seemed to decide that it wasn't worth the headache to stop it.

If the American economy crashes again such acts may gain more sympathy over time. It's a matter of gauging the political climate.

Diversity of Tactics

From the start of the debate, it was clear that we would never reach consensus on ethical and tactical questions surrounding violence and property destruction. The question was what we should do about our divergent opinions. There were really only two options: draft some sort of 'peace pledge' and exclude those who would not adhere to it, or embrace a "diversity of tactics" approach which would allow space for a variety of tactical outlooks to coexist under the Occupy umbrella (though potentially alienate those who abhorred anything that might blur the line of non-violence).

Some organizers, like Cecily McMillan, argued for the importance of a "firm statement of non-violence." Cecily grew up in southeast Texas and spent her summers in Atlanta around John Lewis and Coretta Scott King. She said, "If you don't safeguard your organization or your ideals by saying that you're committed to non-violence, then anything that anybody in your group does is on you."[107] Although there were organizers who agreed with Cecily mixed throughout OWS, they never held enough sway to even take practical steps to formulate and present such a proposal. Certainly documents like the "Statement of Autonomy" passed by the GA in November, 2011 had lines like "we welcome all, who, in good faith, petition for a redress of grievances through nonviolence,"[108] such statements coexisted with DA's commitment to a diversity of tactics (and for those who considered property destruction to be non-violent this wasn't a contradiction at all). As a result of the plurality of voices speaking for OWS and Occupy's increasing decentralization heading into the spring, the movement had the benefits and drawbacks of speaking out of both sides of its mouth at the same time. This made press work much easier because it allowed us to hide behind the language of non-violence when necessary without condemning militant tactics.

In the absence of an enforceable statement of non-violence, diversity of tactics filled in as a way to promote solidarity despite tactical differences. The concept of diversity of tactics developed out of the controversy surrounding the black bloc in Seattle in 1999. As much as many insist that diversity of tactics is not about violence, it was born out of the violence debate. In the wake of the WTO protest, the loose-knit alliance between NGOs, labor unions, environmental groups, anarchists and others was threatened by the potential inability to coexist at large summit protests. In response to this seeming impasse, the notion of diversity of tactics, when respected, allowed for coexistence without public recriminations. The earliest use of the term that I could find was from a statement from the Revolutionary Anti-Capitalist Bloc in anticipation of the April 16, 2000 (A16) protest against the IMF/World Bank in Washington, D.C. saying that they were "open to a diversity of tactics as a means of legitimate defense."[109] However, in April 2000, the French Canadian group CLAC (*Convergence des luttes anti-capitalistes*) was formed in Montreal to organize against Summit of the Americas in Quebec City in April 2001. Influenced by recent conflicts over property destruction within the direct action group known as Salami,[110] these Montreal anti-capitalists played an important role in promoting the diversity of tactics framework across the continent.

Diversity of tactics, a term that many were unfamiliar with only months earlier, made an important contribution to the project of coexistence within Occupy but it also caused problems. Some lamented the degree to which a potentially rich and open conversation about diverse tactics had been reduced to a discussion of property destruction. Dana Balicki (31), a longtime organizer with Code Pink involved in the Press WG, said that she was "interested in the idea of diversity of tactics being a broader conversation as opposed to 'we're gonna go out into the streets. Will we or won't we turn over trash cans?'"[111] Atiq

Zabinski remarked that "I do believe in diversity of tactics and as far as OWS employing them, like Gandhi said about Western Civilization: I think it would be a good idea!"[112] Alexandre Carvalho (29), a Brazilian anarchist doctor who participated in disaster relief efforts in Haiti, deplored our "nauseating poverty of ideas regarding tactics." As one of the organizers of the Arts and Culture WG, Alexandre wanted diversity of tactics to be about as much artistic expression and creative disruptions in daily life as anything else.[113]

But insofar as diversity of tactics related to property destruction, many were concerned about the use of the phrase to justify anything at all. As Matt Presto (25), one of the founding members of the OWS tactical team over the summer of 2011, pointed out, "some people tend to use the term 'diversity of tactics' in a very disingenuous way as a euphemism for 'let's smash some windows.'"[114] Sara Zainab Bokhari told me that in her experience "'diversity of tactics' was a phrase used more to shut people down than it was to truly build people up."[115] As Moira Meltzer-Cohen (35), an organizer with the Legal WG, pointed out, arguments for diversity of tactics became "a method of distinction among the occupiers. Its discursive ... it's a way of setting yourself apart as more 'hardcore.'"[116]

In some conversations, advocates of a diversity of tactics framework wore it as a badge of honor signifying their revolutionary identity. Rather than argue for it from the standpoint of practicality, the concept was sometimes used to justify any independent initiative and summarily dismiss those who disagreed. At times, the anarchist idea of autonomy became a cop-out excuse for avoiding the painful and grueling work of getting a diverse group of people on the same page to act collectively. On a number of occasions, I attended planning meetings for major actions where some anti-authoritarians proposed that we just leave it up to affinity groups and autonomous projects to make things happen on the day of action rather than organize something collectively and allow smaller groups to supplement the day with their independent initiatives.[117] At its worst, the defense of diversity of tactics occasionally took on a *liberal libertarian* character when people would make arguments like "I think it's a good idea for anyone to do whatever it is that they think is a good idea to do." As I explained in Chapter 2, for some it was more important to allow free tactical expression than to compromise for the larger whole. At a larger scale this meant that after a while we dispersed a massive amount of energy and resources into small disconnected actions when we could have been more selective and decided on a couple of big actions that would have generated more popular momentum. As Pamela Hains wrote in 1977 in *Dandelion,* the periodical of Movement for a New Society, "An unspoken 'do-your-own-thingism' has meant that hardheaded decisions about the most effective use of energy have not been made."[118] If we are going to make any progress, we need to be able to critique each other in a compassionate manner within movement circles and get beyond this idea of *tactics as freedom of speech* where any attempt to confine the range of tactical options is interpreted as a denial of one's personal right to express themselves as they please. As Cindy Milstein points out, "when a diversity of tactics notion lacks the anarchist ethic of voluntary association and accountability, and sets some people's desires above the good of others, it should be contested."[119]

Unfortunately, this outlook gave some people a misleading impression of anarchism as the following quote from Jen Waller demonstrates:

> When working within a social movement no one is an island. No one is actually autonomous from the rest of the movement. That's just a fantasy and actually a fallacy of anarchism, or at least people's interpretations of anarchism, because the state sees us all as the same. They see us all as

> subversive and they don't care if I disagree with your tactics. They'll lump us all together as much as they can so they can charge as many of us as possible ... so if you break a window and I'm standing there then I can be charged with the same thing as you.[120]

Jen's comments point to the importance of making sure that militant tactics do not endanger people who did not consent to putting themselves at risk. Over the past several years agreements such as the St. Paul Principles, adopted by organizers for the 2008 RNC protest, and the Pittsburgh Principles, adopted for the G20 Summit Protest in 2009, specified that their diversity of tactics framework would require that "the actions and tactics used will be organized to maintain a separation of time or space."[121] This means that "red actions," to use the parlance of the Global Justice movement, would not be held in the same place or at the same time as "green actions." OWS incorporated elements of this strategy by drafting "action agreements" for several of our major actions. On the leaflet handed out at our weekly "Spring Training Marches" every Friday leading up to May Day 2012 it said "do not instigate physical conflict w/ cops or pedestrians" (which leaves room for self-defense) and "respect diversity of tactics, but be aware of how your actions affect the group." There's never any guarantee that action agreements will be followed, but they set a standard of conduct that most people will respect and they give organizers something to refer to if the media tries to portray them as violent terrorists.

But it's crucial to emphasize that diversity of tactics is a coalition tactic. It's a way for different groups with different agendas to coexist. Within a specific, more closely knit organization or group, it usually makes more sense to come to an agreement about tactics. It's mainly when those distinct groups occupy the same space or struggle that the principle of diversity of tactics becomes most relevant.

Ultimately, the entire conversation comes down to a single question: if some people break a window or engage in militant tactics at a 'nonviolent' event (without harming others) will the organizers publicly condemn them and help the police apprehend them or not? I would hope that most readers would realize that such a condemnation would do more harm than good and give the authorities an opening to divide us and escalate repression. As Amin Husain said "[movement tactics] can't be policed and if you put your energy there you're already distracted."[122]

Reflections on the Black Bloc

Although diversity of tactics allows us to coexist, we mustn't limit ourselves to a tacit acceptance of inept or counterproductive tactics in the absence of larger strategic perspectives. Just because some anarchists form black blocs doesn't mean that it's always, or ever, the most useful thing to do. If we are going to make strides toward building a new world, we need to challenge each other on the efficacy of our tactics and learn from our successes and failures. With that in mind, I'm going to share five short reflections on my experience with black blocs before delving into the history of the tactic to address when it might be useful and when not.

December 1, 1999

My alarm goes off at 6:41 and I roll over in bed savoring another moment of rest before heading off to another day of high school. After a few seconds, I take a step toward the alarm clock sitting on my dresser but I can't believe what I hear on the news update: "Protesters riot and smash windows at World Trade Organization meeting in Seattle!"[123] I had no idea what the World Trade Organization was, or why anyone would hate it enough to smash a bunch of windows, but I knew I had to find out.

September 29, 2001

My fellow organizers at Wesleyan University and I had been planning to go down to Washington, DC for weeks to protest the annual IMF/World Bank meetings when September 11th happened. Instantly, many within our organizing group decided that it was time to mourn rather than protest capitalist globalization. Although it seemed clear to me that the IMF and World Bank were as destructive on September 11th as they had been on the 10th, very few wanted to make the trip down to DC even when the meetings were cancelled and the protest was turned into a pre-emptive anti-war mobilization.

Since some of my friends in the group I travelled to DC with were anarchists, like Abe Walker and Matt Desan, our whole group ended up marching together in the Black Bloc of the Anti-Capitalist Convergence (ACC). However, at the time, I didn't identify as an anarchist or anything else specifically. After the demonstration, I wrote a short piece about the day's events in which I said:

> Although I am certainly no anarchist, I did identify most with the black bloc since they came closest to achieving my political and cultural views. Many of them were crusty punks with patches of familiar bands. I knew many people like them and identified with their frustration.

Though I lacked the perspective to realize it at the time, later I would reflect upon the fact that the very same political/cultural elements of the black bloc that appealed to me alienated many people from different racial and cultural backgrounds.

For what seemed like a couple of hours, riot police encircled our march in front of the World Bank building. For some reason, someone had the foresight to bring along a soccer ball so we set down a few bags and shirts to make goals and we played 'anarchist soccer' without any defined teams or rules.[124] Reading back over my account of playing anarchist soccer on a warm late September afternoon surrounded by riot police at my first large demonstration, I am struck by how similar my tone jubilant tone was to that of young people in Liberty Square in the fall of 2011.

February 15, 2003

As the threat of an American invasion of Iraq grew more imminent (it would start about a month later), February 15th marked the largest day of global protest in world history. In New York, a massive demonstration was planned but organizers couldn't get a permit to march. I showed up dressed in black with a bandana and goggles (in case of pepper spray) in my pocket and looked for other black-clad organizers to join. But I couldn't find them. Thousands of people stretched in every direction and I had no choice but to stay where I was and see how things unfolded. Then something remarkable happened: as police packed more and more people into their protest pens preventing them from marching, the frustration boiled over. Wanting to march, people started to shout at the police and push the barricades. Before I knew it, a diverse crowd of 'everyday' people was pulling over barricades in a tug of war with police and surging past them to take the streets. I did what I could to join the effort and pull over a few here and there, but the crowd's militancy was so contagious that after a while the police gave up.

That evening I wondered whether maybe *sometimes* dressing in black and distinguishing ourselves from the crowd might actually limit the potential spread of militancy in a protest. On that wintry day in February there were no barriers to entry or criteria for participation in confronting the cops. Everyone did it because anyone could do it.

May 21, 2012

Bright lights pour down on me as I stare into a black lens. In my right ear, I hear CNN Newsroom anchor Carol Costello speaking about a group of people in Chicago who were arrested for supposedly planning to firebomb a local Democratic Party office. Although I was told that I was coming into the studio to discuss the ongoing protest against NATO in Chicago, it was clear that I was being taken down the path of sensationalism.

After laying out the details of the case, Costello said that "police are calling them *aaanarchists…*" and asked me if they were part of Occupy (as if I could just refer to some membership roster to check). I responded that I had no idea whether they were part of any group and pointed out that authorities were known for practicing entrapment by providing impressionable young people with weapons and encouraging them to commit crimes (as it turns out, it was another case of entrapment).[125] Then things got pretty surreal for me. Costello said:

Well, Mark, there is a group that play a role in these type of protests. They are called 'Black Bloc.' They're a group of anarchists who taunt police into violence. You see them in the crowds. They have their faces covered with black bandanas so people can't identify them. Is Black Bloc part of the "Occupy" movement?

After having participated in about 10-12 black blocs in New York, DC, Boston, and Ottawa from 2001-2004, it was bizarre to be asked what I thought about them on CNN from someone who clearly assumed that I, dressed in a blue button shirt and khakis, was neither an anarchist nor someone who had been in black blocs. I briefly considered just letting the cat out of the bag, but I knew that doing so would make the entire interview about the black bloc and violence without even mentioning NATO. Therefore, after Costello said that the black bloc had chanted, "kill the police," I said:

Well, you know, certainly the occupy movement is not about killing people. It's NATO that's killing people. We aren't the ones with unmanned predator drones dropping bombs on civilian populations in Afghanistan and Pakistan. So, I think it's important that we realize that there's a reason the media is focusing upon a few scuffles with the police instead of larger systems of economic violence and injustice, because this system is indeed organized crime and we're all the victims, on a global level.[126]

November 17, 2012

Every year the Greek left marches to honor the anniversary of the brutal repression of the 1973 Athens Polytechnic Uprising against the ruling military junta. All of the left groups and parties unfurl their massive banners and march with their flags in the air to stand against a possible return to military rule. Unfortunately, that possibility has loomed large recently given the recent success of the fascist political party Golden Dawn. While visiting my good friends Chris Spannos and Harpreet K. Paul, I got to know a number of organizers with one of the largest Greek anarchist groups, the Alpha Kappa anti-authoritarian movement. On the morning of the 17th, people slowly congregated and set up their banners. Alpha Kappa brought a pile of relatively small black and red and black and green flags attached to long bamboo and wooden sticks, which always have the potential to be more than flagpoles. Some of the Alpha Kappa organizers, especially one guy with a trial coming up, had dressed up more 'conservatively' than usual to avoid being targeted by the police.

When the march started, only a few hours late, we joined the anarchist/anti-authoritarian bloc, which had at least 1,000 people (and a few of the anarchist groups, such as ΕΣΕ the anarcho-syndicalist union, marched with the labor contingent). But it wasn't a black bloc since most people weren't masked and many weren't wearing black. Although people had gas masks in their bags or bandanas in their pockets, they were a precaution in case the police attacked. There was some concern that the police would provoke the march when we entered Syntagma Square, but confrontation didn't materialize and the march ended without incident.

Afterward, I started to walk back to the Alpha Kappa social center *Nosotros*[127] located on the edge of Exarcheia Square in the center of the main anarchist neighborhood of Athens. On the way, I had to pass through several detachments of riot police monitoring the side streets that led into Exarcheia. As I approached the square from the north, I quickly realized that the square was under siege. Masked youth were erecting flaming barricades at the intersections leading into the square as the police held their ground about a block down each street.

One of the remarkable things about Exarcheia Square is that police do not patrol there. My friend Chris had been living there for months and had never seen police walk through that neighborhood. It's just understood that if the police come in they will be attacked. In a context where the links between the police and the Golden Dawn fascists have been thoroughly documented (more than half of cops voted Golden Dawn in the May 2012 election),[128] it's especially important that there is a safe area for immigrants and leftists (you see plenty of both in Exarcheia).

The police were intentionally infringing upon the relative autonomy of the square and the predictable backlash was unfolding. I watched as masked youth prepared molotovs in side alleyways and pulled out little hammers and picks to hack off chunks of concrete from the sidewalks and pull up bricks and cobble stones that they stacked in preparation for the advancing police. Scouts positioned themselves on side streets to relay calls for reinforcements when it looked like the police were going to advance. As the scent of pepper spray wafted through the air, it was really unbelievable to see the entire square itself come to life as an organic geography of resistance. Despite the intensity of the situation, there was a surprising serenity in the energy of the participants because these clashes had become so common that they were almost routine. A number of Greek anarchists I met

I noticed this series of images in Athens in November 2012. They depict the everyday nature of resistance in the age of austerity.

spoke about their frustration with the ritualization of protest, whether general strikes or street fighting, without a sense of moving forward in a tangible revolutionary direction.

I walked back and forth between the barricades observing the cat and mouse game with the police. After a while, there were calls for people to move to the barricade near the anarchist café BOΞ (pronounced 'Vox').[129] I followed a large group over to the intersection and, being that I didn't have a gas mask, a gust of pepper spray smacked me in the face making it nearly impossible to open my eyes. After a few moments, I stumbled back to

Nosotros and someone smeared malox in my eyes to reduce the burning. Shortly after I had been pepper sprayed, the police had broken through the barricades and were flooding the square. While I was having my eyes treated, a number of people fled into *Nosotros* since it was one of the only places with its doors open. But someone had made the mistake of bringing a Molotov into the social center in front of the police. A moment after the Alpha Kappa organizers locked the door, the police started to gather in force outside the building. In the past the cops had fired tear gas canisters onto the roof of the building but they had never tried to enter. At that moment it seemed like a very real possibility. For Greek anarchists the threat of arrest is much more serious than it is for American protesters. For example, on September 30, 2012, 15 participants in one of the regular anti-fascist motorcycle patrols were arrested and tortured by police. They were beaten, burnt with cigarettes and lighters, tasered, sexually humiliated, denied water or a lawyer, and kept awake all night with lights and lasers. Moreover, the police threatened to give their addresses and information to Golden Dawn thugs.[130] So in this case surrender was not an option.

Upstairs in *Nosotros* many Alpha Kappa organizers were very frustrated. One active organizer named Vangelis grumbled about the street clashes and said they were nothing more than "playing with the police." They were not part of any larger strategy; they were predictable, cathartic rituals carried out with special enthusiasm on big days of protest. And this time they risked bringing down serious repression on a well-organized movement embedded in social struggles. The windows and doors were shut and a stack of especially large sticks and clubs were taken out of the closet. One organizer went into the back and put on his motorcycle body armor and a group took up defensive positions on the staircase. After a tense period of uncertainty, the police left.

* * *

Among the self-identified anarchists I interviewed about 4 out of 5 thought that the black bloc could serve a useful purpose in the US if executed properly in the right political context, though many specified that OWS was not such a context. My interviews produced the usual array of arguments for and against the black bloc, but in order to be able to situate my assessment of its potential efficacy, it's important to start out with an understanding of where the tactic came from.

The black bloc (or *schwarze block*) grew out of the movement of the German Autonomen in the 1980s (to clarify, the Autonomen were of mixed genders). Although the term 'black bloc' originated as a derogatory police description of autonomous street tactics, the Autonomen embraced the name.[131] Defying conventional political categorization, German autonomism was a blend of radical feminism, autonomous Marxism, radical ecology, and anarchism. They rejected traditional politics and much of the new left and operated a vast network of alternative institutions, such as cafes, libraries, infoshops, music venues, and squats, through general assemblies and councils. In fact, much of modern small-a anarchist culture can be traced back to prefigurative counter-cultural politics of the Autonomen who saw autonomy as a way to "practice different forms of life in the here and now."[132]

The black bloc had a number of important historical precedents, however. The German autonomists were heavily influenced by the Italian autonomists who organized "nights of fire," involving the simultaneous targeting of several different reactionary locations with coordinated property destruction.[133] In the early 1970s, West German squatters, the political ancestors of the Autonomen, defended their squats in formation while wearing helmets and balaclavas and carrying clubs, reminiscent of a black bloc.[134] But really the phenomenon of radical youth engaging in predominantly non-lethal street battles with the police using clubs and masks/helmets was a hallmark of post-

WWII radicalism. During the 1969 "days of rage" organized by the Weatherman, many marchers wore helmets and committed property destruction. They were influenced by the Japanese Zengakuren, which split into many different revolutionary student groups that marked their distinct identities by wearing different colored helmets.[135] On the cover of his 1971 single "Power to the People" John Lennon wore a Zengakuren helmet.

The general phenomenon of street fighting with helmets or masks and clubs or shields, evident in May 1968 in France for example, could only have emerged under the protection of a nominally 'democratic' public sphere that was compelled to superficially value certain civil and human rights. This range of tactics could really only come into its own once it was clear that killing a protester carried serious political consequences. Looking back in history, we don't see Spanish anarchists organizing a black bloc to resist the Primo de Rivera regime of the 1920s because, even assuming for the sake of argument that it would have made sense to them, they would have been gunned down without remorse. That's certainly not to discount the long history of riots and spontaneous insurrections that have occurred throughout the centuries, but the crucial difference that I'm highlighting here is what is at stake. Standing on a 'first world' picket line in 1890 could get you shot, and it would take a colossal effort to generate the momentum necessary to spark the kind of outrage necessary to affect the government. Undoubtedly, a number of late 19th/early 20th century campaigns managed to generate significant public outcry over police and government atrocities, and that collective pressure played an essential role in developing the popular rights consciousness that provided cover for post-war militant tactics, but it was not the default setting of 'influential' popular opinion. In contrast, throwing a Molotov at a cop in Italy, or throwing a bottle or a rock at a cop in the US, in 1970, 1980 or 2013 would be *relatively* unlikely to get you shot (Carlo Giuliani[136] notwithstanding), and if it did the default societal reaction would be that it was a police over-reaction. That's why they've invested so much money in non-lethal weapons. Therefore, as much as those with insurrectionary politics like to think of the black bloc as an unmediated attack on capital and the state, it relies heavily on a popular rights consciousness standing between the bloc and the police. Any tactic short of armed struggle (and even arguably armed struggle itself, at times) relies on where it's situated in the popular consciousness. I distinguished between throwing a Molotov in southern Europe from throwing a rock in the US because if you were to actually throw a Molotov at a cop in the US most Americans would be fine with the cop shooting you. The fact that the black bloc has much less tactical latitude in the US than elsewhere is a direct consequence of a lower public tolerance for militant protest and, the flip side of the coin, a higher public tolerance for police repression.

The importance of context was evident in a conversation I had over dinner with some Greek anarchists in Athens about the people's Mic. They thought it was the most ridiculous thing they'd ever heard of and couldn't understand how people could make it through an entire general assembly when you have to wait for every word to be repeated several times. I laughed and agreed before pointing out that originally we had a megaphone but the police took it away because we didn't have a permit for amplified sound. Therefore, the people's Mic was a clever adaptation to the situation. But as soon as I finished a bearded comrade called Tzissous blurted out, "But why did you all let the police take the megaphone? Why didn't you just stop them?" Before I could answer, Vangelis at the end of the table put down his white wine mixed with seltzer water (which is apparently popular in Greece for some reason) and said "Because if they fight back they get 25 years in jail." He took the words right out of my mouth. Whereas it was considered *harsh* for a German autonomous militant to get a year in prison for throwing a

Molotov in the mid 80s,[137] today, and especially after September 11th, bumping into a cop can land you in deep shit. That's why it's important to avoid the fallacy of thinking that you can just transplant tactics from other times or places and expect the same results.

It's essential to evaluate political action in its context. If we do that with the original black blocs of the 1980s, we can better understand how and when the tactic can play a productive role in the anarchist project. Here I'll focus on two main examples of the Autonomen use of the black bloc: in the squatters' movement and in anti-racist struggles.

Although the squatters' movement got going under the Autonomen umbrella in the early 80s, it had important precedents with the militant feminist movement of the late 60s. More than most feminist movements of the era, the West German radical feminist movement emphasized autonomy over formal, legalistic equality. They played an important role in prefiguring the Autonomen by establishing a wide circle of social centers in squatted properties working closely with Turkish immigrants long before the rest of the West German Left. Though it ebbed and flowed, the squatters' movement continued through the 70s especially in Frankfurt under the influence of the "Spontis" (spontaneous autonomous direct-actionists) who supported Turkish and Italian immigrant rent strikes. By the early 80s, these various tendencies united under the Autonomen umbrella to organize a vast squatters' movement of 5-8,000 squatters in 370-500 squatted properties in West Germany, about the size of Oregon, under the slogan "no power to anyone." Given the severe shortage of affordable housing, this movement played a critical role in a number of urban areas.[138]

This connection to the community was evident in the widespread collective resistance to the attempted eviction of Hamburg's *Hafenstraße* squat. The squat was originally occupied in 1981 but, despite fending off four separate eviction attempts over the years, in 1986 the squat was under attack by the police. In response to police attacks, the Autonomen organized a march of 10,000 in defense of the squat including a black bloc of 1,500 marching behind a banner that said "Build Revolutionary Dual Power!" At the end of the march, the bloc pushed back the police in heavy street fighting. The next day the black bloc retaliated against the attempted eviction by setting fire to 13 department stores across Hamburg causing about $10 million in damages.[139] Here we can see that a black bloc means something very different when it's formed for the purpose of defending popular institutions that respond to popular needs with widespread public support. The Autonomen were widely known for fighting the police, but they gained working class support for their struggle because they defended a movement that responded to real needs in the community. Moreover, regardless of one's stance on property destruction, its undeniable that causing millions of dollars in damages actually hurts capitalists in a way that purely symbolic window smashing frequently cannot.

During conversations about property destruction at large demonstrations, eventually someone makes the astute comment that if the main goal is to destroy property then why do it in front of so many cops? Why not just come back at night when no one's around? It's true that smashing things at large demonstrations derives its main rationale from the spectacle it creates. But the *Kraakers* of Amsterdam, essentially Dutch Autonomen, took that idea to heart when they carried out actions under the banner of RA RA (Anti-Racist Action Group). In 1985, RA RA initiated a campaign against MAKRO supermarkets to get them to divest from the Apartheid regime of South Africa. Under the cover of darkness, RA RA militants firebombed a number of MAKRO locations causing over 100 million guilders in damages eventually forcing the supermarket chain to divest from South Africa. After that victory, they tried to get Shell to divest from South Africa by carrying out over 100 attacks on Shell, including one night where 37 Shell stations were attacked in Amsterdam alone, but Shell didn't budge.[140] Here property destruction was not a matter of smashing the windows of whichever random corporate target happens to appear; it was a coordinated campaign in direct solidarity with a struggle of anti-racist liberation.

After re-unification, the German Autonomen played an even more direct role in resisting the racism of a Nazi revival. Starting in 1990, fascist and Nazi groups proliferated, increasing their attacks on immigrants. In 1990, the neo-fascist Republican Party got nearly a million votes and in 1993 the constitution was amended to prevent refugees from entering the country. Between 1990-1994, fascists committed more than 80 murders and in 1993 police registered more than 23,000 right wing crimes. It got so bad that Amnesty International issued a report accusing the police of mistreating foreigners and Germany was brought before the UN Human Rights Commission to respond to widespread allegations that it was not protecting immigrants. In this context, the Autonomen, often using black bloc tactics, were the only force on the Left to fight back. Often joining with Turkish youth gangs, the black bloc disrupted a number of Nazi events, including a permitted demonstration in front of the Reichstag.[141] Given that history, it's no surprise that Anti-Racist Action (ARA) groups in the US and Canada were among the first North Americans to adopt the tactic.[142] Swedish anarchist Stina Soderling had a similar perspective on the black bloc:

> When I was living in Sweden I was doing No Borders immigrants' rights activism and we worked a lot with the AntiFa movement ... where [the Black Bloc] was very useful because we had direct confrontations with neo-Nazis and having people that are willing to engage in militia-like tactics is useful in that context.[143]

In some ways the situation in Greece today is similar to newly reunified Germany twenty years ago. With the rise of the fascist Golden Dawn, attacks against immigrants have proliferated with impunity. In response, anti-authoritarians have organized "Anti-Fascist Motorcycle Squads" that patrol immigrant neighborhoods and confront fascists. I had the honor of witnessing one of the patrols as it left the Athens Polytechnic in November 2012. There were about 500 motorcycles with two people apiece dressed predominantly in black carrying black and red and black flags on thick wooden poles. Throughout their patrol, they threw leaflets in the air with slogans like "fascism doesn't die on its own, you have to smash it."[144] As the patrol passed, many immigrants stepped out onto the street to cheer and salute these anti-fascists. At one point, the patrol stopped and together the anti-fascists and immigrants chanted the slogan "The People Never Forget the Fascists/The People Hang the Fascists!" Once again, militant black bloc tactics make sense when they have a clearly expressed social purpose that supports community struggles. My Greek comrades Eliana and Tzissous explained to me that without their "power in the streets" they would be unable to protect their social centers and squats. Eliana said that their violent self-defense is "necessary to build our structures, in demonstrations, in the streets, and in everyday life."

However, there's also another scenario where the black bloc can make sense: when it's urgently necessary to lash out against a notable case of state repression. For example, in 1981 a West German squatter received an especially harsh prison sentence for squatting activities. In response, the Autonomen and supporters jammed the locks of 40 banks and smashed the windows of another 70 in two nights of rioting behind the slogan "You Have the Power, We Have the Night!" In addition they organized surprise riots on main commercial streets causing millions of deutsche marks in damage.[145] One of the most notable recent examples was the 2008 Greek Uprising, which included university occupations and attacks on police stations, in response to the police murder of 15-year-old Alexandros Grigoropoulos.[146] The importance of increasing the social cost of repression transcends the black bloc. I would imagine that for as long as there have been riots they have been recognized as opportunities for collective catharsis. But rioting in response to especially egregious crimes of the state in solidarity with a significant stratum of the community can be an important use of the tactic. Certainly German judges thought twice before sentencing another squatter to a long sentence and Greek cops thought twice before shooting another anarchist kid.

That's why I felt torn about the spectacle of ritualized street fighting that I witnessed in Athens in 2012. On the one hand it runs the risk of stagnating into triviality, or, even worse, bringing down repression on active groups and movements for no reason. But on the other hand, it provides a ready reserve of street power that can be mobilized in an instant to light the flame of resistance. In the context of a potential fascist takeover, I feel better knowing that there are legions of militant anti-fascist youth ready to throw down at a moment's notice. The key is to incorporate that revolutionary passion into bodies of resistance oriented around a more long-term strategy.

Toward the end of the first OWS forum on diversity of tactics and nonviolence in February 2012, we finished with sort of a group open space where people were sitting on the floor and one by one people took turns expressing what they were thinking after our smaller group discussions about tactics. Toward the end of the session I felt like sharing my thought so I got up and made a comment along these lines:

> Most people think holding signs to protest something is stupid. They do. They can't understand why anyone would spend hours walking in a circle chanting the same slogans over and over again when we all know that it usually doesn't

> make a difference because nobody's listening. Within the left we may think that such non-violent tactics are self-evident, but they're not. So it's missing the point to spend all of our time focusing on how most people respond negatively to 'violent' tactics when in fact they tend to respond negatively to all tactics. That is unless they work. People respond to tactics based on whether they work or not and usually the best tactics are non-violent but sometimes they're not so we should evaluate our tactics based on efficacy.

Or something like that. The argument to evaluate tactics based on efficacy is certainly very widespread and obvious, but I think that sometimes leftists discount apathy. They subconsciously discount the rationally apathetic without identifying how they became apathetic in the first place, and then formulate strategies geared toward the sensibilities of the politically engaged middle class progressive; what the Team Colors Collective calls the "imaginary middle."[147] All too often this progressive target audience doesn't even care as much about the efficacy of the tactics used as they do about the tactics' loyalty to the liberal pacifist script.

But as Paul Dalton phrased it, we "should care less about what Whole Foods shoppers think and more about what Walmart shoppers do."[148] And what they want is results. A significant part of the debate over property destruction centers on this question of popular reception. Both sides argue about how working class people and people of color interpret smashing windows or setting fires and both sides accuse the other of being privileged for thinking that subalterns favor or reject aggressive tactics. Surprisingly, there are routinely people on both sides of the debate who think that such large groups of people could have fixed positions one way or the other. Part of the reason for this is that many tend to evaluate tactics in general without situating them in specific situations. So let's take an all too common situation in the US and ask the question. Do working class people and people of color tend to look favorably upon property destruction when it's carried out by a group of young, predominantly white, people who they have never known to have done any productive work in their community against a target that seems to have been chosen at random at a large demonstration against an abstract international financial institution that they may not have heard of? Usually not so much. Echoing this sentiment, Senia Barragan, said that the black bloc can be problematic

> if white anarchist kids are doing it in neighborhoods that aren't theirs. It's different like a few years ago in London where it was mostly young folks of Caribbean and Afro-English descent expressing their rage ... Disenchanted people in their own communities have the right to set shit on fire if they don't get what they fucking need. The black bloc has to really prove its usefulness in order to make itself intelligible in this country since we have a totally different kind of history and relation to organized street protest than say for example Italy, Greece or even Canada. So when Americans see mostly, in this case, young white folks or even if they were predominantly people of color, that would terrify them more, but still when everyday Americans see that walking down the street it's not part of a general social phenomenon they can tap into and say 'oh that's part of social movement or protests' its seen as kind of terroristic and scary.[149]

As Senia points out, we need to recognize the fact that without an immediate rationale or social base, the black bloc is unintelligible in the United States. Sofía Gallisa (25), a Puerto Rican organizer involved with *OWS en Español*, emphasized the importance of context when she said that, "throwing a Molotov cocktail in Mexico is not uncommon. It's not some anarchist fantasy. It's not some mental masturbation. It's very real and a short older lady from some rural town might be seen doing it."[150]

Ronny Nuñez was also of the opinion that without the right context the black bloc could be counterproductive:

> [The black bloc's] not effective because there's this active social meme that violence is bad in absolutely every circumstance and you should never act on it. So it's not a friendly image, it's not something that's gonna win people over ... right now there's not really a purpose to the black bloc. It doesn't really serve our own ends. I think the black bloc should really only be showing up once it gets to the point in which people are of the mindset that 'hey, maybe violence *is* the answer.'[151]

George Machado said that he didn't think that the black bloc was useful

> in the current context at all. I think they're ridiculous ...We don't find ourselves in that context or that climate ... it makes more sense to me to bloc up in bright pink colors than a black bloc ... [but] the second Harlem wants to sack the Upper East Side I'm all about it! Don't even front, I will be right there. Masked up. Done![152]

For George and many other OWS anarchists, the black bloc should be used when it makes sense socially and strategically. With these provisional criteria in mind, it seems like the black blocs that were formed in Oakland in the wake of the police murder of Oscar Grant in 2009 and in defense of the attempted occupation of the convention center on January 28, 2012 made sense. Although I wasn't there and don't know the intricate details of these situations, based on what I've read and heard from comrades they were examples of militant action that situated themselves in relation to the needs of the community (whether to lash out against another racist murder or use vacant property for the public benefit).

But we should remember that black blocs often don't work in the United States. As I participated in more and more of them over the years, it became increasingly clear that they rarely accomplished anything, even on a symbolic level. What was once a surprise tactic became very predicable and containable. In part that was because many were in New York where it was considered a fabulous success if we could make it more than a block down the street without being surrounded by riot police after breaking off from the main march. Probably the most 'successful' black bloc I participated in was in Ottawa at the G8 protest in 2002 where marchers tagged Coca Cola trucks, launched paintballs at corporate edifices with slingshots, and cracked a few windows. In contrast to New York, I was shocked to see how the police largely stood back and let it unfold. Of course, they kept their distance because it was wiser to allow a little property damage that could be cleaned up the next day than risk lawsuits and bad press by starting a conflict. In other words, we weren't actually a threat as much as a logistical nuisance.

I think that so many anarchists are so accustomed to defending themselves against liberal pacifist attacks (sometimes literally) that their outlook gets calcified into a kneejerk justification of any black bloc regardless of its results. As Francis Dupuis-Déri phrased it,

> Black Blocs can become a like a religion, with a desire to display and affirm a political identity that remains pure as long as it is limited to certain ritualized acts, such as spectacular confrontations with the police, confrontations that are valorized in themselves, independent of their political impact. Direct action then becomes a way for the militant to affirm their political identity in the eyes of other militants.[153]

If we are to get beyond that mentality we need to be able to situate our tactics within a larger revolutionary strategy.

No Evolution without Revolution

> "If the goal of a revolution isn't anything but to switch governments, if it is only the taking of power by a political party, whichever it may be, then to us it is a political revolution, in a word a coup d'état ... The Revolution that we want and for which we fight today and tomorrow with all of our forces is the *Social Revolution*. What is the social revolution?—That which abolishes the exploitation of man by man: whether from bosses, militarism, or the State. That which substitutes the government of men by men for the administration of things by the producer. That which in the place of authoritarian and centralized society, institutes the libertarian federalist society."
> —Louis Loréal[154]

> "The only way to understand the system is through conceiving of its destruction."
> —*Quaderni Rossi*[155]

Many scholars have portrayed turn of the 20th century anarchists as millenarian romantics.[156] In their eyes, they were irrational, pre-modern dreamers who naively and religiously imagined that eventually a revolution would come that would wipe away all oppression and domination in one fell swoop leaving only cooperation and solidarity in its wake. In response, a number of historians, including my academic advisor Temma Kaplan, demonstrated that the anarchists of this period were actually rational political actors who valued science and organization.[157] While there were certainly plenty of anarchists with overly simplistic notions of immediate revolutionary transformation, as there were capitalists with overly simplistic understandings of the market, it's clear that the overwhelming thrust of the "mass anarchist"[158] movement favored a dual pronged strategy of generating collective power today in order to be able to smash the state and build the new society tomorrow.

Although modern small-a anarchism is strongly associated with a prefigurative emphasis on developing networks of alternative institutions, classical anarchist movements in a number of countries developed legitimately popular working class cultures that rivaled mainstream culture. In advance of 'the revolution,' anarchists organized schools, daycare centers, libraries, lecture and concert halls, unions, health clinics, industrial and agricultural cooperatives and more. They actually had a very realistic understanding of the need to undertake the painstaking work of building collective power on a daily basis since, as Ba Jin said, "the ideal society will not suddenly appear like a miracle; it comes gradually."[159] In that spirit, the prominent French anarchist Sébastien Faure (1858-1942) wrote that,

> The Social Revolution appears to us as the culminating point and terminus of a more or less long period of education, organization, interior agitation, exterior effervescence, of preparation and training for an action of the masses; we wouldn't know how to conceive of it otherwise.[160]

Faure's quote points to the fact that most anarchists have had a nuanced understanding of the delicate interrelations between revolution and evolution. After all, in his famous *Encyclopedia Britannica* article on "Anarchism," Kropotkin wrote that, "like all evolution in nature, the slow evolution of society is followed from time to time by periods of accelerated evolution which are called revolutions."[161] In 1924 Malatesta also theorized revolution in evolutionary terms:

> Everything in history as in nature occurs gradually. When a dam bursts (that is, very rapidly, though always under the influence of time) it is either because the pressure of the water has become too great for the dam to hold any longer or because of the gradual disintegration of the molecules of which the matter of the dam is made ... We are reformers today in that we seek to create the most favorable conditions and the greatest possible number of responsible and aware people necessary in order to bring about a successful people's insurrection.[162]

In fact, the anarchists of the Spanish section of the First International initially called themselves "evolutionists" rather than "revolutionists" because they wanted to distinguish their vision of constant societal transformation punctuated by moments of rupture from contemporary bourgeois republican aspirations for a political revolution, a superficial coup d'état.[163]

Nevertheless, despite anarchism's appreciation for building the new world in the shell of the old, the vast majority of anarchists have insisted that these steps can't transform society in the absence of a violent conflict with the state, the defender of the capitalist system. Although there have been a number of notable pacifist anarchists, such as Gustav Landauer, Bart de Ligt, Dorothy Day, and Leo Tolstoy (if we have a rather loose conception of anarchism), the main argument about violence throughout the majority of anarchist history has *not* been about whether the movement should be peaceful or violent, but whether class enemies should be attacked by small groups of insurrectionaries or by larger community groups or unions organized into democratic militias (essentially the argument between "insurrectionist" and "mass" anarchists).

Before I continue, it's important to address the popular portrayal of the anarchist as a violent, deviant being has morphed from its 19th century bomb-thrower variant into today's window-smasher caricature. So are anarchists violent? Well, I just finished emphasizing how anarchists usually think that a violent revolution is lamentably necessary, but we certainly aren't violent compared to other political doctrines. As a number of writers have documented,[164] monarchists, conservatives, liberals, nationalists, authoritarian Marxists, fascists and followers of the major religions have been responsible for infinitely more violence than anarchists. If you were to accumulate the entirety of anarchist violence throughout history it would pale in comparison to horrendous scope of modern warfare. So then why has the stigma of violence been attached to anarchists? Because anarchists carry out their acts of self-defense and resistance without the legitimization of the state. It's really as simple as that. How else can you explain a world where architects of war who break international law and murder innocent civilians in the interest of maintaining a vastly unjust world economic system, like Henry Kissinger and Barack Obama, win Nobel *Peace* prizes while those who insist on prioritizing the fulfillment of human need across the planet and smash the implements of war and exploitation are monsters? The discussion isn't really about 'violence' as a neutral category, but political power, which can be used to justify anything.

Historically, the image of the violent anarchist owes much to the relatively brief popularity of "propaganda by the deed" in international anarchist circles in the late 19th century. Although the concept originally described demonstrations of revolutionary praxis through popular insurrection[165] or actions in support of popular struggles, over time its scope was narrowed to isolated attacks on prominent reactionaries, such as politicians and capitalists. The small minority of anarchists that advocated propaganda by the deed, such as Luigi Galleani, thought that these attacks would be "raised to a sacred standard" that would inspire resistance, but, as we know, that didn't happen.[166] Some of the most notable anarchist attacks were against American

President William McKinley, Italian King Umberto I, Austrian Empress Elisabeth, French President Marie François Sadi Carnot, and three Spanish Prime Ministers.[167] Some prominent anarchists, like Kropotkin, supported it initially only to change reverse course when it brought pointless repression without emboldening resistance. In 1880 Kropotkin argued for "permanent revolt in speech, writing, by the dagger and the gun, or by dynamite,"[168] but by 1891 he wrote that "European anarchists imagined that henceforth a handful of zealous revolutionaries, armed with a few bombs, would be enough to make the social revolution ... [but] an edifice built upon centuries of history cannot be destroyed by a few kilos of explosives..."[169] As anarchism entered the 20th century, propaganda by the deed declined while the popularity of anarcho-synidicalism soared. Since then, a number of different political groups have carried out their share of assassinations[170] and there have been plenty of state-sponsored assassinations, but the fact that a minority of anarchists were among the first prominent assassins of the modern period solidified the image of the bomb-throwing anarchist.[171]

Today, especially in the United States, there are far more anarchist pacifists than there were before World War II as a result of the influence of the civil rights movement and other struggles. Anarchist pacifists gravitate toward building alternative institutions, which they hope will gradually transform society over time through education and practical demonstrations of the superiority of anarchist practice. For the anarchist pacifist, if anarchism is the epitome of peace, and the means must reflect the ends, then the means must embody peace. In 1901, Gustav Landauer asked "what has the killing of people to do with anarchism, a theory striving for a society without government and authoritarian coercion, a movement against the state and legalized violence? The answer is: nothing at all."[172] In 1900 Tolstoy wrote that, "all attempts to abolish slavery by violence are like extinguishing fire with fire, stopping water with water, or filling up one hole by digging another."[173] Bart de Ligt made a similar argument in his 1937 *The Conquest of Violence*: "it is impossible to educate people in liberty by force, just as it is impossible to breathe by coal gas. Life must have fresh air. And freedom must be awakened and stimulated by freedom and in freedom. It can never be born of violence."[174]

Is it a contradiction of anarchist values to engage in acts of violence? Is it impossible to "fight fire with fire"? I think the problem with the pacifist argument in this case is that it assumes that the primary anarchist goal is peace, when it's actually justice. Sure, anarchists would ideally prefer a world without violence of any sort, and the elimination of class hierarchy would go a long way toward that goal, but that doesn't mean that an absolute absence of violence would be a defining characteristic of an anarchist society. As I touched upon in the discussion about *liberal libertarianism* and coercion in Chapter 2, if someone tried to burn down someone's house or start a counter-revolution in an anarchist society, they would be met with violence if they didn't stop what they were doing. So actually it's not a contradiction for an anarchist to use violence as a last resort against perpetrators of injustice now or in the future society since the revolution will always be an ongoing process. The pacifist argument sneaks in a pacifist conception of the future society in order to be able to demonstrate the consistency of a pacifist approach to resistance.

Regardless of their tactical outlook, however, almost all anarchists agree that violence is inherently corrosive. Anarchists are the political group most committed to drastically reducing the role of violence in society as quickly as possible since statist ideologies posit the eternal necessity of violence (and often laud it) and orthodox Marxists seek to maintain the repressive capacity of the state after the revolution (and we've seen how long the 'dictatorship of the proletariat' can hang on for). Malatesta argued this point: "What distinguishes the anarchists from all the others is precisely the horror of violence, the desire and the proposal to eliminate violence, material violence, that is, from human affairs."[175] Although Malatesta was an ardent advocate of armed revolution, he devoted a lot of energy to emphasizing the inherently corrosive nature of violence. In an 1895 article in the midst of the propaganda by the deed frenzy, he wrote that violence

> is the most brutal form the struggle between men can assume, is eminently corrupting. It tends by its very nature, to suffocate the best sentiments of man, and to develop all the anti-social qualities: ferocity, hatred, revenge, the spirit of domination and tyranny, contempt of the weak, servility towards the strong ... In short it is our duty to call attention to the dangers attendant on the use of violence, to insist on the principle of the inviolability of human life, to combat the spirit of hatred and revenge, and to preach love and toleration. But to blind ourselves to the true conditions of the struggle, to renounce the use of force for the purpose of repelling and attacking force, relying on the fanciful efficacy of 'passive resistance,' and in the name of a mystical morality to deny the right of self-defense, or to restrain it to the point of rendering it illusionary, can only end in nothing, or in leaving a free field of action to the oppressors.[176]

The Spanish anarchist movement of the 1930s took this point about the corrupting nature of violence so seriously that they decided that only older anarchists should engage in violence. The anarchist youth groups were to refrain from street fighting because they were less politically developed so violence might lead them astray, and, more importantly, violence would inhibit the natural development of libertarian sensibilities and corrupt the youth who were to build the new world. They reluctantly abandoned this stance once the exigencies of the Civil War emerged.[177]

Anarchists have taken violence seriously but, as Malatesta argues, they have generally concluded that the only alternative is servility. As Lucy Parsons (1853-1942), an African-American anarchist who some believe may have been born into slavery, wrote

> Passivity while slavery is stealing over us is a crime … hence most anarchists believe the coming change can only come through a revolution, because the possessing class will not allow a peaceful change to take place; still we are willing to work for peace at any price, except at the price of liberty.[178]

So is this true? Is it impossible to imagine that someday maybe the capitalists and militarists will tell the police to lay down their weapons before they abolish their privilege and join in the collective construction of a new egalitarian world? Didn't Soviet Bloc governments collapse in the late 80s without a violent revolution? Well, in Romania government buildings were torched and Ceaușescu was thrown in front of a firing squad,[179] but generally it's true that they were non-violent. But there haven't been any non-violent *social* revolutions and there couldn't be because those who hold the reigns of the economy and enjoy lives of luxury won't give up their privileges without a fight. They'll concede shifts in governmental form, provide more space for civil rights, or even pay a higher tax rate (while burrowing loopholes), but the fundamental axis of the class struggle cannot be resolved peacefully because they won't let us do it that way. If the revolutionaries of Czechoslovakia or Bulgaria had tried to keep the factories, schools, and town halls for themselves and establish a *libertarian* socialist society, they would have needed more than flowers.

Overall, most OWS anarchists agreed that the creation of a new world would necessitate some sort of violent conflict with the state. Zu Solanas didn't hesitate to say that "the people that have all the power, all the resources, that have armies, like Bloomberg, are not going to be won over."[180] Andrew said:

> I can't imagine because of the history of the world that real opposition and resistance to any sort of powerful force is not going to become violent at some point, which isn't to say that I think that a violent insurrection is something that we need per se but it is something that I logically recognize as a likely escalation of any successful resistance.[181]

But it's important to discard the antiquated idea of the revolution as a single apocalyptic moment. Jonathan Smucker made the following astute observation:

> I think that a lot of peoples' model of revolution is based on anti-monarchy, anti-colonial, and anti-feudal systems. I don't know of a single situation where this model of the violent, or non-violent, overthrow of a government has happened in a democratic country except in the form of right-wing coups ... [with] that model of this kind of 'some day huge confrontation with the state' the question is 'then what?' That model can get a bit into this 'the reality of change and struggle is too messy right now so I am putting it off into some future apocalyptic moment'... [but] society is gonna recreate itself the way it is unless you actually transform values.[182]

Smucker's absolutely right that we need to have a more nuanced understanding of revolution as an ongoing process of building collective power and shifting popular values punctuated by moments of rupture and conflict. A number of interviewees discounted the possibility of a revolution because the state has such powerful weaponry, but that critique assumes a static model of revolution where you have dissidents on one side with rocks and a few pistols and you have the state on the other with unmanned rocket-launching drones. If that were the situation then certainly any hope at insurrection would be hopeless.

But what if it looked more like this: over the years networks and federations of unions, self-managed workplaces, tenants' associations, collective kitchens, free health clinics, and other organs of autonomous resistance that fill in the gaps left by a decaying capitalist system blossom. Maybe there's another economic crash, or government scandal, or incident that damages the public's faith in government even further to the point where those in power feel the need to crack down on the networks of resistance that challenge their legitimacy. This crackdown might win the opposition sympathy and spark pockets of resistance. Some might loot gun shops and take over large public buildings. With the government unable to balance its books, let's say it implements more austerity measures causing mainstream unions to strike. That strike grows into a general strike and the military is called in to force people back to work. But the soldiers are reluctant to open fire, so some desert while other switch sides.

What I'm trying to get at in this imaginary scenario is that if (1) we can build up our collective power to a sufficient degree that our actions articulate an alternative, (2) we use our role in the economic system as leverage to bring the economy to a standstill, and (3) we aren't afraid to defend ourselves and increase the cost of repression for the government (once again leveraging public opinion to gain popular support), then a new world might not be that impossible. But if these imaginary revolutionaries were to lie down before state repression, their hard-won momentum would be wasted. It's true that such a scenario is almost unimaginable in the United States right now, though far less unimaginable in some other places, but given the imminence of ecological catastrophe and global capitalism's inability to infinitely expand we need to start thinking about how we can position ourselves to steer things away from some post-apocalyptic authoritarian regime and toward a genuine libertarian socialism.

And we won't be able to get there if we retreat into insular, counter-cultural bookstores, co-ops, cafes, and community gardens. Such alternatives can be highly valuable in demonstrating the potential of workers' self-management and they can contribute to the formation of networks of resistance, but if they don't engage with the broader population they run the risk of veering into escapism. In Madrid, for example, there is a vast network of "Occupied, Self-managed Social Centers" (CSOA) that have free stores where people can get donated clothing and household items, free language classes, cultural spaces, a woodworking workshop where people can make usable goods out of discarded furniture and they're integrated into popular struggles including the neighborhood assemblies of 15M (aka *indignados*). In Thessaloniki, Greece the Alpha Kappa anti-authoritarian movement is affiliated with a social center called Micropolis that has a daycare center (with a children's chess league), self-defense classes, a pottery workshop, a bar and restaurant with cheap *delicious* lunches (€2), a woodworking facility called "Vida," a lending library, and a store where independent farmers and craftspeople can bring their goods to sell provided that they agree to teach others their craft to build a self managed economy. Micropolis is an example of how alternative institutions can meet our collective needs in the short term while prefiguring the self-managed society, building popular power, and turning the anarchist movement outward.

One of my greatest concerns leaving OWS was that some had come to the conclusion that "mass movements are inherently problematic," that radicals should never work with liberals, and the way forward is to form small groups of like-minded people and simply escape from capitalism. As Jackie Disalvo said, some in Occupy "think you can just withdraw from the power structures and set up your own thing as though Zuccotti were 'socialism in one park.'"[183] But if the withdrawal strategy ever got powerful enough to make a difference the state would lash out forcing us defend ourselves or return to normal. It's about striking the right balance between the two in the context of a popular movement.

Some told me that it really takes the pressure off to be able to go at your own pace and build solid, intentional relationships that truly value the individual without reducing them to a cog in a "mass." In essence, some argued that since capitalism reduces humanity to a formless mass then resistance should head in the opposite direction. It's perfectly fine to form small collectives based on personal or ideological affinity and organize small-scale projects, but in order to engage with working class people with families that don't have a lot of time to devote to politics, large events and organizations are vital. We want to empower people, but it's unrealistic and unfair to expect that everyone will have the same level of commitment. Political work that doesn't leave space for the majority of the population can only be a niche phenomenon. If we turn our backs to society we'll never get anywhere. Prefigurative groups and movements, such as Movement for a New Society and the German Autonomen, ran into trouble when they became too self-referential. One German autonomous writer had this critique of the fetishization of an alternative space or "free space":

> We do not criticize the existence of relatively free spaces, but the concept of 'free space' as a goal. To us, free spaces are but departure points for wider struggles. To merely establish and defend them … is classical reformism! It poses no challenge to the system. In fact, capitalism proves how flexible it is: 'free spaces' are integrated, resistance is channeled, and ghettos are created that have no explosive force. We are left with nothing but playgrounds.[184]

Many Occupy people had an idealized vision of cooperatives as the key to transforming the economy without understanding that in a capitalist system a cooperative is merely a form of self-exploitation (though in that sense usually preferable) since the market system dictates certain levels of productivity and efficiency; levels that corporations will always meet much better than cooperatives since they have no qualms with exploitation. They are a step in the right direction but they cannot substitute for the class struggle. In addition, moving our money from big banks to small ones or credit unions is not withdrawing our consent. It makes a small dent, at best, in large banks without addressing capitalism. It's liberal feel-good politics. Most of the money you spend is going to end up right back in one of those big banks anyway.

If we are going to take the motto "an injury to one is an injury to all" seriously, then we need to create popular federated organs of resistance that value small group initiatives while representing the scale necessary to project our image of a better world for all to see.

Conclusion: "Like Ectoplasm Through a Mist"

Now that the Occupy frenzy has subsided, we can start to think about how the legacy of Occupy Wall Street will influence the future of radical organizing in the United States and beyond. I think Ryan Harvey is absolutely correct to say that, "within political movements in the US, it is hard to imagine hierarchical organizing becoming popular among a generation that was brought into politics through Occupy."[1] In the same way that it was simply assumed among the radical left of the early 2000s that organizing would be horizontal or it would not be at all, over the coming years new activists will incorporate the lessons they've learned from Occupy—and hopefully ditch some of the counterproductive baggage—to renew horizontalism for a new generation.

It's a vitally important process, but unfortunately it's simply not enough. Anarchists and anti-authoritarians need to spread their anti-oppressive and anti-hierarchical values beyond the limited sphere of organizational process to express a comprehensive political vision and forge more solid, long-term projects and entities. Directly democratic procedures and values do not necessarily produce revolutionary outcomes on their own. There were plenty of liberals and moderates who mastered consensus process during their time with Occupy and left with essentially the same 'repeal Citizens United' politics they came in with. Many of those people gleefully twinkling their fingers in the GAs experienced direct democracy as an amusing novelty without any serious thought about its broader application to decision-making at a societal level.

By *Translating Anarchy* to a broad liberal population, we managed to bring thousands of people into contact with anarchistic politics and that experience changed quite a few lives.

But could we have done better than that? Sure, we managed to flavor the political culture of the radical left, but shouldn't we set our sights higher? With only a single table packed with free photocopied pamphlets, the In Our Hearts anarchist collective managed to bring a number of fence-sitters into the anarchist fold. Their presence was invaluable. But what if there had been more well-organized, established anarchist groups, collectives, organizations, publishers, and so forth ready to step in to bolster what I refer to as the third layer[2] of radical messaging? Although the situation and political culture was very different, I think it's instructive to reflect upon the words of the French anarchist Maurice Fayolle looking back at the role of anarchists in May 1968 in France:

> In May-June 1968, we paid a high price for our 15 years of absenteeism and organizational vacuum. The ceaseless activities of a few comrades and a few groups could not make good that deficit. And, at a time when Paris was bedecked with black flags, we glided through these events like ectoplasm through a mist, that is, without reaping all the benefits which other leftist formations drained from them. Had we, at that point, had a worthwhile organization, like the FA [*Fédération Anarchiste*] of the years following the 1939-45 war, with its structures and its weekly newspaper, France today would have over two hundred organized groups and a press with a huge print run, in short, a numerous and very coherent anarchist movement which might make its voice heard in this country.[3]

Now I'm certainly not suggesting that OWS was similar to May '68, a rebellion that actually threatened the government, but when I step back to evaluate the tangible political outcome for the anarchist movement after months spent before a world spotlight with thousands of eager new people beating the doors down to get involved, I get the sinking feeling that to some extent we too "glided through these events like ectoplasm through a mist." We didn't even have any competing leftist formations. The field of political influence was left open to us and we didn't get as much out of it as we should have. If we're serious about building a powerful anarchist movement, then we need to create more alternative institutions and groups that can bring people in and give them an outlet to continue their revolutionary political engagement after the tents come down and the fingers stop wiggling. Because if we don't, most people will understandably just continue to go about their business.

There are a number of reasons why anarchists may not have been optimally prepared to take full advantage of Occupy Wall Street. The most obvious is that no one expected it. As a result procedures, working groups, and other systems of communication were devised without envisioning the scale of participation that would soon overwhelm things. One of the most frequent comments I heard from the non-anarchist(ic) organizers that I interviewed was that they really loved direct democracy and leaderlessness but they didn't see how they could scale up to include large numbers of people across large geographical areas. If we want to project our image of another world we need to be able to adapt with larger structures that at least sometimes operate by majority voting and use recallable delegates to transmit the perspectives of smaller groups. A lot of radicals are drawn to these values but skeptical about their implementation. In response we need to experiment with new forms and structures to take advantage of that vast political opportunity.

Moreover, most anarchists, such as myself, were putting all of their energy into actually organizing the movement. Certainly the priority had to be the movement, but if more groups and collectives were well organized before the movement got going I think participation and spreading anarchist ideas could have been balanced and merged more successfully. A lot of new organizers were inspired by the anarchist ethos and it would have been useful for anarchist organizers to be able to say, 'oh, you're interested in anarchism? Come to our discussion Thursday evening about 'anarchist perspectives on organizing'; or 'maybe you'd be interested in joining our anarchist organization/collective.' I know that a lot of Occupy people cringe at the notion of 'factionalism' within the movement because they have this bizarre, new-age, apolitical, vanilla, individualistic conception of democracy, but factionalism *did* develop, only it was around affinity groups and unarticulated political divisions that expressed themselves in different organizing foci. Rather than mask our divisions we should make them open so that those who agree with us can join us.

Another issue was that while our organizational forms failed to maintain a distinct OWS identity, the individual countercultural identity of 'the Occupier' calcified in a very counterproductive way. Lorenzo Serna said that around the time of Occupy Congress in DC "suddenly there was this idea of an 'Occupier' and this 'Occupier' was a person who was defined … So instead of expanding the movement at that point I kind of felt like we were contracting it..."[4] Similarly, George Machado said that for many, "Occupy became their identity and that identity cemented into something static that looked only a certain way … [they were] constantly thinking about strategies for re-occupation and wanted to shove the label 'Occupy' where it doesn't fit…"[5] Yet, for Justin Stone-Diaz (37) the 'Occupier' identity was very important:

> A good portion, 99% of the people who came to support us were just supporting us. They weren't Occupiers. Becoming an Occupier is a self-determining thing … it's this unquantifiable little mix of things … you can tell when people are just hanging out, people are occupying. There's an element of joy. There's an element of justice.[6]

This related to the tendency of young countercultural 'Occupiers' that were frequently quite new to activism to think that they were more 'hardcore' or 'authentic' than longtime community organizers that didn't sleep in the park. For many, being dirty and sleeping on concrete became the signifier of a true 'Occupier,' and while it's important to take into account that cultural identity played a significant role in giving masses of alienated youth a sense of belonging and importance, it tended to short-circuit the expansion of the movement.

On October 5, 2011, Senia and I were going to sleep in Liberty for the first time. We brought our sleeping bags and set them down somewhere before spending the entire day doing press work for the first big march with the labor unions. By the time 7pm rolled around, I was ready to collapse, but the park was just coming to life. I knew that if I didn't get home to get a decent night's sleep I wouldn't be able to be out there in the morning speaking to literally hundreds of journalists, so we went home. It was certainly the right decision since after a while it was a lot easier to find people interested in sleeping in the park than it was to find people dedicated to completing important logistical tasks in organizing campaigns. About a week later, I was sitting at the press table when one of the more irascible 'Occupiers' who slept in the park but didn't seem to do much of anything else came up to me and berated me for speaking to the press. Fortunately, my years in retail customer service came in handy and I just thanked him for sharing his opinion until he left. But it was a strange environment where people tried to reinforce their outsider status to prove their 'authentic' connection to a mainstream phenomenon. For these reasons, I made a conscious effort to avoid using the term 'Occupier' to refer to OWS organizers throughout the book. I wanted to emphasize the role that these individuals played in a political movement rather than the construction of an exclusive, and at times asocial, cultural identity.

Even those organizers who weren't committed to the 'Occupier' identity were often concerned about sliding out of the inner circles of the fast-paced movement. Therefore, some seemed to spend an inordinate amount of energy focusing their attention inward to maintain their status rather than facing outward to bring more people in. I started my interviews in December 2011 and did quite a few over the first few months of 2012. At that time, I would often conclude my interviews by asking people how much longer they thought OWS would last as a vibrant political force. The most common answer was 'I don't know,' but quite a few said that they were sure it would keep going strong for years into the future. When it all got started, I was pretty positive that it could only survive until the 2012 election cycle devoured it, but the fact that so many thought that Occupy was here to stay shows how a lot of attention that should have been spent on appealing to society was spent on internal maneuvers, since Occupy was thought to be essentially immortal.

On the one hand, many thought that OWS would be around for a long time and therefore didn't concentrate enough on how to make it grow. On the other, some activists have developed a passport stamp mentality oriented around the expectation that organizing is not about building long-term relationships and commitments, but rather about having a long string of diverse and interesting activist experiences to enrich their lives. It's almost gotten to the point where people don't really mind that much when projects, groups, and campaigns fold because they were never expected to last that long to begin with. Part of this trend is a response to an era of precarity that prevents a lot of people from setting down roots long enough to organize serious campaigns. But I've also witnessed a tendency of some anarchists and anti-authoritarians to drop out of groups or projects at the first sign of reformist tendencies in order to preserve their ideological purity rather than stay and fight it out.

I'm not at all saying that most who left OWS fall into this category; everyone had their own reasons and I had to leave the country myself. Some then concluded that the very notion of organizing with non-anarchists under any circumstance is a mistake since they tend to do non-anarchist things. But if we actually want to bring more people over to our side then we need to stand up for our ideas to those who oppose them. That doesn't mean that sticking around in a messed up group is always the right choice. Whether one should take that step depends on the specific nature of the issue and the numbers you have, but I was dismayed by the fact that some anarchists could fold so quickly in a context where their ideas were in the mainstream of the movement. Instead anarchists need to put themselves wherever struggle is manifesting itself, however imperfect it may be. As the Italian anarchist Carlo Cafiero (1846-1892) wrote:

> Every popular movement already carries with it the seeds of the revolutionary socialism: we must take part in it to ensure its growth. A clear and precise ideal of revolution is formulated only by an infinitesimal minority, and if we wait to take part in a struggle which appears exactly as we have imagined it in our minds—we shall wait forever. Don't imitate the dogmatists who ask for the formula before anything else: the people carry the living revolution in their hearts, and we must fight and die with them.[7]

* * *

Some may wonder why I would write a book explicitly about the anarchism of OWS if the entire point that I'm making is that it was strategically useful to refrain from talking openly about anarchism. My reason for writing the book was that I think it's important to emphasize how anarchist ideas relate to each other and support each other as an ideological unit. It's not enough to exclusively focus on direct democracy, or anti-oppression issues, or anti-capitalism without seeing how a holistic opposition to domination must encompass them all. Occupy did a fantastic job of spreading direct democracy, had moderate success at pushing anti-capitalism, but only meager success with anti-oppression work. But the potential risk with the Occupy-ization of politics is that although it had a big tent for many issues to coexist and we often emphasized how they all relate, many lacked the conceptual tools to actually link them together. As a result the typical 'Occupier' left the movement with a tattered checker-board politics. That is to be expected with any mass movement, but if anarchists can articulate a clearer vision of how these different forms of resistance feed off of each other, I think that the next time a similar opportunity arises we can achieve a greater political clarity. I don't think that you necessarily need the term 'anarchism' to do that, but it can help to distinguish an anti-electoral, anti-hierarchical, direct action oriented anti-capitalism from other perspectives on social change. To that end, I wanted to conduct these interviews and put together this book to set the historical record straight about the centrality of anarchism in this historic social movement. While OWS may not have shut down Wall Street, every movement that emerges rekindles the flame of resistance for a new generation and acts as a reminder to future revolutionaries that their struggles are part of a long and robust tradition of resistance.

Undoubtedly, the world is heading into choppy waters over the coming decades and there will be more political openings like Occupy that we need to be ready for. In such uncertain times, we need to be ready with solid organizational bases to work from. Neo-liberal capitalism, increasingly unable to maintain the infinite expansion that it craves, is sputtering from one bailout to the next, and social democratic parties are cowering under the heel of global finance and capitulating to disastrous austerity measures. Increasingly, the unfettered 'free' market and the welfare state, the two dominant visions of society, are crumbling and the people of the world are struggling to forge a new path toward sustainability, equity, and the satisfaction of the needs of all. After the nightmarish histories of the Soviet Bloc and other 'really existing' socialist countries, it's no surprise that the most dynamic social movements of the 21st century have championed horizontalism. More than any time since the 1930s anarchism is at the forefront of the world's revolutionary left. If anarchism is to expand and truly become the "revolutionary movement of the twenty-first century," as Graeber and Grubacic prophesied back in 2004,[8] then we need to work tirelessly to incorporate our anti-authoritarian vision into everyday struggles while also articulating a comprehensive vision of another world. After all, most people would love to live in a world where healthcare is available for everyone, where poverty has been ended and our collective needs are made the highest priority, where democracy and collective decision-making actually mean something and there are no bosses and emperors to tell us what to do, where we develop ways of life that respect the earth and its other inhabitants without commodifying them into extinction, and where our sexual, racial, or gender identities, to the degree that they still exist, have long ceased to become sources of oppression. Considering how many people struggle from paycheck to paycheck and groan under the insurmountable weight of medical, educational, and consumer debt, I know people would jump at the opportunity to live in a world where they got what they needed and contributed what they could… it's just that very few think it's possible.

As the supposedly 'natural' and 'eternal' world of the market crumbles around us, it is our urgent responsibility to articulate an alternative vision and take steps toward its construction in our organizing. In this respect, I think that the study of history is supremely important because it demonstrates an incredibly simple yet profoundly radical truth: the past was thoroughly different from the present in almost every way. In fact, the main constituents of personal identity that we use today didn't exist in the past. Let's take a look at a few examples of the historical construction of 'human nature' through identity including gender, sexuality, race, nationality, and class.

Before World War II, all American babies, regardless of sex, were dressed in little white dresses and in 1927 *TIME* magazine wrote that pink was the appropriate color for baby boys.[9] In the 16th and 17th centuries it was prestigious for elite men to wear high heels throughout Europe and Asia. Take a look at a portrait of Louis XIV, one of the most powerful rulers in history. He wore long flowing curly hair, long flowing velvet robes, heels, and tights.[10] If a 'man' dressed like that today, they'd be ostracized or even physically assaulted in the interest of gender policing. I put 'man' in quotes because many cultures today and in the past have had third genders that are considered neither men nor women, not to mention intersex people. Historically, people who transgress gender norms were thought to have forfeited their claims to their gender anyway so it's certainly a historical construct. Recently, researchers have refuted the idea that men and women are psychologically distinct.[11] If gender was understood so differently in the past and has already undergone so many changes in the last hundred years, then is it so crazy to think that someday we might be able to express ourselves as we please and relegate such a restrictive category to the scrapheap of history?

Prior to the modern era, the concept of homosexuality or 'the homosexual' didn't exist. Sure, people had same-sex relations with each other, but as a category of identity there was no concept that such behavior was only limited to certain people.[12] It was a drastically different way of thinking of sexuality. So if humanity existed for thousands of years without dividing people into sexual species, couldn't we eventually abolish concepts that box our sexual desires into rigid categories and interact with whomever we please free from categorization?

Prior to the colonization of the Americas modern notions of a 'white race' or a 'black race' didn't exist. Whiteness had to be invented and its rationale only really fully emerged once Europeans started to think of themselves as Europeans as they made more contact with the other peoples of the world. As Joel Olson wrote, race was invented in North America "to preserve the land and power of the wealthy ... the planters gave the English certain rights and privileges denied to all persons of African and Native American descent" and out of this division modern notions of race developed.[13] Likewise 'nationalism' is little more than a few hundred years old though it fashioned itself as a natural and eternal collective identity. So if the divisions that plague us today are artificial human constructs, though their manifestations are all too real, then after long arduous campaigns of racial justice and collective struggle is it so strange to imagine that some day we might be able to develop a world where the differences of race and regional origin no longer stimulate hatred or oppression?

And as I discussed in Chapter 2, for the majority of people throughout history the idea of pursuing individual riches at the expense of the community was anathema. Only since the inception of capitalism has the pursuit of profit been so thoroughly naturalized. As Mark Fisher wrote, the prevalent perspective that capitalism is the only economic system that conforms to human nature has produced a phenomenon that he calls "capitalist realism." For Fisher, capitalist realism is "the widespread sense that not only is capitalism the only viable political and economic system, but also that it is now impossible to even *imagine* a coherent alternative to it." As Frederic Jameson and Slavoj Žižek have said, "It's easier to imagine the end of the world than the end of capitalism."[14] Ironically, the popular American television program "Revolution" is about coping with a post-apocalyptic world rather than an actual revolution. The world that we live in today would have been entirely unthinkable to a pre-modern society. Their notions of time, identity, cosmology, history, and even change itself were utterly different. It wasn't until the modern era that the word 'revolution' gained its current connotation of a break with the past toward some new future. Previously it implied a return to the normal, natural state of affairs (re-volution).

It's clear that the only thing that we can know about the future is that it will be different from the present in ways that we cannot even begin to imagine. But staring into that abyss shouldn't cause us existential angst; we should cherish it for what it is: an invitation to join the "angels of bread" in imagining and building a new world.

Notes

Introduction: "Conquerors on Horseback are not Many-Legged Gods"

1 Excerpt from: Martín Espada, "Imagine the Angels of Bread," http://www.martinespada.net/Imagine_the_Angels_of_Br.html.

2 Ruth Milkman, Stephanie Luce and Penny Lewis, "Changing the Subject: A Bottom-Up Account of Occupy Wall Street in New York City," http://sps.cuny.edu/filestore/1/5/7/1_a05051d2117901d/1571_92f562221b8041e.pdf. This study only interviewed 25 core OWS organizers (a couple of whom weren't actually all that involved) and it's sample of 729 interviews were taken from the May Day 2012 coalition march organized by many non OWS groups rather than the OWS event earlier that day at Bryant Park.

3 "Research By and For the Movement: Key Findings from the Occupy Research General Demographic and Participation Survey (ORGS)," in Kate Khatib, Margaret Killjoy, and Mike McGuire eds., *We Are Many: Reflections on Movement Strategy from Occupation to Liberation* (Oakland: AK Press, 2012), 69-73.

4 I am included in the percentages but not the total number of interviews.

Chapter One: Insight from Confusion: The Media and Occupy

1 Newsroom, "Dr. Cornel West elaborates about 'Occupy Wall Street' Protests," *CNN*, Sept. 29, 2011, http://www.cnn.com/video/#/video/bestoftv/2011/09/29/brookewestoccupy-wallstreetprotests.cnn

2 Brian Montopoli, "Poll: 43 percent agree with views of

'Occupy Wall Street,'" *CBS News*, Oct. 25, 2011, http://www.cbsnews.com/8301-503544_162-20125515-503544/poll-43-percent-agree-with-views-of-occupy-wall-street/; and Lucy Madison, "Congressional approval at all-time low of 9%, according to new CBS News/New York Times poll", *CBS News*, Oct. 25, 2011, http://www.cbsnews.com/8301-503544_162-20125482-503544/congressional-approval-at-all-time-low-of-9-according-to-new-cbs-news-new-york-times-poll/?tag=contentMain;contentBody.

3 "Making a Difference," *NBC Nightly News*, http://www.msnbc.msn.com/id/40153870/.

4 During the first week of the occupation, coverage of OWS didn't register in the national monitoring of Pew's Project for Excellence in Journalism, but during the last week in September Occupy coverage was 2% of national news and during the first week of October it was 7%. See Brian Stelter, "Occupy Wall Street Occupies Headlines," *The New York Times*, Oct. 12, 2011, http://mediadecoder.blogs.nytimes.com/2011/10/12/occupy-wall-street-occupies-headlines/.

5 Mark Bray, "Confronting the Many Men in Suits: Rethinking the 'Positive' Coverage of Occupy Wall Street," *Critical Quarterly* 54 (July 2012): 5-9.

6 "Looking deeper into Occupy Wall Street," *CNN Newsroom*, Oct 10, 2011, http://www.cnn.com/video/#/video/us/2011/10/10/nr-granderson-cain-occupy-wall-street.cnn.

7 Sean Hennessey, "Police Respond to OWS Protests," *CBS 2*, Sept. 17, 2012, http://newyork.cbslocal.com/video/7734709-police-respond-to-ows-protests/.

8 Jean K. Chalaby, *The Invention of Journalism* (New York: St. Martin's Press, 1998), 35-40.

9 Martin Conboy, *The Press and Popular Culture* (London: SAGE, 2002), 84.

10 Chalaby, *The Invention of Journalism*, 138.

11 *Ibid.*, 111.

12 Something similar happens with conservative arguments against things like affirmative action. The idea is to construct abstract absolute principles that apply to everyone in all circumstances without reference to their social position or the history that put them there. A radical historicist emphasis on context is fundamentally at odds with Western traditions of disembodied abstract moral legislation.

13 Chalaby, *The Invention of Journalism*, 181.

14 Edward S. Herman and Noam Chomsky, *Manufacturing Consent: The Political Economy of the Mass Media* (New York: Pantheon, 2002), xviii. Second half of the quote from: Kevin Robins and Frank Webster, *Times of the Technoculture* (London: Routledge, 1999), 127.

15 Conboy, *The Press and Popular Culture*, 86.

16 Chalaby, *The Invention of Journalism*, 76.

17 Steve Cuozzo, "Mike is blowing it: No leadership amid Zuccotti mess," *New York Post*, Nov. 11, 2011, http://www.nypost.com/p/news/opinion/opedcolumnists/bloomberg_blinks_nxL3oQ3Xo8NO8FQZFr72CL.

18 "Occupy Wall Street Mobilizes for May Day Protests," *CBS New York*, May 1, 2012, http://newyork.cbslocal.com/video/7105898-occupy-wall-street-mobilizes-for-may-day-protests/.

19 Gadi Wolfsfeld, "Media, Protest and Political Violence: A Transactional Analysis," *Journalism Monographs* 127 (June 1991), 8.

20 Neal Ungerleider, "The Stealth Leaders of Occupy Wall Street," *Fast Company*, Oct. 7, 2011, http://www.fastcompany.com/1785698/stealth-leaders-occupy-wall-street.

21 Arthur S. Brisbane, "Who is Occupy Wall Street?" *The New York Times*, Nov. 12, 2011, http://www.nytimes.com /2011 /11/13/opinion/sunday/who-is-occupy-wall-street. html.

22 Kenneth Rapoza, "The Brains Behind 'Occupy Wall Street,'"

Forbes, Oct. 14, 2011, http://www.forbes.com/sites/kenrapoza/2011/10/14/the-brains-behind-occupy-wall-street-and-where-its-heading/.

23 "Left-Wingers Exploiting Occupy Wall Street Movement?" *Fox News,* O'Reilly Factor, Oct. 28, 2011, http://video.foxnews.com/v/1247450901001/left-wingers-exploiting-occupy-wall-street-movement.

24 Kathryn Blaze Carlson, "Occupy Wall Street plagued by the hierarchy it seeks to destroy," *National Post,* Nov. 25, 2011, http://news.nationalpost.com/2011/11/25/occupy-wall-street-plagued-by-the-hierarchy-it-seeks-to-destroy/.

25 "Occupy Wall Street Political Movement?" *CNN Newsroom,* Oct. 5, 2011, http://www.cnn.com/video/#/video/bestoftv/2011/10/05/am-kazin-occupy-wall-street.cnn.

26 After all, in Spanish the word "real" means both royal and real, while the political theory of power is called Realpolitik.

27 Sean Captain, "Will the Real 99% Please Stand Up?" *Fast Company,* Oct. 21, 2011, http://www.fastcompany.com/1789422/will-real-99-please-stand.

28 "Declaration of the Occupation of New York City," nycga.net, http://www.nycga.net/resources/documents/declaration/.

29 Francis Fukuyama, *The End of History and the Last Man* (New York: Free Press, 1992).

30 Ken Makovsky, "The 'Occupy Wall Street' Communications Gap," *Forbes,* Oct. 25, 2011, http://www.forbes.com/sites/kenmakovsky/2011/10/25/the-occupy-wall-street-communications-gap-3/.

31 Paul West, "Is Occupy Wall Street a Tea Party for Democrats," *Los Angeles Times,* Oct. 6, 2011, http://www.latimes.com/news/nationworld/nation/la-na-occupy-political-20111007,0,6412329.story.

32 David Ariosto, "Obama says protests give voice to

economic frustrations," *CNN*, Oct. 6, 2011, http://articles.cnn.com/2011-10-06/politics/politics_occupy-wall-street_1_protests-tea-party-financial-crisis?_s=PM:POLITICS.

33 This part of the interview didn't make it into the final segment.

34 Jeff Poor, "Maher to leftover Occupy movement 'douchebags': 'Get a job,'" *The Daily Caller*, Feb. 4, 2012, http://dailycaller.com/2012/02/04/maher-to-leftover-occupy-movement-douchebags-get-a-job/.

35 Esmé E. Deprez and Alison Vekshin, "New York Police in Riot Gear Clear 'Occupy' Protesters from Zuccotti Park, *Bloomberg*, Nov. 15, 2011, http://www.bloomberg.com/news/2011-11-15/u-s-mayors-crack-down-on-occupy-wall-street.html.

36 "Left-Wingers Exploiting Occupy Wall Street Movement?" *O'Reilly Factor*.

37 "Bill Maher has a critical message for Occupy Wall Street" *Daily Kos*, June 9, 2012, http://www.dailykos.com/story/2012/06/09/1098677/-Bill-Maher-has-a-critical-message-for-Occupy-Wall-Street.

38 Hugh R. Morley, "Has Occupy Stock Fallen?" *The Record*, Sept. 16, 2012.

39 Michael Howard Saul, "Bloomberg: Occupy Wall Street Can Stay Indefinitely," *Wall Street Journal Blog Metropolis*, Oct. 10, 2011, http://blogs.wsj.com/metropolis/2011/10/10/bloomberg-occupy-wall-street-can-stay-indefinitely/.

40 "Jones: 'You can't evict an idea," *CNN*, Nov. 16, 2011, http://www.cnn.com/video/#/video/us/2011/11/16/nr-intv-van-jones-ows.cnn.

41 "Occupy Wall Street Mobilizes for May Day Protests," *CBS New York*, May 1, 2012, http://newyork.cbslocal.com/video/7105898-occupy-wall-street-mobilizes-for-may-day-protests/.

42 Chrystia Freeland, *CNN Your Money*, Oct. 15, 2011, http://www.cnn.com/video/#/video/bestoftv/2011/10/16/ym-freeland-g.

43 Paul Krugman, "Confronting the Malefactors," *New York Times*, October 6, 2011, http://www.nytimes.com/2011/10/07/opinion/krugman-confronting-the-malefactors.html?_r=2&scp=2&sq=krugman&st=cse.

44 Bray, "Confronting the Many Men in Suits."

45 Tina Susman, "Occupy Wall Street protesters driven by varying goals," *Los Angeles Times*, Sept. 29, 2011, http://articles.latimes.com/2011/sep/29/nation/la-na-wall-street-protest-20110930.

46 "Wall Street protests just Inconvenience?" *CNN American Morning*, Oct. 3, 2011, http://www.cnn.com/video/#/video/us/2011/10/03/am-kosik-occupy-wal.

47 Chalaby, *The Invention of Journalism*, 83.

48 *CNN Your Money*, Oct. 15, 2011, http://www.cnn.com/video/#/video/bestoftv/2011/10/16/ym-freeland-g.

49 Josh Barro, "An Argument Against Taking Occupy Wall Street Seriously," *National Review Online*, Oct. 4, 2011, http://www.nationalreview.com/agenda/279074/argument-against-taking-occupy-wall-street-seriously-josh-barro#.

Chapter Two: "The Bane of Occupy Wall Street": Anarchism and the Anarchistic

1 David Horsey, "Today's anarchists are just brats in black," *Los Angeles Times*, May 22, 2012, http://www.latimes.com/news/politics/topoftheticket/la-na-tt-anarchists-20120522,0,5423459.story.

2 Madeline Nelson, 6/20/12.

3 Justine Tunney, 7/25/12.

4 These are 3 defining features of anarchism but not its entirety.

5 Ravi Ahmad, 8/19/12.
6 Rose Bookbinder, 7/26/12.
7 Karanja Wa Gaçuça, 7/20/12.
8 Dennis Flores, 7/18/12.
9 Richard J. F. Day, *Gramsci is Dead: Anarchist Currents in the Newest Social Movements* (London: Pluto Press, 2005), 20.
10 Cindy Milstein, "'Occupy Anarchism': Musings on Prehistories, Present (Im)Perfects & Future (Im)Perfects," *Outside the Circle*, http://cbmilstein.wordpress.com.
11 In the context of the United States, the term 'libertarian' has come to refer to advocates of a stateless capitalist society, but the term was originally a synonym for 'anarchist' and was used to avoid being censored by the state. In much of the world today, the term 'libertarian' has retained its anarchist associations and in Spanish, for example, *libertario* is interchangeable with *anarquista*. In the 1950s the free-market economist Murray Rothbard started to erroneously equate anarchism with capitalism. He pioneered the use of the term 'libertarian' for free-market capitalism, which led to the contradictory notion of 'anarcho-capitalism.' See Deric Shannon, "Chopping Off the Invisible Hand," in Deric Shannon, Anthony J. Nocella, II, and John Asimakopoulos eds., *The Accumulation of Freedom: Writings on Anarchist Economics* (Oakland: AK Press, 2012), 280. There is no basis to Peter Marshall's claim that anarchists and right-wing libertarians "are members of the same clan" because anti-capitalism is a central feature of anarchism. Peter Marshall, *Demanding the Impossible: A History of Anarchism* (Oakland: PM Press, 2010), xiii.
12 Though only 4 of the 10 Marxists identified with one of the authoritarian schools of Marxism.
13 Day, *Gramsci is Dead*, 218.
14 Quoted in: Alvaro Girón Sierra, *En la mesa con Darwin: evolución y revolución en el movimiento libertario en España*

(1869-1914) (Madrid: Consejo Superior de Investigaciones Científicas, 2005), 5.

15 'Revolution' means different things to different people, and anarchist conceptions of revolution have shifted over time. More attention will be paid to revolution in Chapter 4.

16 Marshall, *Demanding the Impossible*, x.

17 Luke Richardson, 6/26/12.

18 Peter Kropotkin, "Anarchist Communism: Its Basis and Principles," in *Anarchism: A Collection of Revolutionary Writings*, ed. Roger N. Baldwin (Mineola, NY: Dover Publications, 2002), 61.

19 Alexandre Skirda, *Facing the Enemy: A History of Anarchist Organization from Proudhon to May 1968* (Oakland: AK Press, 2002), 9.

20 Marshall, *Demanding the Impossible*, 189.

21 Paul Avrich, "The Legacy of Bakunin," *Russian Review* 29 (April 1970): 129.

22 Although Proudhon was the first person to label himself an anarchist, I consider him more of a proto-anarchist for reasons that will be discussed later.

23 Michael Greenberg, "What Future for Occupy Wall Street?" *The New York Review of Books*, Feb. 9, 2012, http://www.nybooks.com/articles/archives/2012/feb/09/what-future-occupy-wall-street/?pagination=false.

24 Essentially a street theater and arts group in OWS that would add on to other actions as a supplement.

25 Amin Husain, 2/26/12.

26 Mikhail Bakunin, *The Political Philosophy of Bakunin: Scientific Anarchism*, ed. Grigorii Petrovich Maksimov (Free Press, 1953), 288.

27 Carolyn P. Boyd, "The Anarchists and Education in Spain, 1868-1909," *The Journal of Modern History* 48, no. 4 (1976): 125-170.

28 Matthew Thomas, *Anarchist Ideas and Counter-Cultures in*

Britain, 1880-1914: Revolutions in Everyday Life (Burlington, VT: Ashgate, 2005), 207-229.

29 The predominantly anarchist Spanish section of the IWMA, the *Federación Regional Española* (FRE), was founded in 1870 and had a membership of 40,000 by 1873. See Benjamin Martin, *The Agony of Modernization: Labor and Industrialization in Spain* (Ithaca, New York: ILR Press, 1990), 78. After the Bourbon Restoration, however, the FRE had to go underground and never really recovered. When the liberal government came to power in 1881, there was more space for political action and anarchists formed the *Federación de Trabajadores de la Región Española* (FTRE), which had 60,000 members by 1883, but the emergence of anarchist communism, which was then tactically oriented around small, clandestine cells, was influenced by the long period of illegal activity in the 1870s. See George Richard Esenwein, *Anarchist Ideology and the Working-Class Movement in Spain, 1868-1898* (Berkeley, California: University of California Press, 1989), 8.

30 'Propaganda by the Deed' was a term for direct, violent attacks, and often assassinations, directed against class enemies such as politicians or members of the clergy that were intended to inspire revolutionary action on the part of the working poor that witnessed them. More in Chapter 4.

31 Antoni Dalmau, *El Procés de Montjuïc: Barcelona al final del segle XIX* (Barcelona: Editorial Base, 2010), 272.

32 The term "anarcho-syndicalism" was first used by the Russian anarchist Novomirsky during the first decade of the 20th century. See Skirda, *Facing the Enemy*, 76.

33 Yoni Miller, Facebook correspondence, Oct. 5, 2012.

34 E. J. Hobsbawm, *The Age of Empire 1875-1914* (New York: Pantheon Books, 1987), 134.

35 Also, it is important to point out that many anarchists in favor of mass organizing chose to work within mainstream

authoritarian unions in an attempt to democratize them and push them toward more militant action. Some prominent anarchists were not so enamored with syndicalism.

36 Joan Casanovas, *Bread, or Bullets! Urban Labor and Spanish Colonialism in Cuba, 1850-1898* (Pittsburgh: University of Pittsburgh Press, 1998), 146.

37 Michael Schmidt and Lucien van der Walt, *Black Flame: The Revolutionary Class Politics of Anarchism and Syndicalism* (Oakland: AK Press, 2009), 166-68 and 187-8.

38 George Orwell, *Homage to Catalonia* (Houghton Mifflin Harcourt, 1969), 4.

39 Noam Chomsky, *Radical Priorities* (Oakland: AK Press, 2003), 212.

40 Ida Mett, *The Kronstadt Uprising, 1921* (Montreal: Black Rose, 1973), 65.

41 Peter Gelderloos, *Anarchy Works* (The Anarchist Library Anti-Copyright, 2012), 41.

42 Steve Wright, *Storming Heaven: Class Composition and Struggle in Italian Autonomous Marxism* (London: Pluto Press, 2002); George Katsiaficas, *The Subversion of Politics: European Autonomous Social Movements and the Decolonization of Everyday Life* (Atlantic Highlands, NJ: Humanities Press, 1997).

43 Richard Kempton, *Provo: Amsterdam's Anarchist Revolt* (Brooklyn, NY: Autonomedia, 2007).

44 After the anti-authoritarian Mexican Revolutionary leader Emiliano Zapata (1879-1919).

45 After the famous Mexican anarchist Ricardo Flores Magón (1874-1922). See Ricardo Flores Magón, *Dreams of Freedom: A Ricardo Flores Magón Reader*, ed. Chaz Bufe and Mitchell Cowen Verter (Oakland: AK Press, 2005).

46 David Graeber, "The New Anarchists," *New Left Review* 13 (2002): 72.

47 Uri Gordon, *Anarchy Alive! Anti-Authoritarian Politics from*

Practice to Theory (London: Pluto Press, 2008), 23-5.

48 The curious george brigade, *Anarchy in the Age of Dinosaurs*, (Crimethinc, 2003).

49 There is some confusion about the exact contours of "individualist" anarchism. The term "individualist" has been used to describe anti-organizational anarchists but although I disagree with them they are not who I have in mind here. Instead, I refer to those individualists that Malatesta described as having "a care only for their own individuality and never have any hesitation in sacrificing others to it" which he considered a "colossal nonsense." See Skirda, *Facing the Enemy*, 84.

50 Mutualism is an economic theory based on the ideas of Pierre-Joseph Proudhon. Proudhon desired a society of independent craftsmen and workers' collectives that would make use of a mutual-credit bank that would lend money on low interest rates so goods could be exchanged on a free market.

51 Primitivists blame the ills of modern society on technology and want to revert to a hunter-gatherer society.

52 Richard D. Sonn, *Anarchism and Cultural Politics in Fin de Siècle France* (Lincoln: University of Nebraska Press, 1989), 136-7.

53 Rami Shamir, 9/15/12.

54 Harrison 'Tesoura' Schultz, 6/26/12.

55 Jez, 8/27/12.

56 Ed Mortimer, 6/20/12.

57 Nevertheless it is worth pointing out that Rami, Harrison, Jez and Ed are all anti-capitalists in favor of direct democracy so the contrast in emphasis shouldn't be interpreted as a substantially different political outlook.

58 Marshall, *Demanding the Impossible*, 3-4.

59 David Graeber, *Direct Action: An Ethnography* (Oakland: AK Press, 2009), 214-15. Graeber cites a number of stateless

societies: "the Bororo, the Baining, the Onondaga, the Wintu, the Ema, the Tallensi, the Vezo." See David Graeber, *Fragments of an Anarchist Anthropology* (Chicago, Prickly Paradigm Press, 2004), 38.

60 Voltairine de Cleyre, "Anarchism," in ed. Alexander Berkman, *Selected Works of Voltairine de Cleyre* (New York: Mother Earth Pub. Association, 1914), 98.

61 E. J. Hobsbawm, *The Age of Revolution 1789-1848* (New York: New American Library, 1962), 144-5.

62 The famous Chinese anarchist Ba Jin, pseudonym for Li Pei Kan (1904-2005), agreed: "Anarchism is not an idle dream that transcends time. It could not have emerged before the Industrial Revolution, and could not have developed before the French revolution. Many Chinese hold that Lao Tzu and Chuang Tzu were China's [first] anarchists. This is very misleading. Taoism shares nothing with modern anarchism." See Li Pei Kan, "On Theory and Practice," in Robert Graham ed., *Anarchism: A Documentary History of Libertarian Ideas, Volume One: From Anarchy to Anarchism (300CE to 1939)* (Montreal: Black Rose, 2005), 362. I don't think it's always problematic to use a modern term to describe earlier phenomena, as long as the use of such a term lends insight. But when it doesn't there is surely no incentive for its use.

63 Schmidt and van der Walt, *Black Flame*, 34-72.

64 Graeber, *Direct Action*, 216.

65 Although today Ferrer is revered as one of the great anarchists of Spanish history, during his life he was distrusted by Spanish anarchists for being too close to the federal republicans. Ferrer is best known for his work in organizing *La Escuela Moderna*, which promoted secular, libertarian education, but, in part, he funded the school and a number of anarchist newspapers and publishing ventures from stock he purchased in a Barcelona construction

company with capital he acquired when one of his wealthy Parisian students left him half of her estate including bonds and a valuable commercial property. See Joan Connelly Ullman, *La Semana Trágica: estudio sobre las causas socioeconómicas del anticlericalismo en España (1898-1912)* (Esplugues de Llobregat: Ariel, 1972), 168.

66 Thomas, *Anarchist Ideas and Counter-Cultures*, 215.

67 In response the prominent Italian anarchist, Errico Malatesta, wrote an indictment of pro-war anarchists called *Anarchistes de Gouvernements*. Louis Patsouras, *Jean Grave and the Anarchist Tradition in France* (Middletown, NJ: Calson, 1995), 65-6.

68 Just as Marx argued that Bakunin's behavior stemmed from his "Russian blood," Bakunin claimed that the behavior of Marx, Liebknecht and other stemmed from their Jewish identities. This racist behavior was unfortunately prevalent. At the time it was quite common to ascribe personal traits to one's background. Bakunin said that "all nations are equal in my eyes" because each was "a product of historical ethnography and consequently not responsible for either its defaults or merits." So he emphasized that he was "neither the enemy nor the detractor of the Jews" but he, like many, considered race and ethnicity to be social constructs that carried character traits with them. See Mark Leier, *Bakunin: The Creative Passion* (New York: St. Martin's Press, 2006), 247-8.

69 Graeber, *Fragments*, 5.

70 Richard Cleminson, *Anarchism, Science and Sex: Eugenics in Eastern Spain, 1900-1937* (Oxford: University of Bradford Press, 2000); Girón Sierra, *En la mesa con Darwin*, 2005.

71 David Horsey, "Today's anarchists are just brats in black."

72 Alexander Berkman, *Now and After: The ABC of Communist Anarchism* (New York: Vanguard Press, 1929), Introduction, in Anarchy Archives, http://dwardmac.pitzer.edu/Anar

chist_Archives/bright/berkman/comanarchism/whatis_forward.html.

73 Alexandre Carvalho, e-mail correspondence Sept. 30, 2012.

74 Jason Linkins, "Occupy Wall Street: Not Here to Destroy Capitalism, But to Remind Us Who Saved It," *Huffington Post*, Oct. 27, 2011, http://www.huffingtonpost.com/2011/10/27/occupy-wall-street-isnt-h_n_1035988.html.

75 Sally Kohn, "'Occupy Wall Street'—It's Not What They're for, But What They're Against," *FoxNews.com*, Oct. 14, 2011, http://www.foxnews.com/opinion/2011/10/14/understanding-occupy-wall-street/.

76 Michael Schuman, "How to Save Capitalism," *TIME*, Jan. 19, 2012, http://business.time.com/2012/01/19/how-to-save-capitalism/.

77 Richard Quest, "Is Capitalism Outdated in the 21st Century?" *CNN*, Jan. 25, 2012, http://business.blogs.cnn.com/2012/01/25/is-capitalism-outdated-in-the-21st-century/.

78 Chris Moody, "How Republicans are being taught to talk about Occupy Wall Street," *Yahoo! News*, Dec. 1, 2011, http://news.yahoo.com/blogs/ticket/republicans-being-taught-talk-occupy-wall-street-133707949.html.

79 Pew Research Center, Dec. 7-11, 2011, http://www.people-press.org/2011/12/28/little-change-in-publics-response-to-capitalism-socialism/12-28-11-1-2/. A youth unemployment rate of about 17% was certainly a contributing factor. See "Employment and Unemployment Among Youth Survey," Bureau of Labor Statistics, August 21, 2012, http://www.bls.gov/news.release/youth.nr0.htm.

80 Rebecca Smithers, "Almost half of the world's food thrown away, report finds," *The Guardian*, Jan. 10, 2013, http://www.guardian.co.uk/environment/2013/jan/10/half-world-food-waste.

81 David Harvey, "Organizing for the Anti-Capitalist

Transition," Talk given at the World Social Forum 2010, http://davidharvey.org/2009/12/organizing-for-the-anti-capitalist-transition/.

82 Joyce Appleby, *The Relentless Revolution: A History of Capitalism* (New York: W. W. Norton, 2010), 5.

83 Saki Knafo "U. S. Child Poverty Second Highest Among Developed Nations: Report," *Huffington Post*, May 30, 2012, http://www.huffingtonpost.com/2012/05/30/us-child-poverty-report-unicef_n_1555533.html.

84 Christhian Diaz, 9/29/12.

85 Malcolm Moore, "'Mass suicide' protest at Apple manufacturer Foxconn factory," *The Telegraph*, Jan. 11, 2012, http://www.telegraph.co.uk/news/worldnews/asia/china/9006988/Mass-suicide-protest-at-Apple-manufacturer-Foxconn-factory.html#.

86 Of course many would argue that this is not about capitalism, it's about the Chinese government. Yet China, which has long since given up any possible claims of socialism, like all other developing countries, is merely following the logic of capital: if you strip your working class of every shred of dignity and humanity, investors will come.

87 Justin Elliot, "The insane wealth of Walmart's founding family," *Salon*, Dec. 8, 2011, http://www.salon.com/2011/12/08/the_insane_wealth_of_walmarts_founding_family/.

88 That was even below the minimum wage in Bangladesh. See Pallavi Gogoi, "Wal-Mart Supplier Accused of Sweatshop Conditions," *Bloomberg Businessweek*, Oct. 9, 2008, http://www.businessweek.com/stories/2008-10-09/wal-mart-supplier-accused-of-sweatshop-conditionsbusinessweek-business-news-stock-market-and-financial-advice.

89 Ted Steinberg, "Can Capitalism Save the Planet? On the Origins of Green Liberalism," *Radical History Review* 107 (Spring 2010), 20.

90 Larry Lohmann, *Carbon Trading—A Critical Conversation on*

Climate Change, Privatisation and Power (Uppsala, Sweden: Dag Hammarskjöld Foundation, 2006); Tamra Gilbertson and Oscar Reyes, *Carbon Trading: How it Works and Why it Fails* (Uppsala, Sweden: Dag Hammarskjöld Foundation, 2009); Giorgio Trucchi, "Mecanismo de Desarrollo Limpio (MDL): ¿Y los derechos humanos qué?" *Adital: Noticias de América Latina y Caribe,* April 29, 2011, http://www.adital.com.br/site/noticia_imp.asp?lang=ES&img=S&cod=55985.

91 Ahmed Shawki, *Black Liberation and Socialism* (Chiago: Haymarket Books, 2006), 180.

92 JOMO, "Queer Liberation is Class Struggle," *Unity and Struggle,* Jan. 8, 2010, http://gatheringforces.org/2010/01/08/queer-liberation-is-class-struggle/.

93 Michelle Alexander, *The New Jim Crow: Mass Incarceration in the Age of Colorblindness* (New York: New Press, 2010); Jason Lydon, "Tearing Down Walls: Queerness, Anarchism and the Prison Industrial Complex," in C. B. Daring, J. Rogue, Deric Shannon, and Abbey Volcano eds., *Queering Anarchism: Addressing and Undressing Power and Desire* (Oakland: AK Press, 2013).

94 J. Kojo Livingston, "A Black Person is Killed by Police Every 36 Hours," *Politic365,* Sept. 29, 2012, http://politic365.com/2012/09/29/study-a-black-person-is-killed-by-police-every-36-hours/.

95 Michael Albert, "Life After Capitalism—And Now Too," *ZNET,* Dec. 10, 2004, http://www.zcommunications.org/life-after-capitalism-and-now-too-by-michael-albert.

96 Drew Hornbein, 9/15/12.

97 Jillian Buckley, 9/25/12.

98 E. J. Hobsbawm, *The Age of Capital 1848-1875* (New York: Charles Scribner, 1975), 3.

99 Quest, "Is Capitalism Outdated in the 21st Century?" Churchill said, "Democracy is the worst form of

government, except for all those other forms that have been tried from time to time."

100 Deric Shannon, Anthony J. Nocella, II, and John Asimakopoulos, "Anarchist Economics: A Holistic View," in Shannon et. al. eds. *The Accumulation of Freedom*, 18.

101 Jonathan Smucker, 7/17/12.

102 Schmidt and van der Walt, *Black Flame*, 21.

103 Leslie Derfler, *Paul Lafargue and the Founding of French Marxism 1842-1882* (Cambridge, Mass: Harvard Universty Press, 1991), 74.

104 Francisco Madrid and Claudio Venza, eds. "Principios Revolucionarios." In *Antología documental del anarquismo Español: organización y revolución: de la Primera Internacional al Proceso de Montjuic (1868-1896)* (Madrid: Fundación de estudios libertarios Anselmo Lorenzo, 2001), 312.

105 Berkman, *Now and After*, Chapter 1.

106 Leier, *Bakunin*, 110.

107 It's important to clarify that the Soviet-style countries that have been referred to as 'communist' were never, even by their own admission, communist; they were run by communist political parties. Their leaders considered the eventual emergence of a stateless, classless, communist society to be their ultimate goal. However, based on the Marxist conception of the stages of revolution, these parties were still using the 'dictatorship of the proletariat' against their class enemies and building the economy to be able to produce the surplus necessary for communism and the eventual withering of the state.

108 According to Max Nettlau, the phrase "anarchist communism" was first written in a pamphlet entitled "*Aux travailleurs manuels partisans de l'action politique*" written in 1876 by Francois Dumartheray who was a friend of Élisée Reclus. See Esenwein, *Anarchist Ideology*. 107. Cafiero was influenced by the hybrid collectivist/communist pamphlet

of 1876 "Ideas on Social Organization" by Bakunin's disciple James Guillaume. See Nunzio Pernicone, *Italian Anarchism, 1864-1892* (Princeton, NJ: Princeton University Press, 1993), 111-112.

109 Collectivism held on longer in Spain where collectivists engaged in bitter polemics with anarchist communists into the 1890s. In large part this is because anarchists remained influential in the Spanish labor movement in the 1880s while they were marginalized from it elsewhere.

110 Temma Kaplan, *Anarchists of Andalusia 1868-1903* (Princeton, NJ: Princeton University Press, 1977), 138.

111 Michael Albert, *Parecon: Life After Capitalism* (New York: Verso, 2003).

112 Girón Sierra, *En la mesa con Darwin*.

113 Emma Goldman, "Anarchism: What it Really Stands For," *Anarchy Archives*, http://dwardmac.pitzer.edu/anarchist_archives/goldman/aando/anarchism.html.

114 Keith Thomas, *The Ends of Life: Roads to Fulfilment in Early Modern England* (Oxford: Oxford University Press, 2009), 80.

115 *Ibid.*, 111.

116 Graeber, *Fragments*, 16-17.

117 Oscar Wilde, "The Soul of Man under Socialism," 1891, *Marxists.org*, http://www.marxists.org/reference/archive/wilde-oscar/soul-man/index.htm. Emma Goldman loved this quote too. See Goldman, "Anarchism: What it Really Stands For."

118 Sparrow Ingersoll, 6/20/12.

119 Yotam Marom, 7/11/12.

120 Sara Zainab Bokhari, 7/11/12.

121 Linnea M. Palmer Paton, 1/23/12.

122 Lauren Digioia, 6/19/12.

123 Tashy Endres, 12/20/11.

124 Greg Sharzer, *No Local: Why Small-Scale Alternatives Won't Change the World* (Winchester, UK: Zero Books, 2012).

125 Edward Abbey, *A Voice Crying in the Wilderness (Vox Clamantis in Deserto): Notes from a Secret Journal* (New York: St. Martin's Press, 1991). Thanks to William Haywood Carey for suggesting this quote.

126 Shawn Carrié, 8/9/12.

127 In fact, quite a few OWS anarchists told me that the experience of living in collective houses was among their first experiences of direct democracy (especially the consensus process) and anarchism.

128 Anthony!, 8/6/12.

129 Stokely Carmichael explained the importance of consensus in SNCC: "Close majority votes won't work because what if the minority seriously disagrees? Nobody is gonna risk his or her life for a program or policy with which he or she seriously disagrees." See Stokely Carmichael with Ekwueme Michael Thelwell, *Ready for Revolution: The Life and Struggles of Stokely Carmichael (Kwame Ture)* (New York: Scribner, 2003), 300.

130 MNS was a revolutionary pacifist network of collectives that existed from 1971-1988. Andrew Cornell, *Oppose and Propose!: Lessons from Movement for a New Society* (Oakland: AK Press, 2011).

131 AIDS Coalition to Unleash Power (ACT UP) was a direct action coalition in the 80s and 90s.

132 Earth First! is a largely anarchist militant environmentalist network.

133 Graeber, *Direct Action*, 234-6. Food Not Bombs is a network of people, mostly anarchists, who feed the homeless, often using food that would have otherwise been thrown away.

134 Zak Solomon, 2/21/12.

135 Josh Harkinson, "Meet Professor Occupy," *Mother Jones*, March/April 2012, http://www.motherjones.com/politics/2012/03/lisa-fithian-occupy-wall-street-teaching-civil-disobedience.

136 Lisa Fithian, 8/31/12.

137 Errico Malatesta, "Majorities & Minorities, and other essays" in ed. Verne Richards, *Malatesta: Life and Ideas* (London: Freedom Press, 1965).

138 Skirda, *Facing the Enemy*, 18-19.

139 David Graeber, 8/23/12.

140 Brett G., 6/27/12.

141 Kurt Andersen, "TIME Person of the Year: The Protester," *TIME*, Dec. 14, 2011, http://www.time.com/time/specials/packages/article/0,28804,2101745_2102132_2102373-1,00.html.

142 David Graeber, "On Playing by the Rules—The Strange Success of #OccupyWallStreet," *Naked Capitalism*, Oct. 19, 2011http://www.nakedcapitalism.com/2011/10/david-graeber-on-playing-by-the-rules---the-strange-success-of-occupy-wall-street.html.

143 Isham Christie, 12/5/12.

144 Lorenzo Serna, 6/19/12.

145 Jackie Disalvo, 7/19/12.

146 Max Berger, 10/5/12.

147 Jonathan Smucker, 7/17/12.

148 José Whelan, 8/29/12.

149 Brittany Robinson, 8/12/12.

150 Michael Premo, 8/31/12.

151 Brett G., 6/27/12.

152 Marisa Holmes, "The Center Cannot Hold: A Revolution in Process," in Khatib et. al. eds., *We Are Many*, 157. Marisa Holmes, 2/4/12.

153 Graeber, *Direct Action*, 43.

154 Holmes, "The Center Cannot Hold," in Khatib et. al. eds., *We Are Many*, 155.

155 Anthony!, 8/6/12.

156 Ari Cowan, 2/11/12.

157 Beth Bogart, 1/23/12.

158 William Haywood Carey, 7/12/12.

159 Michael Premo, 8/31/12.

160 Tashy Endres, 12/12/11.

161 This concept is distinct from the "anarcho-liberal" described by Bhaskar Sunkara because the *liberal libertarian* tends to be less explicitly ideological and more interested in free expression and a lack of constraint than the "anarcho-liberal" which seems to be more of a clear mix of actively ideological interpretations of anarchism and liberalism. See Bhaskar Sunkara, "The 'Anarcho-Liberal,'" *Dissent*, Sept. 27, 2011, http://www.dissentmagazine.org/blog/the-anarcho-liberal.

162 Justin Strekal, 7/8/12.

163 Priscilla Grim, 7/25/12.

164 William Haywood Carey, 7/12/12.

165 I'm arguing that liberal libertarians make the mistake of condemning all coercion and authority, regardless of who it is directed against. This is the same mistake that Friedrich Engels wrongfully accused anarchists of in his 1872 "On Authority." Engels misleadingly claimed that the "anti-authoritarians" were opposed to authority even being imposed on capitalists in a revolutionary context where in fact they were arguing against internal hierarchical authority and the state. As history showed, they weren't opposed to using violent means to defeat their enemies. Engels wrote: "A revolution is certainly the most authoritarian thing there is; it is the act whereby one part of the population imposes its will upon the other part by means of rifles, bayonets, and cannon…" Friedrich Engels, "On Authority," *Marxists.org*, 1872, http://www.marxists.org/archive/marx/works/1872/10/authority.htm.

166 William Haywood Carey, 7/12/12.

167 Schmidt and van der Walt, *Black Flame*, 70.

168 Jackie Disalvo, 7/19/12.

169 Atiq Zabinski, 6/27/12.
170 Holmes, "The Center Cannot Hold," in Khatib et. al. eds., *We Are Many*, 174.
171 Justine Tunney, 7/25/12.
172 Kanene, 8/2/12.
173 Negesti, 2/8/12.
174 Sonny Singh, 12/20/12.
175 Manissa McCleave Maharawal, "So Real It Hurts," in Khatib et. al. eds., *We Are Many*, 174.
176 Nicole Carty, 7/19/12.
177 Terry, 8/27/12.
178 Joel Olson, "Whiteness and the 99%," in Khatib et. al. eds., *We Are Many*, 46.
179 Sonny Singh, "Occupying Process, Processing Occupy: Spokes Council Musings by one POC," in Amy Schrager Land and Daniel Lang/Levitsky eds., *Dreaming in Public: Building the Occupy Movement* (Oxford: New Internationalist, 2012), 121-4.
180 S., 6/24/12.
181 Singh, "Occupying Process," in Schrager Land et. al. eds., *Dreaming in Public*, 124.
182 Sumumba Sobukwe, 12/20/11.
183 Yotam Marom, 7/11/12.
184 Cornell, *Oppose and Propose!*, 47.
185 Holmes, "The Center Cannot Hold," in Khatib et. al. eds., *We Are Many*, 157.
186 Cecily McMillan, 8/6/12.
187 Colby Hopkins, 6/20/12.
188 Julianne Pepitone, "Why Occupy Wall Street isn't about a list of demands," *CNN Money*, Oct. 12, 2011, http://money.cnn.es/2011/10/12/technology/occupy_wall_street_demands/index.htm.
189 Stina Soderling, 6/25/12.
190 William Jesse, 7/25/12.

191 Amin Husain, 2/26/12.

192 Timothy Eastman, 6/27/12.

193 Sam Corbin, 7/10/12.

194 David Korn, 2/26/12.

195 Tim Fitzgerald, 8/12/12.

196 Brett G., 6/27/12.

197 Errico Malatesta, "An Anarchist Programme," in Richards ed., *Errico Malatesta,* 196.

198 For a critique of this perspective in an Occupy context see: Yotam Marom, "Rome Wasn't Sacked in a Day: On Reform, Revolution, and Winning," in Khatib et. al. eds., *We Are Many*, 417-423.

199 David Graeber, "Occupy Wall Street's Anarchist Roots," *Al Jazeera,* Nov. 30, 2011; Graeber, "Situating Occupy," Adbusters, Dec. 2, 2011; Graeber, "Occupy's Liberation from Liberalism: the Real Meaning of May Day," *The Guardian,* May 7, 2012.

200 Dan Berrett, "Intellectual Roots of Wall St. Protest Lie in Academe: Movement's Principles Arise from Scholarship on Anarchy," *The Chronicle of Higher Education* , Oct. 16, 2011, http://chronicle.com/article/Intellectual-Roots-of-Wall/129428/; Thomas Meaney, "Anarchist Anthropology," *The New York Times,* Dec. 8, 2011, http://www.nytimes.com/2011/12/11/books/review/anarchist-anthropology.html?adxnnl=1&pagewanted=all&adxnnlx=1346877429-ELOeF5pZaDopIsjDfoaRcg&_r=0.

201 Drake Bennett, "David Graeber, the Anti-Leader of Occupy Wall Street," *Businessweek,* Oct. 26, 2011, http://www.businessweek.com/magazine/david-graeber-the-antileader-of-occupy-wall-street-10262011.html.

202 Frank Santo, "Raging, Well-Manicured Fists: Sitting in with the Practical Anarchists of NYC Reading Group," *New York Daily News,* Feb. 28, 2012, http://www.nydailynews.com/blogs/pageviews/2012/02/raging-well-manicured-fists-

sitting-in-with-the-practical-anarchists-of-nyc-readin.

203 Jonathan Chait, "Obama's Unlikely Anarchist Friends," *New York Magazine*, Oct. 4, 2011, http://nymag.com/daily/intel/2011/10/obamas_unlikely_anarchist_frie.html.

204 Jack Mirkinson, "Reuters' Occupy Wall Street Story Draws Fire for George Soros Connection," *Huffington Post*, Oct. 13, 2011, http://www.economicpolicyjournal.com/2011/10/george-soros-connection-to-occupy-wall.html.

205 *O'Reilly Factor*, Oct. 5, 2011.

206 Michael Gerson, "As radicalism creeps in, credibility retreats from OWS," *Washington Post*, Nov. 7, 2011, http://www.washingtonpost.com/opinions/as-radicalism-creeps-in-credibility-retreats-from-ows/2011/11/07/gIQA866IxM_story.html.

207 James Miller, "Will Extremists Hijack Occupy Wall Street?" *New York Times*, Oct. 25, 2011, http://www.nytimes.com/2011/10/26/opinion/will-extremists-hijack-occupy-wall-street.html.

208 Marty Linsky, "Occupy Wall Street is going nowhere without leadership," *CNN*, Oct. 27, 2011, http://articles.cnn.com/2011-10-27/opinion/opinion_linsky-occupy-wall-street-leadership_1_grievance-consensus-change?_s=PM:OPINION.

209 Stefan Fink, 6/27/12.

210 Glenn Beck interviews Buck Sexton, *The Blaze*, April 25, 2012, http://www.theblaze.com/stories/beck-the-blazes-buck-sexton-expose-the-real-forces-behind-occupy-wall-street/.

211 *Ibid.*

Chapter Three: Translating Anarchy

1 Guy Steward, 7/12/12.

2 "Meet the Occupy Wall Street protesters," *CNN Money*, Oct.

5, 2011, http://money.cnn.com/galleries/2011/news/1110/gallery.occupy_wall_street/6.html.

3 Jen Waller, 6/25/12.

4 Sam Corbin, 7/10/12.

5 Michael Premo, 8/31/12.

6 Sparrow Ingersoll, 6/20/12.

7 Senia Barragan, 8/11/12.

8 Malcolm Nokizaru, 7/10/12.

9 Aaron Bornstein, 6/26/12.

10 This really happened after the more than 700 arrests on the Brooklyn Bridge on October 1, 2011.

11 It's important to note that age statistics are based on the ages of the organizers when they were interviewed which was 3-17 months after Sept. 17, 2011 depending on when the interview was conducted. The majority of interviews were over the summer of 2012 so the average age on Sept. 17 would likely be about a half year younger.

12 Winnie Wong, 9/3/12.

13 The *Brigate Rosse,* or Red Brigades, was a Marxist urban guerrilla group active in Italy in the 1970s and 80s. See Robert C. Meade, *Red Brigades: The Story of Italian Terrorism* (New York: St. Martin's Press, 1990).

14 The Provos were countercultural anarchists in the Netherlands in the 1960s. See Kempton, *Provo.*

15 Linette Lopez, "A Massive Union Just Decided to Side with the Wall Street Protesters," *Business Insider,* Sept. 29, 2011, http://www.businessinsider.com/a-massive-union-just-voted-to-side-with-the-wall-street-protesters-2011-9.

16 Rosie Gray, "How Occupy Wall Street Got Hoaxed: The Email From Radiohead's 'Manager,'" *Village Voice Blogs,* Oct. 1, 2011, http://blogs.villagevoice.com/runninscared/2011/10/occupy_wall_street_radiohead.php.

17 Out of a sincere and legitimate attempt to democratize art and communication many radicals have gone too far in

priding themselves in amateurish propaganda that doesn't even attempt to reach a broader audience. Of course there's a time and place for all forms of writing, but as the Welsh rock band Mclusky sang in "You Should be Ashamed, Seamus": "What's the point of do it yourself when it looks so shitty/ these kids can't even feed themselves."

18 This sign was one of the OWS signs featured on the cover of issue 4 of the *Occupied Wall Street Journal*.

19 Beth Bogart, 1/23/12.

20 Malcolm Harris, "Occupied Wall Street: Some Tactical Thoughts," *Jacobin*, Sept. 27, 2011, http://jacobinmag.com/2011/09/occupied-wall-street-some-tactical-thoughts/.

21 Axle, 6/25/12. Crass was the seminal English anarcho-punk band of late 70s-early 80s.

22 Bootz, 1/25/12.

23 S., 6/24/12.

24 Jo Robin, 8/4/12.

25 Sergio Jimenez, 8/31/12.

26 Maria "Sarge" Porto, 8/9/12. Some of the OWS medics had military nicknames like "Sarge" for Sergeant or "Captain."

27 Mark Adams, 2/26/12.

28 Andrew, 8/7/12.

29 The values and phrases that these organizers have used with the public do not represent the entirety of what anarchism means to them. They are merely points of emphasis that came to mind during the interviews as examples.

30 Patrick Bruner, 2/4/12.

31 Of course the First International did vote on some rather specific political positions concerning property and electoral politics, for example, but Bakunin saw it as ideally functioning as a broad labor organization. See Skirda, *Facing the Enemy*, 24-5.

32 Gabriel Kuhn and Siegbert Wolf, "Introduction," in Gabriel

Kuhn ed. and trans., *Gustav Landauer, Revolution and Other Writings: A Political Reader* (Oakland: PM Press, 2010), 31-33.

33 Errico Malatesta, "Syndicalism and Anarchism," 1925, *marxists.org,* http://www.marxists.org/archive/malatesta/1925/04/syndic1.htm.

34 Ward S. Albro, *Always a Rebel: Ricardo Flores Magón and the Mexican Revolution* (Fort Worth, TX: Christian University Press, 1992).

35 Jacinto Barrera Basols, Correspondencia 2: 1919-1922 (México, DF: Fondo Editorial Tierra Adentro, 2000), 468. Notes 30 and 31 are cited in Chuck Morse, "Magonismo: An Overview" New Formulation, 2:2, http://www.newformulation.org/4Morse.htm.

36 During its first three years Common Ground had over 23,000 volunteers making it "the largest functioning organization based on anarchist ideals in the United States since the IWW" according to co-founder Scott Crow. See Scott Crow, *Black Flags and Windmills: Hope, Anarchy and the Common Ground Collective* (Oakland: PM Press, 2011), 137 and 159.

37 Here, I am not attempting to wade into the debates about class classification. It's true that the term 'middle class' is often used to obscure class conflict and divide the working class. In this instance I am simply noting that my quality of life as a child was qualitatively different than that of many working class people who struggle to get by. But this raises the larger question of the class composition of OWS. I didn't do a class breakdown of the organizers interviewed for several reasons. First, so many people had left their jobs, or were in between jobs, or working odd jobs in order to be able to participate. So the class status of some organizers was in temporary flux. Second, though I could have inquired about their class backgrounds, so many Americans think of almost everyone as the 'middle class' that it would

have been very inexact. Moreover, many may not have been honest about coming from affluent families. Nevertheless, my qualitative impression was that organizers came from a wide variety of class backgrounds. The main pattern that I noticed was that most were university educated, often from prestigious institutions.

38 Examples of prominent anarchists with backgrounds in the middle class or intelligentsia: Mikhail Bakunin, James Guillaume, Luigi Galleani, Pyotr Kropotkin, Ricardo Flores Magón, Errico Malatesta, Louise Michel, Élisée Reclus, Shifu, Ervin Batthyány, and John Creaghe. Examples of prominent anarchists from the popular classes include: Peter Arshinov, Alexander Berkman, Buenaventura Durruti, Emma Goldman, and Nestor Makhno. See Schmidt and van der Walt, *Black Flame*, 272.

39 I loved the Rage Against the Machine video for "Guerrilla Radio" which was a satire of the popular minimalist GAP commercials instead featuring sweatshop workers.

40 "American Apparel Exposed," *Clamor*, Fall 2006, Issue 38, http://clamormagazine.org/issues/38/aa/index.php.

41 Greg Sharzer, *No Local*.

42 Saul Alinsky, *Rules for Radicals: A Practical Primer for Realistic Radicals* (New York: Vintage Books, 1972), xix.

43 For Betsy Leondar-Wright, "essential weirdness" includes those traits that people you are organizing with may be turned off by but are important to maintain. For George Lakey, an example of "essential weirndess" would be presenting oneself as openly gay even if the neighborhood you were trying to organize was largely homophobic. "Inessential weirdness" might for some include certain kinds of clothing or cultural behaviors. See Cornell, *Oppose and Propose!*, 182-3. In contrast some queer Israeli Palestine solidarity activists have said that "in the territories we usually go back to the closet" since their sexuality might

impair their ability to work with some Palestinians. As opposed to Lakey, these activists might consider their sexuality to be "inessential weirdness" in this context. See Gordon, *Anarchy Alive!*, 146.

44 In parliamentary systems, such as those in Europe, small parties can win seats to parliament. Yet, as I will discuss in Chapter 4, any political party, regardless of politics, is ultimately constrained by the market.

45 Among others, I read Gerald Brenan, *The Spanish Labyrinth: An Account of the Social and Political Background of the Civil War* (Cambridge: Cambridge University Press, 1950); Gastón Leval, *Collectives in the Spanish Revolution* (London: Freedom Press, 1975); Sam Dolgoff, *The Anarchist Collectives: Workers' Self-management in the Spanish Revolution, 1936-39* (New York: Free Life Editions, 1974); José Peirats, *Anarchists in the Spanish Revolution* (Detroit: Black & Red, 1974); Robert W. Kern, *Red Years/Black Years: A Political History of Spanish Anarchism, 1911-1937* (Philadelphia: Institute for the Study of Human Issues, 1978).

46 This is my interpretation of some overarching points that we shared. These were not points that the group formally adopted in that format.

47 From the Preamble to the Constitution of the Industrial Workers of the World, http://www.iww.org/en/culture/official/preamble.shtml.

48 This framework has been championed by both authoritarian Soviet-style communists and libertarian communists, including many anarchists. A key difference is that anarcho-communists aim to implement this egalitarian framework as soon as possible, while the Soviets argued that it was first necessary to have a long transitional period under 'the dictatorship of the proletariat,' which actually did not allow much space for the proletariat to govern at all.

49 The "revolutionary watchword" of the IWW is "Abolition of

the Wage System" which implies a communist position. See the Preamble to the Constitution of the Industrial Workers of the World, http://www.iww.org/en/culture/official/preamble.shtml.

50 Some right wing libertarians and Ron Paul supporters would show up now and then especially toward the beginning, but I never met a single right wing libertarian who played an active role in organizing anything. I would mention their presence when describing the ideological plurality of the movement to appeal to the American liberal fetishization of 'non-ideological' popular discontent.

51 King argued in 1968 that the United States had "socialism for the rich and free enterprise for the poor." See Michael Eric Dyson, "King's Light, Malcolm's Shadow," *The New York Times*, Jan. 18, 1993, http://www.nytimes.com/1993/01/18/opinion/king-s-light-malcolm-s-shadow.html.

52 Voltairine de Cleyre, "Direct Action," in Berkman ed., *Selected Works*, 231.

53 Released on Sept. 30, 2011.

54 It's no longer threatening to talk about 'revolution' since everything from a new model of blender to different style of jeans is labeled 'revolutionary.' So most people picking up the paper weren't thinking that many Occupy organizers actually wanted a real revolution.

55 Dated Oct. 8, 2011.

56 Priscilla Grim, 7/25/12.

57 *Ibid*. Likewise, I tried to be presentable by wearing khakis and a buttoned shirt. I'm not saying that we should all dress like businesspeople at all, but it was useful for OWS to have some people playing the part of the straight-laced, 'average' person because, whether we like it or not, some people will only respond to that image of 'respectability.'

58 Amelia, 8/4/12.

59 Justine Tunney, 7/25/12.

60 The Situationist International (1957-1972) was a small but influential European avant-garde libertarian Marxist network of artists and intellectuals focused primarily on the relationships between capitalism and aesthetics in the context of post-war consumer alienation.

61 Isham Christie, 12/5/12.

62 Amin Husain, 2/26/12.

63 Yates told me that he was in "a transitional phase" moving from NGO politics toward a greater appreciation of anarchism and an anti-capitalist stance "in principal" despite advocating "some form of Left Keynsian reconstruction" in practice. He said that, "I used to be really skeptical of anarchism" but has come to better appreciate it through Occupy. Yates McKee, 6/19/12. Similarly, Laura explained that one of the most powerful elements of OWS was how it radicalized many people, such as herself. She did not identify with a specific ideology and said she was "still learning" but she said that she opposed capitalism as it currently exists, advocated direct democracy, and decided not to vote for Obama in 2012. Laura Gottesdiener, 9/24/12.

64 Suzahn Ebrahimian, 1/11/12.

65 In the second edition, Marina Sitrin argued that "The State, whether capitalist or socialist cannot be the emancipatory agent of change." Gayatri Chakravorty Spivak wrote that "General Strikes are always against 'Wall Street' or capitalism." Also, the piece on the Student Debt Strike had anti-capitalist messaging.

66 This action was in solidarity with a West Coast Occupy port shutdown protesting the exploitative role of a Goldman Sachs subsidiary in a trucker labor dispute.

67 The premise was based on an article by Matt Taibbi in *Rolling Stone*. Taibbi wrote that Goldman Sachs "is a great vampire squid wrapped around the face of humanity, relentlessly jamming its blood funnel into anything that smells

like money." See Matt Taibbi, "The Great American Bubble Machine," *Rolling Stone*, July 9, 2009, http://www.rollingstone.com/politics/news/the-great-american-bubble-machine-20100405.

68 I don't think that radical flair kept people away. The decline in attendance was inevitable as long as we weren't actually part of many concrete organizing initiatives.

69 Scott Horsley, "The Income Gap: Unfair, Or Are We Just Jealous?" *NPR*, Jan. 14, 2012, http://m.npr.org/story/145213421. "Hell no, we won't go" was an anti-war slogan during the Vietnam War.

70 Brian Stelter, "Camps are Cleared, but '99 Percent' Still Occupies the Lexicon," *New York Times*, Nov. 30, 2011, http://www.nytimes.com/2011/12/01/us/we-are-the-99-percent-joins-the-cultural-and-political-lexicon.html?_r=0.

71 William Alden, "Is Occupy a Fad?" *New York Times Deal B%k*, Sept. 18, 2012, http://dealbook.nytimes.com/2012/09/18/morning-agenda-is-occupy-a-fad/.

72 Jesse Greenspan, "Occupy Wall Street aims at comeback," *Metro*, Sept. 16, 2012, http://www.metro.us/newyork/local/article/1152167—occupy-wall-street-aims-at-comeback.

73 As of 2009. See: "Wealth Inequality," *inequality.org*, http://inequality.org/wealth-inequality/.

74 David Graeber, 8/23/12; Adam Weinstein, "'We Are the 99 Percent' Creators Revealed," *Mother Jones*, Oct. 7, 2011, http://www.motherjones.com/politics/2011/10/we-are-the-99-percent-creators.

75 Chris, 2/4/12.

76 Suzy Khimm, "Who are the 1 percent?" *The Washington Post*, Oct. 6, 2011, http://www.washingtonpost.com/blogs/wonkblog/post/who-are-the-1-percenters/2011/10/06/gIQAn4JDQL_blog.html.

77 Morrigan Phillips, "Room for the Poor," in Khatib et. al.

eds., *We Are Many*, 145.

78 Olivia, 12/20/12.

79 Brett G., 6/27/12.

80 Elizabeth Arce, 8/13/12.

81 Ben Reynoso, 6/25/12.

82 Luke Richardson, 6/26/12.

83 Madeline Nelson, 6/20/12.

84 Ronny Nuñez, 8/14/12.

85 Austin became so passionate about emphasizing the role of the police in maintaining class rule that he helped organize late-night rap battles at Union Square where rappers would rap against the police who had come out to keep watch over the Union Square occupation.

86 Austin Guest, 7/27/12.

87 George Machado, 7/11/12.

88 Stacey Hessler, 7/24/12.

89 Rowland Miller, 7/25/12.

90 Nicholas "OWS Tea", 12/6/12.

91 Louis Jargow, 8/4/12.

92 Tim Fitzgerald, 8/12/12.

93 Mike Andrews, 2/4/12.

94 Ba Jin was the pseudonym of Li Pei Kan. In the same article, he also added that "In sum, if we throw ourselves into China's revolutionary torrent, although we are unable to fully realize anarchist society overnight, we may bring the Chinese people closer to the ideal of anarchism, and bring more anarchist influence to the movement. This would certainly be a much better attitude than looking on unconcerned and making indiscreet criticisms." Li Pei Kan, "On Theory and Practice," in Graham ed., *Anarchism: A Documentary History*, 364.

95 Zak, 1/25/12.

96 Writers for the 99%, *Occupying Wall Street: The Inside Story of an Action that Changed America* (New York: OR Books, 2011),

64.

97 In my experience, I was just as likely to chat with liberals who were dressed like hippies and banging away in the drum circle as I was to find them in khakis holding a sign about Citizens United.

98 Zak, 1/25/12.

Chapter Four: Why We Need a Revolution or: Beyond "Socialism in One Park"

1 Tess Cohen, 8/30/12.

2 Nicholas "OWS Tea," 12/6/12.

3 Brett G., 6/27/12.

4 Mirza Shahzad Akbar, "The folly of drone attacks and U.S. strategy," *CNN*, Oct. 4, 2012, http://www.cnn.es/2012/10/04/opinion/pakistan-drone-attacks-akbar/index.html.

5 Peter Bergen, "Obama ramps up covert war in Yemen," *CNN*, June 12, 2012, http://www.cnn.es/2012/06/11/opinion/bergen-yemen-drone-war/index.html.

6 Simon Rogers, "US drone strikes listed and detailed in Pakistan, Somalia and Yemen," *The Guardian*, August 2, 2012, http://www.guardian.co.uk/news/datablog/2012/aug/02/us-drone-strikes-data.

7 Conor Friedersdorf, "How Team Obama Justifies the Killing of a 16-Year-Old American," *The Atlantic*, Oct. 24, 2012, http://www.theatlantic.com/politics/archive/2012/10/how-team-obama-justifies-the-killing-of-a-16-year-old-american/264028/. Moreover, whereas during the Bush administration the National Counterterrorism Center (NCTC), which oversees the various CIA and Pentagon "kill lists," was "barred from storing non-terrorist-related information about innocent Americans for more than 180 days…it is now free to do so." See Glenn Greenwald, "Obama moves to make the War on Terror permanent," *The*

Guardian, Oct. 24, 2012, http://www.guardian.co.uk/commentisfree/2012/oct/24/obama-terrorism-kill-list?CMP=twt_gu.

8 Ingrid Formanek and Dana Ford, "U.S. steps up involvement in Mali," *CNN,* Jan. 28, 2013, http://edition.cnn.com/2013/01/26/world/africa/mali-unrest; Eric Schmitt, "New Drone Base in Niger Builds U.S. Presence in Africa," *New York Times,* Feb. 22, 2013, http://www.nytimes.com/2013/02/23/world/africa/in-niger-us-troops-set-up-drone-base.html?pagewanted=all&_r=0.

9 Avni Patel, "Obama Waives Child Soldier Ban in Yemen and Congo," *ABC News,* Oct. 5, 2011, http://abcnews.go.com/Blotter/obama-waives-child-soldier-ban-yemen-congo/story?id=14663930.

10 "NDAA," *American Civil Liberties Union,* http://www.aclu.org/blog/tag/ndaa.

11 Jim Abrams, "Patriot Act Extension Signed by Obama," *The Huffington Post,* May 27, 2011, 2013, http://www.huffingtonpost.com/2011/05/27/patriot-act-extension-signed-obama-autopen_n_867851.html.

12 It's important to remember that the "Secret Service does not just protect the president and vice president. Rather, the agency has the responsibility for protecting the president, vice president and their immediate families; former presidents, vice presidents and certain family members; certain foreign dignitaries; major presidential and vice presidential candidates (within 120 days of an election); and other individuals as designated by a presidential executive order. If any of these individuals are temporarily visiting a location, this law kicks in." See Gabe Rottman, "Ready to Occupy? What You Need to Know about H.R. 347, the 'Criminalizing Protest' Law," *ACLU,* April 26, 2012, http://www.aclu.org/blog/free-speech/ready-occupy-what-you-need-know-about-hr-347-criminalizing-protest-law.

13 Gabriel Lerner, "How Many People Have Really Been Deported Under Obama?" *The Huffington Post*, March 3, 2012, http://www.huffingtonpost.com/2012/03/01/deportation-numbers-obama_n_1314916.html.

14 Josh Eidelson, "Obama to unions: See you later," *Salon*, Feb. 15, 2012, http://www.salon.com/2012/02/15/obama_to_unions_see_you_next_year/.

15 David Dayen, "Wall Street wins again," *Salon*, Feb. 13, 2013, http://www.salon.com/2013/02/13/wall_street_wins_again/.

16 Jamie Crawford, "Fact Check: Has Obama 'not signed one new free-trade agreement'?" *CNN*, Oct. 9, 2012, http://www.cnn.es/2012/10/08/politics/fact-check-romney-trade/index.html.

17 Victor Medina, "College students learn of Obama's secret Pell Grant cuts," *examiner.com*, Nov. 15, 2012, http://www.examiner.com/article/college-students-learn-of-obama-s-secret-pell-grant-cuts.

18 Nicole Carty, 7/19/12.

19 Suzanne Goldenberg, "Revealed: the day Obama chose a strategy of silence on climate change," *The Guardian*, Nov. 1, 2012, http://www.guardian.co.uk/environment/2012/nov/01/obama-strategy-silence-climate-change.

20 Derek Thompson, "Reality Check: Obama Cuts Social Security and Medicare by Much More Than the GOP," *The Atlantic*, April 11, 2013, http://www.theatlantic.com/business/archive/2013/04/reality-check-obama-cuts-social-security-and-medicare-by-much-more-than-the-gop/274919/; Matt Stoler, "The progressive case against Obama," *Salon*, Oct. 27, 2012, http://www.salon.com/2012/10/27/the_progressive_case_against_obama/.

21 Lisa Fithian, 8/31/12.

22 Stoler, "The progressive case against Obama."

23 Pete Dutro, 7/10/12.

24 Glenn Greenwald, "Repulsive progressive hypocrisy,"

Salon, Feb. 8, 2012, http://www.salon.com/2012/02/08/repulsive_progressive_hypocrisy/.

25 Edward Needham, 6/26/12.

26 Jordan Fabian, "Obama: More Moderate Republican than Socialist," *ABC News*, Dec. 14, 2012, http://abcnews.go.com/ABC_Univision/Politics/obama-considered-moderate-republican-1980s/story?id=17973080.

27 'Guitarmy' was a term used for the various musically oriented OWS marches where marchers were encouraged to march with guitars or other instruments and play songs together. Occasionally, as on May Day 2012, Tom Morello participated. Goldi, 8/10/12.

28 Atiq Zabinski, 6/27/12.

29 Sam Corbin, 7/10/12.

30 Aaron Bornstein, 6/26/12.

31 Jake DeGroot, 2/26/12.

32 Stan, 6/27/12.

33 Isham Christie, 12/5/12.

34 Drew Hornbein, 9/15/12.

35 Ethan, 8/27/12.

36 Stoller, "The progressive case against Obama."

37 Gina Rodríguez-Drix, "From Havana to Obama, Four Years Without Drinking the Kool-Aid," http://ginamariela.com/2012/10/22/from-havana-to-obama-four-years-without-drinking-the-kool-aid/.

38 Ryan Conrad ed., *Against Equality: Queer Critiques of Gay Marriage* (Lewiston, ME: Against Equality Press, 2010).

39 Bill Livsey, 6/19/12.

40 "Presidential Race," *CBS News*, http://www.cbsnews.com/election-results-2012/president.shtml.

41 "2000 Presidential Election," http://www.archives.gov/federal-register/electoral-college/2000/popular_vote.html.

42 Roger J. Sullivan, *Immanuel Kant's Moral Theory* (Cambridge: Cambridge University Press, 1989), 365.

43 Immanuel Wallerstein, "Upsurge in Movements Around the Globe," in Khatib et al. eds., *We Are Many*, 110.

44 Mark Mazower, *Dark Continent: Europe's Twentieth Century* (New York: Random House, 1999), 188-208.

45 Zu Solanas, 2/11/12.

46 http://crimethinc.com/tools/downloads/pdfs/dont_just_vote.pdf.

47 Voltairine de Cleyre, "Direct Action," in *Selected Works of Voltairine de Cleyre*, 221.

48 Kubo Yuzuru, "On Class Struggle and the Daily Struggle," in Graham ed., *Anarchism: A Documentary History*, 380-1.

49 Graeber, *Direct Action*, 203.

50 Jerry Goralnick, 2/8/12.

51 CJ Holm, 1/10/12.

52 Sara Zainab Bokhari, 7/11/12.

53 Gordon, *Anarchy Alive!*, 15-16.

54 Eduardo González Calleja, *La razón de la fuerza: orden público, subversion y violencia política en la España de la Restauración (1875-1917)* (Madrid: Consejo Superior de Investigaciones Científicas, 1998), 245; Esenwein, *Anarchist Ideology*, 44.

55 Over 80,000 people in Catalunya and Andalucía, later the hotbeds of Spanish anarchism, were organized into the Democratic *choza* structure during this period. See Kaplan, *Anarchists of Andalusia*, 58.

56 Aaron Black, 7/11/12.

57 Henry "Hambone" Harris, 7/24/12.

58 Candice M. Giove, "'They took my place! Single dad trying to take back home occupied by OWS," *New York Post*, Jan. 15, 2012, http://www.nypost.com/p/news/local/brooklyn/ows_home_invasion_z9ApqDP6Q0boFviq8CjvAL.

59 Will Gusakov, 7/15/12.

60 Beka Economopoulos, 1/21/13.

61 Jonathan Smucker, 7/17/12.

62 Beka Economopoulos, 1/21/13.

63 http://www.trinitywallstreet.org/about/real-estate.

64 Andrew, 8/7/12.

65 Katie Davidson, 8/22/12. When Mark was imprisoned during the summer of 2012, a bunch of Occupy people maintained a 24-hour sleep-in protest on the sidewalk outside of Trinity Church that lasted well beyond Mark's eventual release.

66 Will Gusakov, 7/15/12.

67 Josh Ehrenberg, 6/26/12.

68 Laura Gottesdiener, 9/24/12.

69 Drew Hornbein, 9/15/12.

70 Chris Hedges, "The Cancer in Occupy," *truthdig*, Feb. 6, 2012, http://www.truthdig.com/report/item/the_cancer_of_occupy_20120206/.

71 David Graeber, "Concerning the Violent Peace-Police: An Open Letter to Chris Hedges," *n+1*, Feb. 9, 2012, http://nplusonemag.com/concerning-the-violent-peace-police.

72 David Graeber, 8/23/12.

73 Luke Richardson, 6/26/12.

74 Rachel Donadio, "In Italy, Rioting Leads to Recriminations," *New York Times*, Oct. 16, 2011, http://www.nytimes.com/2011/10/17/world/europe/in-italy-rioting-leads-to-recriminations.html?_r=0.

75 Patrick Bruner, 2/4/12.

76 Rachel Herzing and Isaac Ontiveros, "Reflections from the Fight Against Policing," in Khatib et al. eds., *We Are Many*, 218.

77 http://occupywallst.org/article/solidarity-sunday/.

78 Graeber, "Concerning the Violent Peace Police"; Don Gato, "'To be fair he is a journalist': a short response to Chris Hedges on the Black Bloc," *libcom.org*, Feb. 8, 2012, http://libcom.org/library/be-fair-he-journalist-short-

response-chris-hedges-black-bloc; Peter Gelderloos, "The Surgeons of Occupy," *Counterpunch*, Feb. 9, 2012, http://www.counterpunch.org/2012/02/09/the-surgeons-of-occupy/.

79 For example, the Egyptian black bloc that burst onto the scene in early 2013 to join anti-government protesters had very diverse politics and some strong reformist and liberal tendencies. See Joshua Stephens, "Representation and the Egyptian Black Bloc: The Siren Song of Orientalism?" *Jadaliyya*, Mar. 1, 2013, http://www.jadaliyya.com/pages/index/10411/representation-and-the-egyptian-black-bloc_the-sir.

80 Hedges, "The Cancer in Occupy."

81 Ruth Ben-Ghiat, *Fascist Modernities: Italy, 1922-1945* (Berkeley: University of California Press, 2004), 157. It's also not a new way of describing the black bloc. In 2001, Agence France Presse journalist Christian Spillmann called the black bloc the *"véritable cancer du mouvement"* referring to the Global Justice movement. See: Francis Dupuis-Déri, *Les Black Blocs: La liberté et l'égalité se manifestent* (Lyon: Atelier de création libertaire, 2005), 16.

82 Chris Hedges, "The Greeks Get It," *truthdig*, May 24, 2010, http://www.truthdig.com/report/item/the_greeks_get_it_20100524/. Both Ward Churchill and Peter Gelderloos speak about the common pacifist hypocrisy of condemning revolutionary violence at home while praising it abroad. Though Hedges doesn't identify as a pacifist, his contradictory comments bear evidence of such pacifist NIMBY hypocrisy. See Ward Churchill, *Pacifism as Pathology: Reflections on the Role of Armed Struggle in North America* (Oakland: AK Press, 2007), 46, 77-80; Peter Gelderloos, *How Nonviolence Protects the State* (Cambridge, Mass: South End Press, 2007), 40.

83 This occurred in Oakland on Oct. 25, 2011 during the raid of

Oscar Grant Park when a group of 'non-violent' protesters tried to make a "citizen's arrest" on someone who was simply verbally defending the right of self-defense, and again on Nov. 2, 2011 when 'non-violent' protesters attacked those committing property destruction of corporate targets. See Emily Brissette and Mike King, "Overcoming Internal Pacification: The Uncompromising Faith of Fanaticism," in Khatib et al. eds., *We Are Many*, 196-7.

84 Dave Haack, 7/15/12.

85 Christine Crowther, 8/26/12.

86 Henry "Hambone" Harris, 7/24/12.

87 Michael Levitin, 8/4/12.

88 David Van Deusen and Xavier Massot, *The Black Bloc Papers: An Anthology of Primary Texts from the North American Anarchist Black Bloc 1988-2005* (Shawnee Mission, KS: Breaking Glass Press, 2010), 45.

89 Shane Gill, 2/12/12.

90 Reporters will even perform the linguistic gymnastics of calling a police shooting a "police involved shooting" to further distance the police from violence.

91 "Occupy Wall Street Protesters: We Are Americans," *ABC World News with Diane Sawyer*, Oct. 2, 2011, http://abcnews.go.com/US/occupy-wall-street-protesters-americans/story?id=14652698#.UEkL_Y7A3Yo. Sofía Gallisa told me how some of her Mexican comrades were appalled that the protestors on the bridge didn't try to push through the police lines. "We can't believe you guys just stood there," they said. Sofía Gallisa, 7/12/12.

92 Brissette and King, "Overcoming Internal Pacification," in Khatib et al. eds., *We Are Many*, 195.

93 Betsy Catlin, 9/5/12.

94 Patrick Bruner, 2/4/12.

95 Sam Corbin, 7/10/12.

96 Sparrow Ingersoll, 6/20/12.

97 Ashen Ruins, "Against the Corpse Machine: Defining a Post-Leftist Anarchist Critique of Violence," 2002.
98 Anthony!, 8/6/12.
99 Axle, 6/25/12.
100 Goldi, 8/10/12.
101 Ingrid Burrington, 6/27/12.
102 Will Gusakov, 7/15/12.
103 Michael Levitin, 8/4/12.
104 Mariano Muñoz-Elias, 8/4/12.
105 Ari Cowan, 2/11/12.
106 Fanshen, 8/8/12.
107 Cecily McMillan, 8/6/12.
108 "Statement of Autonomy," in Khatib et al. eds., *We Are Many*, 369.
109 Van Deusen and Massot, *The Black Bloc Papers*, 56.
110 On March 15, 2000 COBP (*Collectif opposé à la brutalité policière*) organized an anti-police brutality march in Montreal that ended with over 100 arrests and attacks on McDonalds and various banks. In response, Salami leaders condemned the property destruction causing many to quit Salami. See Dupuis-Déri, *Les Black Blocs*, 48-51.
111 Dana Balicki, 6/20/12.
112 Atiq Zabinski, 6/27/12.
113 Alexandre Carvalho, 7/27/12.
114 Matt Presto, 2/4/12.
115 Sara Zainab Bokhari, 7/11/12.
116 Moira Meltzer-Cohen, 8/6/12.
117 Here I'm not referring to the actions on September 17, 2012, which were coordinated through an affinity group spokescouncil. In that case, a larger plan was organized that affinity groups could plug into rather than simply trusting in the fact that autonomous groups would, of their own fragmented initiative, throw something together.
118 Cornell, *Oppose and Propose!*, 46.

119 Cindy Milstein, *Anarchism and its Aspirations* (Oakland: AK Press, 2010), 135.

120 Jen Waller, 6/25/12.

121 St. Paul Principles: http://rnc08report.org/archive/224.shtml.

122 Amin Husain, 2/26/12.

123 That's a paraphrased version of what I heard.

124 Some European anarchist groups and unions have their own soccer leagues, like the French CNT and the Athens antifa network, and they take it more seriously.

125 Kris Hermes, "The NATO 5: Manufactured Crimes Used to Paint Political Dissidents as Terrorists," *Huffington Post*, Jan. 25, 2013, http://www.huffingtonpost.com/kris-hermes/the-nato-5-terrorism-charges_b_2552554.html.

126 *CNN Newsroom*, May 21, 2012, http://transcripts.cnn.com/TRANSCRIPTS/1205/21/cnr.01.html. This transcript has a lot of typos so I corrected the quotes above. Also I couldn't help throwing in a Refused quote where I substituted in "this system" for "capitalism" in "capitalism is, indeed, organized crime and we're all the victims."

127 *Nosotros* is the Spanish word for "we" and was the name of the famous affinity group of the FAI, which included Buenaventura Durruti, Juan García Oliver, and Francisco Ascaso. Earlier manifestations of Durruti's affinity group were called *Los Solidarios* and *Los Justicieros*. See Abel Paz, *Durruti in the Spanish Revolution*, trans. Chuck Morse (Oakland: AK Press, 2006).

128 "Half of Greek cops go ultra-nationalist at elections," RT , May 16, 2012, http://rt.com/news/greek-police-vote-nazis-350/; Aris Chatzistefanou, "Golden Dawn has infiltrated Greek police, claims officer," *The Guardian*, Oct. 26, 2012, http://www.guardian.co.uk/world/2012/oct/26/goldendawn-infiltrated-greek-police-claims.

129 *BOΞ* is a newly squatted anarchist café that dedicates all of its proceeds to political prisoners around the world.

Throughout Exarcheia there are a wide variety of self-managed cooperatives.

130 Maria Margaronis, "Greek anti-fascist protesters 'tortured by police' after Golden Dawn clash," *The Guardian*, Oct. 9, 2012, http://www.guardian.co.uk/world/2012/oct/09/greek-antifascist-protesters-torture-police.

131 Dupuis-Déri, *Les Black Blocs*, 21.

132 Geronimo, *Fire and Flames: A History of the German Autonomist Movement* (Oakland: PM Press, 2012), 103.

133 Meade, *Red Brigades*,184. Similarly, the "red handkerchiefs" were squads of Italian workers who intimidated management while wearing masks to cover their identities in the late 60s/early 70s. See Katsiaficas, *The Subversion of Politics*, 21.

134 Geronimo, *Fire and Flames*, 56.

135 Nakanishi Masahiro, "Kakumaru: Analysis of an Ultra-Radical Group," in Stuart J. Dowsey ed., *Zengakuren: Japan's Revolutionary Students* (Berkeley: Ishi Press, 1970), 223.

136 Carlo Giuliani was an Italian anarchist who was killed by the police at the G8 summit protest in Genoa in 2001.

137 Katsiaficas, *The Subversion of Politics*, 178-9.

138 *Ibid.*, 63-93; Geronimo, *Fire and Flames*, 54.

139 Katsiaficas, *The Subversion of Politics*, 128.

140 *Ibid.*, 119.

141 *Ibid.*, 161-174.

142 The black bloc was first used in the United States by a small group at the Pentagon on Oct. 17, 1988 in protest against death squads in El Salvador. Next there was a bloc of 50 at an Earth Day event on Wall Street in April 1990, one during a Gulf War protest in Jan. 1991 organized by the Love & Rage anarchist group, more at protests against the 500th anniversary of Columbus's voyage in 1992, one at the DNC protest in Chicago in 1996, and another at a Philadelphia march for Mumia Abu-Jamal in 1999. See Van Deusen and

Massot, *The Black Bloc Papers*, 34-7. In Canada black blocs were formed by Toronto ARA against Nazis protecting a conference of the Front National français in 1993. See Dupuis-Déri, *Les Black Blocs*, 23.

143 Stina Soderling, 6/25/12.

144 This line comes from a song by Maria Dimitriadou.

145 Geronimo, *Fire and Flames*, 101.

146 The street he was murdered on now bears his name.

147 Team Colors Collective, "Messy Hearts Made of Thunder: Occupy, Struggle, and Radical Community Organizing," in Khatib et al. eds., *We Are Many*, 404.

148 Paul Dalton in Khatib et al. eds., *We Are Many*, 191.

149 Senia Barragan, 8/11/12.

150 Sofía Gallisa, 7/18/12.

151 Ronny Nuñez, 8/14/12.

152 George Machado, 7/11/12. Actually a "Pink Bloc was formed in Prague at the IMF protest in 2000. See Graeber, "The New Anarchists," 67.

153 Dupuis-Déri, *Les Black Blocs*, 77.

154 Louis Loréal, "Defense Revolutionnaire," in Sébastien Faure ed., *Encyclopédie Anarchiste* (Paris: La Librairie Internationale, 1934), 507-8.

155 Wright, *Storming Heaven*, 29.

156 Although I'm particularly familiar with the Spanish literature, Spain has been the main battleground for this debate. Historians who have made the millenarian argument include: Eric Hobsbawm, *Primitive Rebels* (1959) and *Revolutionaries* (1973); Constancio Bernaldo de Quiros, *El Espartaquismo Agrario Andaluz* (1919); Franz Borkenau, *The Spanish Cockpit* (1937); Gerald Brenan, *The Spanish Labyrinth* (1943); J. Diaz del Moral, *Historia de las Agitaciones Campesinas Andaluzas* (1929); Edward Malefakis, *Agrarian Reform and Peasant Revolution in Spain* (1970); and Stanley G. Payne, *The Spanish Revolution* (1970). See Martha Grace

Duncan, "Spanish Anarchism Refracted: Theme and Image in the Millenarian and Revisionist Literature," *Journal of Contemporary History* 23, no. 3 (1988): 323-346.

157 Kaplan, *Anarchists of Andalusia.*

158 Following Schmidt and van der Walt's distinction between "mass anarchism" and "insurrectionist anarchism" as the two main strands of the Broad Anarchist Tradition. See Schmidt and van der Walt, *Black Flame,* 20.

159 Li Pei Kan, "On Theory and Practice," in Graham ed., *Anarchism: A Documentary History,* 362.

160 Sébastien Faure, "Violence Anarchiste (La)" in Faure ed., *Encyclopédie Anarchiste,* 2874.

161 Peter Kropotkin, "Anarchism," in Baldwin ed., *Anarchism,* 286. During this period many anarchists thought that a revolution was necessary to clear away obstacles to the natural evolution of the human species in a rather literal sense but modern anarchists have abandoned such a literal interpretation of the evolution/revolution relationship. See Girón Sierra, *En la mesa con Darwin,* 46.

162 Errico Malatesta, "Anarchism and Reforms," in Vernon Richards ed., *The Anarchist Revolution: Polemical Articles 1924-1931* (London: Freedom Press, 1995), 81.

163 Girón Sierra, *En la mesa con Darwin,* 69.

164 Dupuis-Déri, *Les Black Blocs,* 35; Marshall, *Demanding the Impossible,* ix.

165 Early advocates of propaganda by the deed, like Malatesta, had insurrections like the 1877 Benevento Affair in mind. In his influential 1877 essay "Propaganda by the Deed," Paul Brousse cited the Paris Commune of 1871 as an example. See Paul Brousse, "Propaganda by the Deed," in Graham ed., *Anarchism: A Documentary History* ,150.

166 Schmidt and van der Walt, *Black Flame,* 131.

167 In 1901 McKinley was shot by the American anarchist Leon Czolgosz. In 1878 anarchist Giovanni Passanante failed in

his attempt to assassinate Umberto I before Gaetano Bresci (who had been living in Paterson, NJ) shot him in 1900. In 1898 Italian anarchist Luigi Lucheni stabbed the Empress in Geneva. In 1894 French President Sadi Carnot was stabbed by Italian anarchist Sante Geronimo Caserio in Lyon. In 1897 Spanish Prime Minister Antonio Cánovas del Castillo, known oppressor of the Cuban resistance and the anarchist movement, was shot by Italian anarchist Michele Angiolillo. In 1912 PM José Canalejas y Méndez was shot by the Argentine anarchist Francisco Pardiñas. In 1921 PM Eduardo Dato was shot by Pedro Mateu, Luis Nicolau and Ramón Casanellas. Tsar Alexander II of Russia was assassinated in 1881 by the Russian group Narodnaya Volya (The People's Will) but they weren't anarchists. That assassination did, however, greatly influence the appeal of propaganda by the deed for some anarchists.

168 Schmidt and van der Walt, *Black Flame*, 132.

169 Skirda, *Facing the Enemy*, 55.

170 Marxist examples include the *Brigate Rosse* in Italy and the *Rote Armee Fraktion* in Germany.

171 Richard Jensen estimates that between 1880-1914 at least 160 people died and 500 were injured from anarchist attacks outside of Russia (where the early twentieth century was basically a constant civil war whether explicitly or implicitly). Propaganda by the deed occurred in 16 countries during this period: Italy, France, Belgium, Spain, Portugal, Switzerland, Britain, Germany, Austria-Hungary, Russia, USA, Sweden, Denmark, Argentina, Australia, and possibly Turkey. See Richard Bach Jensen, "The International Campaign Against Anarchist Terrorism 1880-1930s," *Terrorism and Political Violence* 21, no. 1 (2009): 90.

172 Gustav Landauer, "A Few Words on Anarchism," in Kuhn ed. and trans., *Gustav Landauer Revolution and Other Writings*, 85.

173 Leo Tolstoy, "On Non-violent Resistance," in Graham ed., *Anarchism: A Documentary History*, 157.
174 Bart de Ligt, "The Conquest of Violence," in Graham ed., *Anarchism: A Documentary History*, 449.
175 Errico Malatesta, "Anarchy and Violence," in Richards ed., *The Anarchist Revolution*, 59.
176 Errico Malatesta, "Violence as a Social Factor," in Richards ed., *The Anarchist Revolution*, 160-3.
177 Jordi Getman-Eraso, "Too Young to Fight: Anarchist Youth Groups and the Spanish Second Republic," *Journal of the History of Childhood and Youth* 4.2, (2011): 282-307.
178 Lucy Parsons, "The Principles of Anarchism," in Gale Ahrens ed., *Lucy Parsons: Freedom, Equality & Solidarity, Writings and Speeches, 1878-1937* (Chicago: Charles Kerr, 2003), 31.
179 Timothy Garton Ash, *The Magic Lantern: The Revolution of '89 Witnessed in Warsaw, Budapest, Berlin, and Prague* (New York: Random House, 1990), 20.
180 Zu Solanas, 2/11/12.
181 Andrew, 8/7/12.
182 Jonathan Smucker, 7/17/12.
183 Jackie Disalvo, 7/19/12.
184 Geronimo, *Fire and Flames*, 105.

Conclusion: "Like Ectoplasm Through a Mist"

1 Ryan Harvey, "Occupy Before and Beyond," in Khatib et. al. eds., *We Are Many*, 124.
2 The first layer was outward facing communication such as the website, paper, and contact with the mainstream media while the second layer was composed of publications like Tidal designed for an already intrigued audience.
3 Skirda, *Facing the Enemy*, 179.
4 Lorenzo Serna, 6/19/12.

5 George Machado, 7/11/12.

6 Justin Stone-Diaz, 7/19/12.

7 Carlo Cafiero, "Action," in Graham ed., *Anarchism: A Documentary History*, 153.

8 David Graeber and Andrej Grubacic, "Anarchism, Or the Revolutionary Movement of the Twenty-First Century," *ZNET*, Jan. 6, 2004, http://www.zcommunications.org/anarchism-or-the-revolutionary-movement-of-the-twenty-first-century-by-david-graeber.

9 Jeanne Maglaty, "When Did Girls Start Wearing Pink?" *Smithsonian*, April 8, 2011, http://www.smithsonianmag.com/arts-culture/When-Did-Girls-Start-Wearing-Pink.html.

10 William Kremer, "Why did men stop wearing high heels?" *BBC*, Jan. 25, 2013, http://www.bbc.co.uk/news/magazine-21151350.

11 Eric W. Dolan, "Study debunks notion that men and women are psychologically distinct," *The Raw Story*, Feb. 4, 2013, http://www.rawstory.com/rs/2013/02/04/study-debunks-notion-that-men-and-women-are-psychologically-distinct/.

12 The first theorist of homosexuality was Karl Heinrich Ulrichs who first elaborated his theory from 1864-65. See Hubert Kennedy, "Karl Heinrich Ulrichs, First Theorist of Homosexuality," in Vernon A. Rosario ed., *Science and Homosexualities* (New York: Routledge, 1997).

13 Olson, "Whiteness and the 99%," in Khatib et. al. eds., *We Are Many*, 47.

14 Mark Fisher, *Capitalist Realism: Is There No Alternative?* (Winchester, UK: Zero Books, 2009), 2.

List of OWS Organizers Interviewed by First Name (with date of interview)

Aaron Black, 7/11/12.
Aaron Bornstein, 6/26/12.
Alexander Penley, 2/26/12.
Alexandre Carvalho, 7/27/12.
Amelia, 8/4/12.
Amelia Dunbar, 9/15/12.
Amin Husain, 2/26/12.
Amy, 7/24/12.
Andrew, 8/7/12.
Anthony!, 8/6/12.
Anthony Robledo, 6/20/12.
Ari Cowan, 2/11/12.
Ashley, 8/20/12.
Atiq Zabinski, 7/27/12.
Audrea Lim, 7/18/12.
Austin Guest, 7/27/12.
Axle, 6/25/12.
Bear Wisdom, 1/25/12.
Becky, 6/26/12.
Beka Economopoulos, 1/21/13.
Ben Reynoso, 6/25/12.
Beth Bogart, 1/23/12.
Betsy Catlin, 9/5/12.
Bill Dobbs, 12/18/12.
Bill Livsey, 6/19/12.
Bootz, 1/25/12.
Bre, 8/1/12.
Brendan Burke, 6/19/12.
Brett G., 6/27/12.
Brittany Robinson, 8/12/12.
Camille Raneem, 1/22/13.
Cara, 8/8/12.
Cari Machet, 12/20/11.
Caroline Lewis, 2/26/12.
Cecily McMillan, 8/6/12.
Chris, 2/4/12.
Chris Longenecker, 1/18/12.
Christhian Diaz, 9/29/12.
Christine Crowther, 8/26/12.
Christopher Brown, 8/20/12.
CJ Holm, 1/10/12.
Colby Hopkins, 6/20/12.
Cory Thompson, 9/15/12.
Dana Balicki, 6/20/12.
Dave Haack, 7/15/12.
David Graeber, 8/23/12.
David Korn, 2/26/12.
Debra Thimmesch, 6/20/12.
Dennis Flores, 7/18/12.
Diego Ibañez, 8/10/12.
Doug Ferrari, 7/19/12.
Drew Hornbein, 9/15/12.
Dylan, 7/16/12.
Ed Mortimer, 6/20/12.
Edward Needham, 6/26/12.
Elizabeth Arce, 8/13/12.
Eric, 12/20/12.
Eric Carter, 7/20/12.
Ethan, 8/27/12.
Evan Wagner, 8/20/12.

Fanshen, 8/8/12.
Felix Riveria-Pitre, 7/19/12.
George Machado, 7/11/12.
Georgia, 7/21/12.
Goldi, 8/10/12.
Greg Horwitch, 10/4/12.
Guy Steward, 7/12/12.
Harrison 'Tesoura' Schultz, 6/26/12.
Henry Harris ("Hambone"), 7/24/12.
Ingrid Burrington, 6/27/12.
Isham Christie, 12/5/12.
Jack Boyle, 6/20/12.
Jackie Disalvo, 7/19/12.
Jake DeGroot, 2/26/12.
Jason Ahmadi, 12/8/11.
Jay, 8/20/12.
Jeff Smith, 1/23/12.
Jen Waller, 6/25/12.
Jerry Goralnick, 2/8/12.
Jez, 8/27/12.
Jillian Buckley, 9/25/12.
Jo Robin, 8/4/12.
Jonathan G., 6/27/12.
Jonathan Smucker, 7/17/12.
José Martín ("Chepe"), 8/31/12.
José Whelan, 8/29/12.
Josh Ehrenberg, 6/27/12.
Josh Lucy, 7/16/12.
Julien Harrison, 10/2/12.
Julieta Salgado, 7/25/12.
Justin Stone-Diaz, 7/19/12.
Justin Strekal, 7/8/12.
Justin Wedes, 6/19/12.
Justine Tunney, 7/25/12.
Kanene, 8/2/12.
Karanja Wa Gaçuça, 7/20/12.
Katie Davidson, 8/22/12.
Kira Annika, 7/25/12.
Kobi, 7/10/12.
Laura Durkay, 1/18/12.
Laura Gottesdiener, 9/24/12.
Lauren Digioia, 6/19/12.
Leina Bocar, 7/18/12.
Liesbeth Rapp, 1/22/13.
Linnea M. Palmer Paton, 1/23/12.
Lisa Fithian, 8/31/12.
Lorenzo Serna, 6/19/12.
Louis Jargow, 8/4/12.
Luke Richardson, 6/26/12.
Madeline Nelson, 6/20/12.
Malcolm Nokizaru, 7/10/12.
Malory Butler, 2/26/12.
Manissa Maharawal, 7/26/12.
Maria Porto "Sarge", 8/9/12.
Mariano Muñoz-Elias, 8/4/12.
Marina Sitrin, 2/27/13.
Marisa Holmes, 2/4/12.
Mark Adams, 2/26/12.
Matt Presto, 2/4/12.
Max Berger, 10/5/12.
Megan Hayes, 7/18/12.
Michael Fix, 12/3/12.
Michael Levitin, 8/4/12.
Michael Premo, 8/31/12.
Mike Andrews, 2/4/12.
Moira Meltzer-Cohen, 8/6/12.

Moses, 11/1/12.
Nastaran Mohit, 7/10/12.
Negesti, 2/8/12.
Nelini Stamp, 10/4/12.
Nicholas "OWS Tea", 12/6/12.
Nick Mirzoeff, 1/30/13.
Nicole Carty, 7/19/12.
Nina Mehta, 9/25/12.
Olivia, 12/20/12.
Pablo Benson, 7/18/12.
Pam Brown, 6/27/12.
Patricia González-Ramirez, 8/22/12.
Patrick Bruner, 2/4/12.
Pete Dutro, 7/10/12.
Priscilla Grim, 7/25/12.
Rami Shamir, 9/15/12.
Ravi Ahmad, 8/19/12.
Ray, 7/23/12.
Rebecca Manski, 6/27/12.
Richard Machado, 7/11/12.
Ronny Nuñez, 8/14/12.
Rose Bookbinder, 7/26/12.
Rowland Miller, 7/25/12.
S., 6/24/12.
Sam Corbin, 7/10/12.
Sam Wood ("Captain"), 7/19/12.
Sandra Nurse, 8/18/12.
Sara Zainab Bokhari, 7/11/12.
Sean McAlpin, 12/20/12.
Senia Barragan, 8/11/12.
Sergio Jimenez, 8/31/12.
Shane Gill, 2/12/12.
Shawn Carrié, 8/9/12.
Sofía Gallisa, 7/18/12.
Sonny Singh, 12/20/12.
Sparro Kennedy, 7/27/12.
Sparrow Ingersoll, 6/20/12.
Stacey Hessler, 7/24/12.
Stan, 6/27/12.
Stefan Fink, 6/27/12.
Stina Soderling, 6/25/12.
Sully Ross, 12/20/12.
Sumumba Sobukwe, 12/20/11.
Suzahn Ebrahimian, 1/11/12.
Tashy Endres, 12/20/11.
Terry, 8/27/12.
Tess Cohen, 8/30/12.
Thorin Caristo, 12/12/12.
Tim Fitzgerald, 8/12/12.
Timothy Eastman, 6/27/12.
Tom Hintze, 9/12/12.
Vanessa Zettler, 8/11/12.
Victoria Sobel, 7/10/12.
Will Gusakov, 7/15/12.
William Haywood Carey, 7/12/12.
William Jesse, 7/25/12.
William Scott, 12/3/11.
Winnie Wong, 9/3/12.
Winter, 7/11/12.
Yates McKee, 6/19/12.
Yoni Miller, 7/25/12.
Yotam Marom, 7/11/12.
Zak, 1/25/12.
Zak Soloman, 2/21/12.
Zoltán Glück, 7/26/12.
Zu Solanas, 2/11/12.

Bibliography

Abbey, Edward. *A Voice Crying in the Wilderness (Vox Clamantis in Deserto): Notes from a Secret Journal*. New York: St. Martin's Press, 1991.

Albert, Michael. *Parecon: Life After Capitalism*. New York: Verso, 2003.

Albro, Ward S. *Always a Rebel: Ricardo Flores Magón and the Mexican Revolution*. Fort Worth, TX: Christian University Press, 1992.

Alexander, Michelle. *The New Jim Crow: Mass Incarceration in the Age of Colorblindness*. New York: New Press, 2010.

Alinsky, Saul. *Rules for Radicals: A Practical Primer for Realistic Radicals*. New York: Vintage Books, 1972.

Appleby, Joyce. *The Relentless Revolution: A History of Capitalism*. New York: W. W. Norton, 2010.

Avrich, Paul. "The Legacy of Bakunin." *Russian Review* 29, (April 1970): 129-142.

Bakunin, Mikhail. *The Political Philosophy of Bakunin: Scientific Anarchism*. Edited by Grigorii Petrovich Maksimov. Free Press, 1953.

Ben-Ghiat, Ruth. *Fascist Modernities: Italy, 1922-1945*. Berkeley: University of California Press, 2004.

Berkman, Alexander. *Now and After: The ABC of Communist Anarchism*. New York: Vanguard Press, 1929.

Boyd, Carolyn P. "The Anarchists and Education in Spain, 1868-1909." *The Journal of Modern History* 48, no.4 (1976): 125-170.

Bray, Mark. "Confronting the Many Men in Suits: Rethinking the 'Positive' Coverage of Occupy Wall Street." *Critical Quarterly* 54, (July 2012): 5-9.

Brenan, Gerald. *The Spanish Labyrinth: An Account of the Social and Political Background of the Civil War*. Cambridge: Cambridge University Press, 1950.

Carmichael, Stokely with Ekwueme Michael Thelwell. *Ready for Revolution: The Life and Struggles of Stokely Carmichael (Kwame Ture)*. New York: Scribner, 2003.

Casanovas, Joan. *Bread, or Bullets! Urban Labor and Spanish Colonialism in Cuba, 1850-1898*. Pittsburgh: University of Pittsburgh Press, 1998.

Chalaby, Jean K. *The Invention of Journalism*. New York: St. Martin's Press, 1998.

Chomsky, Noam. *Radical Priorities*. Oakland: AK Press, 2003.

Churchill, Ward. *Pacifism as Pathology: Reflections on the Role of Armed Struggle in North America*. Oakland: AK Press, 2007.

Cleminson, Richard. *Anarchism, Science and Sex: Eugenics in Eastern Spain, 1900-1937*. Oxford: University of Bradford Press, 2000.

Cleyre, Voltairine de. *Selected Works of Voltairine de Cleyre*. Edited by Alexander Berkman. New York: Mother Earth Pub. Association, 1914.

Conboy, Martin. *The Press and Popular Culture*. London: SAGE, 2002.

Conrad, Ryan ed. *Against Equality: Queer Critiques of Gay Marriage*. Lewiston, ME: Against Equality Press, 2010.

Cornell, Andrew. *Oppose and Propose!: Lessons from Movement for a New Society*. Oakland: AK Press, 2011.

Crow, Scott. *Black Flags and Windmills: Hope, Anarchy and the Common Ground Collective*. Oakland, PM Press, 2011.

Curious George Brigade, The. *Anarchy in the Age of Dinosaurs*. Crimethinc, 2003.

Dalmau, Antoni. *El Procés de Montjuïc: Barcelona al final del segle XIX*. Barcelona: Editorial Base, 2010.

Daring, C. B., J. Rogue, Deric Shannon, and Abbey Volcano eds. *Queering Anarchism: Addressing and Undressing Power and Desire*. Oakland: AK Press, 2013.

Day, Richard J. F. *Gramsci is Dead: Anarchist Currents in the Newest Social Movements*. London: Pluto Press, 2005.

Derfler, Leslie. *Paul Lafargue and the Founding of French Marxism 1842-1882*. Cambridge, MA: Harvard University Press, 1991.

Dolgoff, Sam. *The Anarchist Collectives: Workers' Self-management in the Spanish Revolution, 1936-39*. New York: Free Life Editions, 1974.

Dowsey, Stuart J. ed. *Zengakuren: Japan's Revolutionary Students*. Berkeley: Ishi Press, 1970.

Duncan, Martha Grace. "Spanish Anarchism Refracted: Theme and Image in the Millenarian and Revisionist Literature." *Journal of Contemporary History* 23, no. 3 (1988): 323-346.

Dupuis-Déri, Francis. *Les Black Blocs: La liberté et l'égalité se manifestent*. Lyon: Atelier de creation libertaire, 2005.

Esenwein, George Richard. *Anarchist Ideology and the Working-Class Movement in Spain, 1868-1898*. Berkeley, California: University of California Press, 1989.

Faure, Sébastien. *Encyclopédie Anarchiste*. Paris: La Librarie Internationale, 1934.

Fisher, Mark. *Capitalist Realism: Is There No Alternative?* Winchester, UK: Zero Books, 2009.

Flores Magón, Ricardo. *Dreams of Freedom: A Ricardo Flores Magón Reader*. Edited by Chaz Bufe and Mitchell Cowen Verter. Oakland: AK Press, 2005.

Fukuyama, Francis. *The End of History and the Last Man*. New York: Free Press, 1992.

Garton Ash, Timothy. *The Magic Lantern: The Revolution of '89 Witnessed in Warsaw, Budapest, Berlin and Prague*. New York: Random House, 1990.

Gelderloos, Peter. *How Nonviolence Protects the State*. Cambridge: South End Press, 2007.

___. *Anarchy Works*. The Anarchist Library Anti-Copyright, 2012.

Geronimo. *Fire and Flames: A History of the German Autonomist Movement*. Oakland: PM Press, 2012.

Getman-Eraso, Jordi. "Too Young to Fight: Anarchist Youth

Groups and the Spanish Second Republic." *Journal of the History of Childhood and Youth* 4.2 (2011): 282-307.

Gilbertson, Tamra and Oscar Reyes. *Carbon Trading: How it Works and Why it Fails*. Uppsala, Sweden: Dag Hammarskjöld Foundation, 2009.

Girón Sierra, Álvaro. *En la mesa con Darwin: evolución y revolución en el movimiento libertario en España (1869-1914)*. Madrid: Consejo Superior de Investigaciones Científicas, 2005.

González Calleja, Eduardo. *La razón de la fuerza: orden público, subversion y violencia política en la España de la Restauración (1875-1917)*. Madrid: Consejo Superior de Investigaciones Científicas, 1998.

Gordon, Uri. *Anarchy Alive! Anti-Authoritarian Politics from Practice to Theory*. London: Pluto Press, 2008.

Graeber, David. "The New Anarchists." *New Left Review* 13, (2002): 61-73.

___. *Fragments of an Anarchist Anthropology*. Chicago: Prickly Paradigm Press, 2004.

___. *Direct Action: An Ethnography*. Oakland: AK Press, 2009.

Graham, Robert ed. *Anarchism: A Documentary History of Libertarian Ideas, Volume One: From Anarchy to Anarchism (300CE to 1939)*. Montreal: Black Rose, 2005.

Herman, Edward S. and Noam Chomsky. *Manufacturing Consent: The Political Economy of the Mass Media*. New York: Pantheon, 2002.

Hobsbawm, E. J. *The Age of Revolution 1789-1848*. New York: New American Library, 1962.

___. *The Age of Capital 1848-1875*. New York: Charles Scribner, 1975.

___. *The Age of Empire 1875-1914*. New York: Pantheon Books, 1987.

Jensen, Richard Bach. "The International Campaign Against Anarchist Terrorism 1880-1930s." *Terrorism and Political Violence* 21, no. 1 (2009): 89-109.

Kaplan, Temma. *Anarchists of Andalusia 1868-1903*. Princeton, NJ: Princeton University Press, 1977.

Katsiaficas, George. *The Subversion of Politics: European Autonomous Social Movements and the Decolonization of Everyday Life*. Atlantic Highlands, NJ: Humanities Press, 1997.

Kempton, Richard. *Provo: Amsterdam's Anarchist Revolt*. Brooklyn, NY: Autonomedia, 2007.

Kern, Robert W. *Red Years/Black Years: A Political History of Spanish Anarchism, 1911-1937*. Philadelphia: Institute for the Study of Human Issues, 1978.

Khatib, Kate, Margaret Killjoy, and Mike McGuire eds. *We Are Many: Reflections on Movement Strategy from Occupation to Liberation*. Oakland: AK Press, 2012.

Kropotkin, Peter. *Anarchism: A Collection of Revolutionary Writings*. Edited by Roger N. Baldwin. Mineola, NY: Dover Publications, 2002.

Land, Amy Schrager and Daniel Lang/Levitsky eds. *Dreaming in Public: Building the Occupy Movement*. Oxford: New Internationalist, 2012.

Landauer, Gustav. *Gustav Landauer, Revolution and Other Writings: A Political Reader*. Edited and Translated by Gabriel Kuhn. Oakland: PM Press, 2010.

Leier, Mark. *Bakunin: The Creative Passion*. New York: St. Martin's Press, 2006.

Leval, Gastón. *Collectives in the Spanish Revolution*. London: Freedom Press, 1975.

Lohmann, Larry. *Carbon Trading—A Critical Conversation on Climate Change, Privatisation and Power*. Uppsala, Sweden: Dag Hammarskjöld Foundation, 2006.

Madrid, Francisco and Claudio Venza eds. *Antología documental del anarquismo Español: organización y revolución: de la Primera Internacional al Proceso de Montjuic (1868-1896)*. Madrid: Fundación de estudios libertarios Anselmo Lorenzo, 2001.

Malatesta, Errico. *Malatesta: Life and Ideas*. Edited by Verne

Richards. London: Freedom Press, 1965.

___. *The Anarchist Revolution: Polemical Articles 1924-1931*. Edited by Vernon Richards. London: Freedom Press, 1995.

Marshall, Peter. *Demanding the Impossible: A History of Anarchism*. Oakland: PM Press, 2010.

Martin, Benjamin. *The Agony of Modernization: Labor and Industrialization in Spain*. Ithaca, NY: ILR Press, 1990.

Mazower, Mark. *Dark Continent: Europe's Twentieth Century*. New York: Random House, 1999.

Meade, Robert C. *Red Brigades: The Story of Italian Terrorism*. New York: St. Martin's Press, 1990.

Mett, Ida. *The Kronstadt Uprising, 1921*. Montreal: Black Rose, 1973.

Milstein, Cindy. *Anarchism and its Aspirations*. Oakland: AK Press, 2010.

Orwell, George. *Homage to Catalonia*. Houghton Mifflin Harcourt, 1969.

Parsons, Lucy. *Lucy Parsons: Freedom, Equality & Solidarity, Writings and Speeches, 1878-1937*. Edited by Gale Ahrens. Chicago: Charles Kerr, 2003.

Patsouras, Louis. *Jean Grave and the Anarchist Tradition in France*. Middletown, NJ: Calson, 1995.

Paz, Abel. *Durruti in the Spanish Revolution*. Translated by Chuck Morse. Oakland: AK Press, 2006.

Peirats, José. *Anarchists in the Spanish Revolution*. Detroit: Black and Red, 1974.

Pernicone, Nunzio. *Italian Anarchism, 1864-1892*. Princeton, NJ: Princeton University Press, 1993.

Robins, Kevin and Frank Webster. *Times of the Technoculture*. London: Routledge, 1999.

Rosario, Vernon A. ed. *Science and Homosexualities*. New York: Routledge, 1997.

Schmidt, Michael and Lucien van der Walt. *Black Flame: The Revolutionary Class Politics of Anarchism and Syndicalism*.

Oakland: AK Press, 2009.

Shannon, Deric, Anthony J. Nocella, II, and John Asimakopoulos eds. *The Accumulation of Freedom: Writings on Anarchist Economics*. Oakland: AK Press, 2012.

Sharzer, Greg. *No Local: Why Small-Scale Alternatives Won't Change the World*. Winchester, UK: Zero Books, 2012.

Shawki, Ahmed. *Black Liberation and Socialism*. Chicago: Haymarket Books, 2006.

Skirda, Alexandre. *Facing the Enemy: A History of Anarchist Organization from Proudhon to May 1968*. Oakland: AK Press, 2002.

Sonn, Richard D. *Anarchism and Cultural Politics in Fin de Siècle France*. Lincoln: University of Nebraska Press, 1989.

Steinberg, Ted. "Can Capitalism Save the Planet? On the Origins of Green Liberalism." *Radical History Review* 107 (Spring 2010): 7-24.

Sullivan, Roger J. *Immanuel Kant's Moral Theory*. Cambridge: Cambridge University Press, 1989.

Thomas, Keith. *The Ends of Life: Roads to Fulfilment in Early Modern England*. Oxford: Oxford University Press, 2009.

Thomas, Matthew. *Anarchists Ideas and Counter-Cultures in Britain, 1880-1914: Revolutions in Everyday Life*. Burlington, VT: Ashgate, 2005.

Ullman, Joan Connelly. *La Semana Trágica: estudio sobre las causas socioeconómicas del anticlericalismo en España (1898-1912)*. Esplugues de Llobregat: Ariel, 1972.

Van Deusen, David and Xavier Massot eds. *The Black Bloc Papers: An Anthology of Primary Texts from the American Anarchist Black Bloc 1988-2005*. Shawnee Mission, KS: Breaking Glass Press, 2010.

Wolfsfeld, Gadi. "Media, Protest and Political Violence: A Transactional Analysis." *Journalism Monographs* 127, (June 1991).

Wright, Steve. *Storming Heaven: Class Composition and Struggle in*

Italian Autonomous Marxism. London: Pluto Press, 2002.
Writers for the 99%. *Occupying Wall Street: The Inside Story of an Action that Changed America*. New York: OR Books, 2011.

Contemporary culture has eliminated both the concept of the public and the figure of the intellectual. Former public spaces – both physical and cultural – are now either derelict or colonized by advertising. A cretinous anti-intellectualism presides, cheerled by expensively educated hacks in the pay of multinational corporations who reassure their bored readers that there is no need to rouse themselves from their interpassive stupor. The informal censorship internalized and propagated by the cultural workers of late capitalism generates a banal conformity that the propaganda chiefs of Stalinism could only ever have dreamt of imposing. Zer0 Books knows that another kind of discourse – intellectual without being academic, popular without being populist – is not only possible: it is already flourishing, in the regions beyond the striplit malls of so-called mass media and the neurotically bureaucratic halls of the academy. Zer0 is committed to the idea of publishing as a making public of the intellectual. It is convinced that in the unthinking, blandly consensual culture in which we live, critical and engaged theoretical reflection is more important than ever before.

9781782791263